Peace is Her Song

Everything that has voice
sing for peace,
speak for peace,
given chance, given choice,
work for peace,
write for peace,
resonating everywhere,
echoing our common care:
everything that has voice,
sing for peace!

Verse 1 from 'Everything That Has Voice' ('Sing for Peace'), written in 2003, first published in Shirley's American collection *Touch the Earth Lightly* to a tune by Marty Haugen and in *Hope is our Song*, to a tune by Colin Gibson.

Peace is Her Song

*The life and legacy of
hymn writer
Shirley Erena Murray*

Anne Manchester

Philip
Garside
Publishing Ltd.

Paperback International edition 2024:
ISBN 9781991027825

Also available
New Zealand paperback: ISBN 9781991027818
Paperback print-on-demand USA: ISBN 9798328781503

PDF: ISBN 9781991027832
ePub / Kindle / Mobi: ISBN 9781991027849

Philip Garside Publishing Ltd
39 Sydenham Street, Northland,
Wellington 6012
Aotearoa New Zealand

sales@philipgarsidebooks.com
www.philipgarsidebooks.com

With thanks to the Justice-Compassion Trust Aotearoa New Zealand, the New Zealand Hymnbook Trust and the Central Presbytery of the Presbyterian Church of Aotearoa New Zealand for funding publication.

Front cover photograph:
White Poppy by Martin Ophuc, Pixabay

Shirley and her husband John had a lifelong commitment to the White Poppies for Peace movement. This dates back to 1933 and remembers all the casualties of war, promotes peace and commits to finding non-violent solutions to conflict.

Back cover photograph of Shirley Murray in 2009:
Alastair Murray

Contents

Introduction

Two major motivations drove Shirley Erena Murray to begin writing her songs of peace, justice and hope in the 1970s. Firstly, she wanted to undergird the progressive theology of her husband John Murray, a Presbyterian minister, who struggled Sunday by Sunday to find hymns of contemporary relevance. Secondly, she sought to support the work of Amnesty International.

Over four decades she produced close to 400 hymns, around half of them published in the five collections of the New Zealand Hymnbook Trust. More than 300 appeared in the six collections of her hymns published by Hope Publishing Company in the United States. Shirley's hymns now appear in more than 30 major denominational hymnals across North America. Many more are included in Scottish, English and Asian collections, and are regularly found in Australian, Canadian and South American hymnals. They have been translated into many languages, including Braille and sign language. As her American publishers say: "She has truly become one of the most influential international hymn text writers of our time."[1]

Shirley says the reason she began to write hymns grew out of the ethos of being a New Zealander. "We have an attitude of 'do it yourself' – a kind of pioneer spirit which is not intimidated by too much tradition and actually welcomes inventiveness. It seemed to me that the [traditional] hymns we sang had no resonance with the world I lived in."[2]

Shirley wanted to reflect her own southern hemisphere environment and its concerns. She also wanted to make connections with Māori culture and to express the visions and hopes of her own society.

Her hymn writing aimed to reflect everyday experience, locally, nationally and globally. And she sought language that was simple, direct and pithy, giving a "jolt of reality".[3]

Shirley's hymns were also a kind of spiritual autobiography – a phrase used in the introduction to her fourth Hope publication *A Place at the Table*. In an earlier Hope publication, she wrote: "I began writing for my own clarification. For me it is writing myself into faith."[4]

Shirley understood who she was. "She spent her life reflecting on her own experience deeply and then finding exactly the right words to reflect that – the mark of a true poet."[5]

So many of her hymns were prompted or inspired by personal experience. Shirley makes it clear to readers and singers where she stands theologically. As retired Methodist minister Terry Wall writes, "each of her hymn texts nails her theological colours to the mast".[6] And the theology we sing, we remember.

In 2021, New Zealand's most well-known theologian, Sir Lloyd Geering, then aged 103, compared the legacies of Shirley and her husband John, both recognised for their leadership and prophetic gifts: "John made a huge contribution to the life of St Andrew's on The Terrace in central Wellington. He ensured the church made its presence felt in the city, but in the end Shirley's contribution as a hymn writer was greater and perhaps longer lasting. John was always very proud of her.

"Through her imagery and the themes she explored – peace, ecology, social justice – she pushed the church to become relevant to the secular world, with an emphasis on humanism, particularly in the figure of Jesus. Her impact on the church, both nationally and internationally, was significant. She is without doubt our greatest hymn writer."[7]

Emeritus professor Colin Gibson, Shirley's principal musical collaborator, has described Shirley's work as bringing fresh life to a jaded church. "She challenged old traditions and brought into existence a new body of work that will always hold an honoured place in our cultural heritage."[8]

Others have noted her contribution to inclusive language in the church. Through her texts and skilful use of language, she created new imagery for God.

Shirley wanted to write truly inclusive hymns that encompassed not just gender, but people of all sorts and conditions – solo parents or the differently-abled, for instance. She looked for hymns that could be sung at interfaith gatherings. It was clear to her that new hymns that addressed our understanding of life now, that could sing out our deepest emotions, from hope to despair, were desperately needed. So too were hymns on peace for people living in a post-nuclear age. What about hymns that "connected the Passion story with the worldwide, daily torture of prisoners of conscience or carols that linked the Christmas story with the tide of refugees"?[9]

She was also a trailblazer with so many of her themes, becoming one of the leading writers covering the care of creation in hymnody. "She could do the expansive and the tiny – could be very intimate too, without sentimentality."[10]

For Anglican priest Ian Render, her legacy is the establishment of the sense of the church in the southern hemisphere. "She unapologetically wrote so it reflected our lived experience, including the bicultural, seasonal and social justice issues we face. She enabled us to look at ourselves compassionately but critically and she gave us language for God that liberated us from patriarchy. These were her great gifts."

Colin Gibson, a Methodist layman and former professor of English at the University of Otago in Dunedin, has further highlighted Shirley's themes: "The search for peace, justice and human rights, inclusiveness, the honouring of women and the feminine element in spirituality, celebration of the natural world and the New Zealand environment, a call to social responsibility and a life of faith lived out with compassion and hopefulness."[11]

Seeking peace is at the heart of Shirley's understanding of Christian faith. "Almost everything I have written revolves ultimately round the concept of peace in all its many manifestations."[12]

And peace for Shirley meant something much more creative and powerful than opposition to war. "Everything radiates from it. Peace is environmental care, it's the atmosphere and ambience in which good and great things happen. Lack of peace equals hunger, domestic violence and abuse of children, and fragile human relationships."[13]

New Zealand composer Jenny McLeod, another of Shirley's musical collaborators, has said that who you are matters as much as what you create.[14] Such a statement could certainly apply to Shirley.

From her earliest years, Shirley impressed all who knew her – it was almost as if people came under her spell. Aged nine, she made a deep impression on her teacher Alex Bremer. He could see that, even at that young age, Shirley was committed to making the world a better place. He admired her youthful poetry and urged her to continue writing.

At Southland Girls' High School, principal Muriel May and Shirley formed a close bond, as Shirley did with the friends she made during these years. They were lifelong.

Shirley was 16 when she met and vanquished John Murray in a French-speaking competition in Dunedin. John had expected to win but Shirley herself turned out to be the prize. Everybody, it seemed, envied John.

Almost without exception, those interviewed for this book – collaborators, friends, former parishioners and family members – remarked on Shirley's warmth and compassion; her supportive approach to people; her lack of ego; her intelligence; her enthusiasm and simplicity; her ability to draw people to her. "She understood a God big enough for everyone and everything."[15]

Almost the only time people remember her being really riled was when someone dared to change the words of one of her hymns without seeking permission, or when John or someone else she loved was treated unfairly. And of course, nothing stirred her emotions more deeply than social injustice.

I, too, have come under Shirley's spell, particularly the spell created by her beautiful words – though I am also lucky enough to have known her personally. Like so many others I have spoken to, it has been her hymns and the theology they espouse that have kept me in the church when disappointment with the institution and some of its decisions might so easily have driven me away. Canadian hymn writing collaborator Ron Klusmeier talks of Shirley weighting the love side of the church for him as he wrestled with feelings of both love and hate for the institution. I can certainly relate to that.

About this book

It was after attending Shirley's funeral in the Kāpiti Uniting Church north of Wellington, on 31 January 2020, that I first envisaged becoming Shirley's biographer. It was there that I overheard Colin Gibson, who had delivered such an eloquent and memorable eulogy, discussing the need for someone to write such a book. Someone a bit younger than himself, he said. I fitted the first criterion, but other more important factors appeared to make me a suitable candidate – my background as a journalist (particularly on the former Presbyterian/ Methodist publication *Crosslink*) and editor, a writer of three books (two for children and a memoir), the fact I had known Shirley personally and had always loved and admired her hymns. Having run the idea past several key people and receiving Colin's blessing, I then set out on a five-year journey of research and writing to finally reach publication in 2024.

Along the way I have interviewed around 40 of Shirley's close friends and family, including hymn writing collaborators in New Zealand and overseas. *Music in the Air: Song and Spirituality*, a journal published between 1996 and 2015, has been a rich resource, as have Sheila Irwin's audio interviews recorded between 2001 and 2002 on behalf of the Association of Presbyterian Women.

In 1996, Hope Publishing Company in the United States videoed an interview with Shirley about her hymn writing influences – I was given complete access to this. And in 2006, both she and John were interviewed as part of the St Andrew's on The Terrace oral history project. The last video recording she made was in 2014, when Ron Klusmeier interviewed both Shirley and John at their home in Raumati Beach.

In addition to all these interviews, written and recorded, Shirley wrote for her family, during her final years, the story of her early life. I have also been privy to a number of emails and letters. Such treasures are a boon for the biographer. For this reason, the first three chapters of the book are taken largely from Shirley's account, with only very light editing and some additions from other sources. As much as possible, then, I have let Shirley tell her own story.

In the first four chapters, all the indented paragraphs are additional information supplied by the author. This style is reversed in Part II, chapters five to seven, where indented paragraphs become Shirley's words.

John's voice is also very strong, particularly in chapters describing the history of the New Zealand Hymnbook Trust (NZHBT). Then there are the voices of people who worked with Shirley, in particular her first great collaborator and mentor Colin Gibson. Without Colin's remarkable companion to the Trust's publications, *Knowing the Song*, I would have floundered. This book became my bible in researching Shirley's hymnody.[16]

Blessed by such riches, I have become a curator as much as a writer, weaving together many contributions – particularly from Shirley herself – then presenting the material in such a way that her life and work become seamless and accessible.

Each chapter begins with a verse from one of her hymns, highlighting the theme of that chapter and tracking her spiritual and theological journey. The majority of the texts of hymns quoted or referred to can be found on the Hope Publishing website (www. hopepublishing.com). These can be downloaded, for personal use only, free of copyright restrictions.

One aspect of Shirley's personality not yet mentioned is her playfulness and delight in nonsense rhymes and poems. For that reason, I leave the last word to her on the techniques of writing a good hymn.

> *A hymnwriter's task takes temerity,*
> *dexterity shot with sincerity,*
> *but do lots of pruning*
> *and endless retuning*
> *before you are sung by posterity.*[17]

Notes

1 Murray, S.E. (2019) Foreword. *Life into Life*. Hope Publishing Company.

2 Wootton, J. (2010) *This Is Our Song: Women's Hymn-Writing*. Eugene, Oregon: Wipf and Stock, p296.

3 Wootton, 2010, p297.

4 Murray, S.E. (2003) Foreword. *Faith Makes the Song*. Hope Publishing Company.

5 Roger Wiig. Interview with the author, 27 May 2022.

6 Wall, T. (2022) *Hymnwriters Downunder: Methodists sing the praise of God in Aotearoa New Zealand*. Tuakau Union Parish, p33.

7 Lloyd Geering. Interview with the author, 20 February 2021.

8 Gibson, C. (2004) Thank you, Shirley and John. *Music in the Air*, Summer.

9 Murray, S. (1996) Company of Clowns and Cripples: Personal Confession about Writing Hymn Texts. *Music in the Air*, Summer.

10 Ian Render. Interview with the author, 27 February 2023.

11 Gibson, C. (2021) *Knowing The Song: A Companion to the Publications of the New Zealand Hymnbook Trust from 1993 to 2009 together with the New Zealand Supplement to With One Voice (1982)*. The New Zealand Hymnbook Trust in association with Philip Garside Publishing Ltd, p341.

12 Wootton, 2010, p301.

13 Bell, G. (2014) In Conversation with … John and Shirley Erena Murray. *Sine Nomine*. Newsletter for the Southern Ontario Chapter of the Hymn Society of the United States and Canada.

14 Meehan, N. (2013) *Jenny McLeod: A Life in Music*. Wellington: Te Herenga Waka University Press, p11.

15 Ian Render. Interview with the author, 27 February 2023.

16 Gibson, 2021.

17 Video interview with Shirley, 12 July 1996, by Sam Young and George Shorney. Shirley says her little bit of doggerel was inspired by "a merry conversation" with American musician and composer Austin Lovelace in 1992.

Part I – Early Life

1 – In the beginning

Life into life, the threads are woven,
parent and child,
partner and friend;

tokens of love received and given:
joy at each birth,
grief at each end.

God of all time, all loves, all living,
hear as we bring our hearts' thanksgiving.[1]

This chapter is drawn largely from Shirley's account of her early life, which she wrote in her later years for her family. Here, she explains her family background and what it was like growing up in the 1930s in a three-generation household in Invercargill. Interwoven are excerpts from an interview for the Association of Presbyterian Women, conducted by Sheila Irwin on 7 November 2002.

When my maternal grandmother, Emma Stuart Ferguson, died in 1952, I realised there were lots of questions I had never asked. She died in her 84th year, just before my 21st birthday. Her unmarried name was Emma Stuart Thomson.

What was it like to have been born in Invercargill, the southernmost city of the South Island of New Zealand, in 1868? What was her family of brothers like (she was the only girl, apart from two stepsisters) and who was her mother, really?

Her mother's name was Emma too. Great-grandmother Emma married a young Scotsman called John Bowie Lindsay whom she met on the immigrant ship *Persian*. They married in Hobart, Tasmania, at

St George's Anglican Church in 1858, when the ship stopped off on its way to New Zealand.

They had two sons, and after a separation for unknown reasons, Emma became known as Mrs Thomson, 'wife' of John Logan Thomson, a printer, with whom she had four sons and a daughter, my grandmother. Possibly this informal marriage was because divorce was costly and difficult then, and the nearest courthouse was in Dunedin.

My Nana, Emma's daughter, was a sharp-tongued, contentious old lady. She had lived in our house all my life, along with my bachelor uncle, Jack, aka John Stanley Ferguson, an old Gallipoli soldier.

Nana (pronounced as in 'banana'), or Emma Ferguson, was relatively tall, with a sort of bony elegance and longish face. Her eyes were hazel, her hair was usually swept up on top and assisted to seem thicker by a little pad (which looked like a dead mouse when placed on her dressing table). Her hands were knotted and veined with arthritic joints, as mine are now. She almost always wore black dresses and sensible lace-up black shoes with solid heels. There were also the wrinkly lisle stockings.

Her best outfit was always her black sealskin fur coat, which had brown tonings on its large collar. And there was always a hat, spiked with formidable hat pins, without which she did not leave the house. She would dole out chocolates, which tasted of mothballs, to her visiting grandchildren, as my cousin remembers.

She was musical, as was all the family, and she often sang – mostly snatches of old parlour songs or dismal-sounding hymns such as 'Shall We Gather at the River?' and old American Sankey and Moody choruses. She had been brought up in the Wesleyan tradition, sang in the choirs, and warned us all against ever joining the Primitive Methodists.

I have her signature on the Women's Suffrage Petition to Parliament, at which stage she was living in Leet Street, and all her women neighbours seemed to have signed as well.

Nana had certain ideas which made life difficult for the household. She did not trust electricity and wandered around in the night with a candle ("Here comes Lady Macbeth," my father would groan), becoming a fire risk as she aged.

She cooked very badly; everything being overcooked by sitting on the coal range for hours. Think mince and cabbage. She helped my mother in doing vegetables and such things, and sat by the kitchen fire for a great deal of the day, so there was no escaping her comments on you and everything else.

One of the few times I remember, and it was very fraught, was when my mother's youngest brother Robert was killed in a diving accident in Burnham Camp during the war, and a cortège of the family drove off to Christchurch.

Looking at the photos of Nana as a younger woman, I always wondered why she married a widower with several children, two quite young daughters as well as three older sons? What was it about Alexander Ferguson that might have charmed her?

Alexander had emigrated from Inverness, Scotland, as a young man of about 22 (b. 1853) and was a watchmaker/jeweller by trade. His first wife was Helena Geary, whose Christian name turned into Erena in Māori (more about that to come).

His passion was music and especially the brass band repertoire, although he also played the double bass in the civic orchestra, and later conducted his own orchestra, giving each of his offspring an instrument to master. Jack had the clarinet, Bill, Alex and Archie the violins, Neil and Don the cornet or some other brass, and my mother the piano, as practice accompanist.

Alexander became a noted soloist on the euphonium and toured the world with a specially chosen New Zealand brass band. In all this, he seemed to leave home with a certain insouciance and let the family fend for themselves. He died in 1925, the year my parents married.

Three generations together

My father, John Walter Cockroft, was alternately maddened and philosophic about the presence of his mother-in-law. It was the economy of the time that forced our three-generation household to live together. I think it must have been the Great Depression of the 1930s that meant selling off the first home my parents had owned in Pomona Street, south Invercargill. When my father's employment in the mail room of the Post Office was cut to half-time, my grandmother and uncle were part of the reorganisation. I was born in the middle of this, in 1931.

My mother, called 'Rena' or 'Rene', had been the only daughter in the second Ferguson family. Born in 1897, she always disliked her Māori name Erena, and changed it to suit. It was also not fashionable to use Māori names at that time. The story goes that after she was born ('on the wash house floor'), grandfather was celebrating over a few whiskies with his friend and drinking partner Tōpi Pātuki, of local Stewart Island notability. [Tōpi Pātuki, of Ngāi Tahu, had interests in both Rakiura and Ruapuke Islands.] Asking what the new baby was to be called, Tōpi suggested she be named after Alexander's wife Helena, which in Māori transliterated into Erena. My grandfather had forgotten Helena was the name of his first wife. What my grandmother, Emma, thought, I never knew. She was certainly not consulted.

But I have always been proud of having Erena as my middle name, and pleased that two of my granddaughters, Rachel (Alastair and Lynda's daughter) and Isabella (Rob and Christine's daughter) have it too.

My mother was of a generation of bright girls who had to leave school after the age of 14 to get a job. She became a typist secretary, eventually personal assistant to J.C. Thomson, of the soft drink empire in Otago and Southland.

How she met Dad, I don't know, but they married in Knox Church, Dunedin, on 13 April 1925. Why Dunedin, I wonder? Running away from a big family wedding? Mum used to refer to the sad fact that many of her close girlfriends, who might have been her bridesmaids, had died in the 1918 'flu epidemic.

There are photos of my parents on holiday on Stewart Island, a favourite place. Mum was a sociable, cheerful sort of person, used to dealing with brothers and good at 'making do', a practice which guided most of her life. She had thick dark wiry hair when young, and interesting blue eyes with a yellow mix. She was very slim in her younger years and had been referred to as 'a yard of pump water', though I think of her as short and slightly plump.

She was an avid reader of novels. She loved movies, cards and going to the races with friends. She became a keen lawn bowls player, which somewhat astonished my father, already a good player. She became the president of the ladies' bowling club and a life member. She loved hats and after her death, we found dozens and dozens tumbling out of her wardrobe. She was kind and loving, and a good mother in quite difficult circumstances.

Dad, always called 'Johnny' by my mother, was a gregarious, humorous sort of fellow, loved singing and loved alcohol (mostly sherry and beer) a bit too much. He had brown eyes and brown hair tinged with red. From him, I learned the parlour songs and popular ballads which he sang, accompanied by my mother. He was a good whistler and had a pleasing baritone voice.

My mother was caught between dealing with her mother, bringing up her children and 'managing' my father's forays into over-drinking or being unwell, as he sometimes was because of a severe kind of arthritis and the medication he took for this. Nevertheless, my father took a keen interest in sport, two of the wider family of Cockrofts having made it to All Blacks. Dad played lawn bowls for many years. He loved the radio and took small bets on horses most Saturdays.

As time went on, his neck became quite crooked (torticollis) and his hands so arthritic that he could not write except with a special ink pen. He taught himself to type and did quite well at it. I still have some of the letters he wrote to me as a student.

His sense of humour and generally positive attitude to life allowed him to overcome the fact that, had my mother been willing to move to other places, he would have advanced to better positions in the Post Office. As it was, he was stuck in Invercargill and became more and more of a risk, wobbling along on his bicycle and not always well enough to turn up at work.

At one point, my parents acquired a second-hand Vauxhall, which my mother learned to drive, but after one scary episode, trying to reverse into a main street, she gave up. Since Dad did not learn, that was that.

Home life

When my brother John Bruce and I were children, we lived in a rented house at 216 Spey Street, opposite Kingsland's biscuit factory and near Middle School. Then the family managed to buy an eighth-acre section opposite the Water Tower in Elles Road (later called Queen's Drive) and built a brick house there. This was an enormous enterprise for them, and when the last of the family died, my mother was still paying off that mortgage.

My parents kept a wonderful and productive garden – Mum in the flower department and Dad in the vegetable, as was the way then. We lived on the garden produce, especially potatoes, parsnips, carrots and peas. There were blackcurrant and gooseberry bushes at the end of the garden, and plenty of lettuces and silverbeet. My father's attempts at growing asparagus never prospered in that climate. He kept a few hens at one stage, and a 'log' of their egg production, which was never impressive.

Mum had 'green fingers' and was never averse to nipping bits from the Rose Gardens or swapping cuttings with friends. Roses were her speciality. She loved her garden, which was also an escape from the house and my grandmother's constant bickering. There was an ongoing feud between my grandmother and the older lady next door, Mrs Hallimore, who was a devoted Roman Catholic and of Irish extraction.

Some of the steamiest arguments over the fence were about dreadful Catholics and awful Protestants. One day a friend and I looked inside the door of St Mary's Basilica, but we were too scared to go in. We didn't know what to do with the water in the little stoup at the door.

My music teacher had been taught by Catholics and she told me about the Catholics before I went to Dunedin. It was an Irish/Scots as much as a religious divide. Catholic girls went to St Catherine's in Invercargill.

My mother was a good baker but loved buying cakes from the local bakeries and teashops that existed then. She also loved going to auctions and had a fine eye for a bargain. Because there was no spare money, she seemed to be incredibly good at being resourceful and turning her hand to various things.

Nana usually cooked for Uncle Jack, who was the full-time earner and upon whom she doted. Since my father was employed by the Post Office in the mail room, he worked shifts, and so he often ate at different times from the rest of us. He might be seen having 'tea' when we arrived home from school. Dinner, as with most families then, happened at midday. It was thought odd to be otherwise. Uncle Jack would come home from his office for dinner every day between 12 and 1pm.

> Barbara Clark, a volunteer archivist at Southland Girls' High School and a former teacher at the school, recounted an amusing story about Jack Ferguson – Shirley's charming, but ratbag uncle, who was so very proud of his niece:
>
> "I have first-hand knowledge of Shirley's genetic disposition for hymn writing, as I once told her. Jack, who loved whisky and tended to overdo it, was a family friend and my 'adopted' uncle. He tried to lead me astray by teaching me a rather unorthodox Sunday school hymn. 'Jesus wants me for a sunbeam. Jesus wants me for a sunbeam. Jesus wants me for a sunbeam and a bloody good sunbeam I'll be.'
>
> "My mother was horrified and needed to 'unteach' me! I told Shirley about this in a note to her in 2009. In her reply, she suggested she might teach the 'work' to her grandchildren!"

My brother Bruce was two years younger than I was, a good sportsman at rugby and cricket from early on, and then a keen golfer. He married Patricia Grisbrook-Hills, who came to Invercargill with her family from South Africa, a place virtually unknown to us in those days.

Bruce joined the office of the Southland Frozen Meat Company and became a marketer for New Zealand lamb and beef. Later, he and Pat moved to Hastings and joined Richmond's, who sent him round the world promoting New Zealand meat, particularly in the Middle East and the United States. He would joke about the 'rag heads' (sic) he had to deal with, and the halal conditions to be observed.

The biggest thrill for Bruce and me as kids was a trip in Uncle Jack's Chevrolet on a Sunday afternoon. [See photo p95.] We would take off in a cloud of dust round the country roads near Invercargill. Such cars had a generously wide running board which you could jump onto and ride at lower speeds. I can always summon up the interesting smell of that car, with its leather seats and aroma of ever-present whisky, kept in a bottle under the rug in the back seat.

I don't remember great gatherings at Christmas. It was a low-key affair, with Bruce and me given only humble presents, e.g. an orange in a pillowcase. I had very few birthday parties.

When I was ten, I signed a pledge against drinking liquor. The wine served in church communion was almost non-alcoholic. Mother was not a drinker but liked a small sherry on occasions. You knew drinking was a bad thing, but every time there was a party or a funeral, there was always alcohol around. A cousin and I would drain the glasses when the adults weren't around – we thought the taste was ghastly.

Most important to us as kids was the capacity to ride and own a bike. That was freedom, possibility and the only means of escape! I was given my first bike when I was nine. It was a re-painted, dark red number called Peanut and one of my memorable thrills. Invercargill may have been flat, but it was seared by a biting east wind which could chill to the bone. The distance to Southland Girls' High School in south Invercargill could seem very long in bad weather.

I took a bike with me to Dunedin when I became a student, even though the topography was more challenging, but its main help was to get me to music lessons at St Dominic's Convent, a fair ride from the university area.

Because both my parents came from large families, there were always plenty of visits from relatives, especially on the Ferguson side. Sunday family visits were almost duty visits.

My father's family, the Cockrofts, originally came from Yorkshire but emigrated from Scotland. Adin Cockroft, my grandfather, married into a farming family from Waikaka Valley near Gore. He was a railway man and drove trains from Lumsden, where the family lived. My father, Johnny, born in 1895, became a messenger boy to do with telegraphs on the railway and eventually joined the Post Office. All the brothers joined some form of public service.

Our paternal grandmother was Annie McKenzie, née Mackay. My father spoke of her with great fondness. As a little girl, she had emigrated from rural Scotland with her brother, Donald. She and Adin had eight children. The first of the five sons, also named Adin, died of tuberculosis in his late teens. Annie died of the same disease, aged about 47, leaving this large family to be brought up mainly by the eldest daughter, Elizabeth (Auntie Bessie).

While Grandfather Cockroft was alive, we would be taken to see him – old and bedridden. He had been looked after by an unmarried niece called Dora. We also visited Auntie Bessie, now and then, on a Sunday afternoon. Her house was so scrupulously clean, we feared to move in it. Bessie became a Baptist and it was she who gave me my first Bible.

Notes

1   Verse 1, 'Life into Life, the Threads are Woven', written in 2007, as an expression of thanksgiving for life. It was published in 2009 in *Hope is our Song*, with music by Colin Gibson, and in her 2008 American collection *Touch the Earth Lightly*, with music by Jane Marshall.

2 – Growing up

Come, celebrate the women
who brought the Church to birth!
the gentle revolution
that shall transform the earth:

whose faith was salt and leaven,
whose hearts and minds were free,
and this was their direction –
to peace and unity.[1]

Some of this chapter is drawn from Shirley's account of her early life. It covers church and schooling experiences from the late 1930s to late 1940s, and some of her forays into poetry writing. Interspersed is material from the Association of Presbyterian Women (APW) interviews, 26 November 2001 and 7 November 2002, along with a variety of other sources.

None of my family were churchgoers during the time Bruce and I grew up. Dad had had a changing allegiance as a young man, going to whatever church had the best choir, but that was all. He had a good baritone voice. My grandmother and mother had also sung in church choirs of the Wesleyan kind. It was felt to be a good thing to send us off to the nearest Sunday school, which just happened to be Methodist.

So it was that we went every Sunday afternoon and then later, on to Bible class. I enjoyed the friends I made at Central Methodist Church, especially Faith Skene, who was one of a large family and also in my class at Southland Girls' High School (SGHS). Faith is a lifelong friend to this day and was the bridesmaid at our wedding. She married Bill Williamson. [Faith, whom Shirley nicknamed Fayo, died in 2022, aged 92.]

During my primary school years, I sometimes went to First Presbyterian Church for the evening service. My clearest memory is of the evening sun streaming through the stained-glass windows to the singing of 'Hail, gladdening light, of His pure glory poured…' We shared a lot of intergenerational singing at this time, but I usually had little idea what I was singing about.

Bible class camp at Easter (sometimes at Greenhills on the way to Bluff and later student camps at Pounawea) was a highlight. There was lots of social and spiritual energy. Our commitment centred around the crucifixion and our sins being forgiven.

The climax of the Sunday school year was the anniversary service. We learnt plays, sang, got a new dress and had ribbons in our hair. There were jellies and coloured cordials and food. Prizegiving included certificates for memory work and seals for learning the golden rule – 'Do unto others, as you would have them do unto you'. I am forever grateful I was made to memorise things – scripture, poetry, statements, quotations. It's a teaching tool par excellence.

> Shirley also wanted to get points, prizes and her name in the paper by contributing to the Little Pakehas Page, published in the *Southland Daily News* on Saturday night.

I sent in horrifically awful poems when I was quite young. Most kids' efforts were published. I would have been seven or eight. Uncle Jack was the manager of the *Southland Daily News*, and his friend, the lady editor of the Little Pakehas Page. Uncle Jack encouraged me to contribute and maybe gave me a penny or two. I also liked rhythm and rhyme, tying language together. My poetry might have been doggerel, but it had to have rhymes. It was sheer imitation of other forms. I stopped contributing by the age of ten or 11.

> One of Shirley's last contributions to the Little Pakehas Page was a poem about Christmas, perhaps the start of her later commitment to explore this most sung festival of the year. She kept a yellowing clipping of this poem her whole life.

Christmas time's the height of fun
Joy and cheer for everyone,
'Tis the children's great delight,
Gazing at shop windows bright.
Fascinated they will stand
In a Christmas Fairyland,
Hoping Father Christmas brings
Some of those enticing things.

Gifts are smuggled safe away,
Until comes that glorious day,
When these parcels are revealed,
Showing what they've long concealed.
Laughter dances everywhere,
Carols chime upon the air.
We exchange glad greetings gay,
For the coming Christmas Day.

I had been 'adopted' by an elderly Scottish couple, Mary and William Thomson, who lived in McMaster Street, and had no children of their own. They allowed me to do their 'messages' for them on my bike, and gave me many treats, including sweeties and pocket money. It was they who played and sang Scottish songs (Will played a fiddle) and introduced me to the Presbyterian culture of Scotland. I went with them to the St Andrew's Scottish Society gatherings where Burns suppers and the ritual of the haggis became familiar. What I most enjoyed was the singing of Scots songs and the poetry readings. Highland dancing was not a feature here but was always part of the Southland agricultural shows and dancing competitions.

I became a junior Sunday school teacher at Central Methodist Church, along with my friend Faith, probably recycling Bible stories. We were both about 14. Goodness knows what I knew to teach! Faith was good at arts and crafts, and I provided the prattle. We really had no idea what we were teaching. I can still see the faded pictures we used.

The arrival of new minister Robert Thornley became important to me as a teenager. He had had the experience of world travel, was a thoughtful and intelligent preacher and inspired me to much activity, including Easter camps and Bible class debates (anything to beat the dominant Presbyterians!).

The most important outcome of this was that he nominated me to go to the churches' first National Ecumenical Youth Conference, held at Blenheim in 1948. Because of our ages – I was not quite 17 – Robert had to bend the rules a little to help us attend. It changed our lives.

There I got a glimpse of what was outside Invercargill and what was happening around the world in terms of ecumenical enthusiasm. This ideal has never left me, despite the subsequent crumbling away of all the churches and the lack of any real unity.

Bible class was the focus of much social life, also Girl Guides. Bible class included dances in the church hall, though the Presbyterians did not dance. I also went to ballroom dancing classes once a week during my secondary school years.

Robert and his wife Dorothy were formative people for me – they were absolute phenomena, after so many dull ministers. They were young and energetic, and had come back from biking through Europe just before the Hitler regime. Faith and I became the permanent babysitters for their young children. The oldest, John, became the editor of [the biannual journal] *Music in the Air*. They widened our horizons, opening up an exciting world beyond Invercargill. In contrast, my mother was anchored to the south and never wanted to go anywhere else, though my father had travelled before marrying.

Dorothy had a huge influence on me. As a young mother she wore slacks at home, wedgie shoes, and was informal in her dress. She didn't worry about hats and gloves and continued to teach maths while having the last of her five children. She simply went on with her intellectual life and wasn't too bothered about what didn't get done. This impressed me tremendously. She was a keen teacher and was always trying to help people get on. The ladies of the parish may not have appreciated her in the beginning, but wartime changed women.

> Robert Thornley died on 1 November 2002. Shirley was not able to attend his funeral in Northland, but wrote a heartfelt letter to his son, John, soon after his death. Robert, Dorothy and their children had epitomised for her, at that time, 'the ideal family'.

"I feel an ongoing sense of gratitude which has never left me since I was a young person, being shown a wider world by both your parents. It is a rare and wonderful thing to have mentors like them, and to be given a sense of direction for the rest of one's days ...

"It was through Robert that I was introduced to the ecumenical movement, was given a pride in my Methodist tradition but the sense that there was more to discover ... I now know I was being tutored by a very fine teacher, as well as someone for whom the arts and music were essential soul food."

Shirley's involvement in Central Methodist Church life was clearly a busy one:

We had debating competitions with the Presbyterians. Both Faith and I enjoyed this. We felt we were the poor, small denomination in Southland. We had to hold our heads up for the sake of John and Charles Wesley – Methodism needed us! One topic, rather trivial as I remember, was: Was it essential to wear your best clothes to church on Sunday? We took the negative and won.

My friends were all from different denominations, and at ages 16 and 17, we all went to each other's First Communions [confirmations]. I remember feeling nervous going into an Anglican church. Our headmistress, Muriel May, became an Anglican and wore a little veil at her First Communion. She invited her 7th form along to witness the ceremony at St John's.

Schooling

Invercargill Middle School, in Spey Street, had a remarkable headmaster, George Griffiths. He loved music and insisted on teaching the tonic sol-fa system as a way to learn tunes by ear. I have much to thank him for in this. He ran a good ship in hard times during the war. My standards two and three teacher was a young man, Alex Bremer, who encouraged me to write poems. When he went off to do war service, I was desolated. Then he was killed. He wrote me a letter from the front, which I still treasure, encouraging me to keep writing.

Greenhills
2 / 10 / 40

Dear Shirley,

I just want to thank you for the especially good efforts you made whilst in my room.

You see, it's so cheering to know that people like you are in the room, working quietly, being bright and generally making the world a better place to live in. Just promise me that you will continue being the same splendid little girl, and that will be all I shall need to be sure that our fight is a just one.

Here is an excellent definition I found the other day. "Poetry is the blossom and the fragrancy of all human knowledge, human thoughts, human passions, emotions, language." Try to remember that part, and when you publish your book of poems, remember me, then send me a copy.

Yours sincerely,
Alex Bremer

The rationing we were exposed to was pretty generous. We were encouraged to be patriotic and to send things to pen friends in Britain, e.g. soap and chocolate. I was keen on pen pals. In my teenage years, a great appeal went out from young Polish airmen in Britain for young women pen pals in New Zealand. I would write in a very romantic vein. These young guys hoped that one day they might be sent to New Zealand and be rescued from where they were. I had one who I was sure would be the great love of my life.

Rationing for clothes was stressful. Mother, who was not a great sewer, had to make things out of old overcoats. Everything else went into army uniforms. Father, who was too old and not fit enough for service, was a local warden. Towards the end of the war, he dug a trench in the back garden because of the imminent invasion of the Japanese, which we believed would happen. Gas masks and trenches were more like symbols of protection and never put into practical use.

School life revolved around war efforts and raising money for soldiers, particularly during lunch hours and playtimes. We knitted khaki mittens and scarves, sold soup at school – tomato soup cans, with lots of milk – and raised pennies by holding concerts during lunchtimes. I had two older cousins on my father's side whose fiancés were pilots and were killed during the Battle of Britain. And my mother's youngest brother died of an accident at Burnham Camp.

I was dux of the school in 1943 and went on to SGHS, along with my best buddy, Lindsey Harrington. I had met Lindsey through Girl Guides, though she went to a different primary school. We became the senior guides in the Rangers Company and for a while, ran proceedings. [The guiding movement was also active at SGHS, with 39 members and six patrols in 1945.] We clicked, stayed close friends and ended up rooming together at St Margaret's College in Dunedin. Our lives were intertwined thereafter.

Principal Muriel May had the capacity to terrify and her imprint on the school was impressive. She loved English literature and Shakespeare, taught both very well, was an idiosyncratic professional and steered the school through the war years with aplomb and style. I was eager to please, started off well and quickly discovered I was at home with words but not much good with maths, science or geography.

Shirley was a regular contributor to the school magazine. "This had quite a high standard and you had to be quite sophisticated to get into it," she said. As a third-former, she had this droll contribution published:

The Spider and the Fly

"Will you come into my schoolroom?" the teacher said to me,
"'Tis the sweetest little classroom you could ever wish to see;
The way to fame and knowledge is up this cold stone stair,
And whoever climbs this pathway will be very happy there."

"Pray don't persuade me, teacher," I firmly did reply,
"Your gloomy, bare, old classroom I happened to espy,
And what I saw did shock me. The pupils sitting there
Looked quite distraught and worried, with ink blots everywhere.

"I will not enter, thank you, for I am much too wise,
I won't become a scholar in your Realm of Paradise.
Oh no, you can't enrol me in your golden book of fame,
For whoever climbs that pathway will ne'er return the same."

Three years later, Sonnet to My School Hat, encapsulates Shirley's love of the absurd.

Sonnet to My School Hat

(as done by William S.)

When I have seen by Time's fell hand defaced
The rich proud cost of outworn hats I know,
I see that thou could'st never be replaced
While I survive to wear them, mon chapeau.

To me, fair Friend, you never can be old
But as you were when first your form I eyed
You are not still. Four winters cold
Have taken shape away and hue beside.

Shall I compare thee to a summer's day?
Thou art less lovely, I confess, but still
Though rough winds shake thy beauty as they may
Th'elastic holds thee on, let come what will.

This though is as a death, which cannot choose
But weep to have that which it fears to lose.

Other school activities included joining the choir, later becoming part of the special sextet, and drama, mainly Shakespeare.

In September 2009, Shirley sent several memorabilia to the school archives, enclosing a letter to then principal Yvonne Browning. The package included a short autobiography of her life and a copy of her 'Hymn for Anzac Day', published in 2008. "SGHS was an incredibly significant part of my life," she wrote. "All my lifelong friends were made at SGHS … One of these friends is former Principal, Elizabeth Clarkson [née Deaker]."

She writes of her debt to the principal of her time, Miss Muriel May, "who insisted I go further and try for a secondary school teachers' bursary (then newly created) which set me up for life and made university possible".

Miss May also made a huge impression on Shirley's lifelong friend Pamela Norris (later Laytham). She often spoke of being part of an inner circle of senior pupils. Shirley called it 'a Miss Jean Brodie type of thing', where Miss May cultivated girls whom she believed could be scholarship winners. Pamela remembered being invited into Miss May's study where this special group of girls could discuss their futures and learn the art of cigarette smoking.

"Muriel smoked Sobranies, a sophisticated European brand of slim, brown cigarettes," said Pamela's daughter Jacqué Mandeno. "She taught them that, as young ladies, they could do whatever they liked. They could smoke, go to university, make their own choices. This Invercargill friendship group lasted their whole lives."

Shirley continues:

Books were very important – we were great library users. Father and mother were always reading books of some sort or another. I always had access to story books and poetry books. I particularly liked the poetry books. I got books as prizes all the way through high school. One was a book by a New Zealand poet, Gloria Rawlinson – she impressed me at the time. But I couldn't latch onto *Alice in Wonderland*. I liked fairy stories and had a collection I read for years. I loved the comic *Felix the Cat*. As soon as I could read, I was left to read by myself.

By her third year at high school, Shirley was given time off to do extra music and Latin instead of maths. She won the speech prize as a third-former and later, the Shakespeare Reading Prize.

Shirley became head prefect in 1948, her upper sixth year. During her time at the school, assemblies were semi-religious occasions, with the head prefect given the role of placing the large Bible on the lectern and often reading from it. Girls would process in carrying their copies of *Hymns of the Kingdom*. Assemblies would include at least one hymn and would end with the singing of the Lord's Prayer. Shirley was often the piano accompanist.

In 1948, the Great Trek and Long March occurred. This was when the school relocated from the corner of Forth and Ness Streets to its new site in Tweed Street, where it continues. The event was even captured on film. During the Great Trek, girls carried a chair each to the new school, while others transported the 3000 library books on their bicycles. Senior chemistry pupils were given the solemn responsibility of carrying the dangerous chemicals over to the new school. And at the head of the procession was Shirley, along with Miss May and her staff.

Moving to a large, light, wooden building was wonderful – it was so different from the old concrete building and prefabs that were dumped on our old site during the war.

When the school was officially opened by the Minister of Education [Terry McCombs], I represented the voice of the students on the local radio station, 4YZ. That was quite formidable and a hugely new experience.

Learning music

When I was seven, I began piano lessons with Mrs Boyd, along Elles Road. Mrs Boyd was convent-trained and a firm teacher who insisted on my doing exams (always Royal Schools of Music, not Trinity College until later). Her fees were two guineas a term, a sum my parents had to find on their limited income. I hated taking home the bill.

So, I progressed up the grades until I was about 11, when I went on strike. My mother wisely let me be for a year and then Mrs Boyd persuaded me to keep on going. This was fortuitous because music became a subject in the new School Certificate curriculum and was an advantage to me. I changed to Trinity College and did the Teachers' ATCL when I was 16, in the same year as doing University Entrance (which was then accredited).

I never enjoyed performing but loved accompanying songs (as I did with John in our early days) and have always loved finding songs and hymns to play. This stood me in good stead in our first parish in Taihape, where I was often the only organist. Good tunes in any style are a marvellous thing to me.

My last year at SGHS was very busy, with scholarship exams at the end of it and the hope of a secondary school teachers' bursary, which I did get, and which paid more than a scholarship. This was a huge relief, since I had no other way of going to university. This paid my fees and gave me an allowance of £112 a year. This covered my board at St Margaret's [residential college] and train travel home in the holidays. When it came time to leave, Uncle Jack and Nana gave me £100, which made the difference between total penury and being as poor as the other students.

Although Shirley had enjoyed her school days in Invercargill, she was clearly keen to leave the city as soon as possible. In an APW interview, she credits Muriel May with encouraging her to go to the University of Otago. "She was ambitious for her girls and wanted them to get scholarships and bursaries." Her father, Shirley said, had jacked up a job for her as a trainee secretary at State Insurance, as he fully expected her to "get married anyway". Miss May, in an unusual gesture, even visited Shirley's parents to persuade them that that was not what she should be doing. Considering her parents' "great insecurity about money because they did not have much of it", it was an enormous relief to them and to her when she won a teachers' bursary. Shirley was the first at the school to get this newly-fledged grant.

In her testimonial for Shirley, written near the end of 1948, Muriel May's last paragraph reads:

"If Miss Cockroft were a boy, she would probably be nominated as a Rhodes Scholar. As a Post-Primary Teachers' Bursar, she would work with intelligence and enthusiasm, and to every activity in which she engaged, she would bring charm and co-operation."

The terms of the bursary were that Shirley had to achieve a degree up to master's, go for a year to Teachers' College and repay the money by teaching for the number of years she had trained. As a woman, she was allowed to cancel the repayment if she got married. Oh that she had known what this might mean!

Notes

1   Verse 1, 'Come, Celebrate the Women', written in 1979 as a reaction to the 1923 hymn, 'Let Us Now Praise Famous Men', by Ralph Vaughan Williams. It was published in Shirley's 1987 private collection and in her first publication with Hope, *In Every Corner Sing*, where Shirley notes: "To me, it is basic to remember that movements for peace and unity have always been strongly supported and often initiated by women."

3 – Meeting John Murray

This thread I weave,
this step I dance,
this stone I carve
this ball I bounce,
this nail I drive,
this pearl I string
this flag I wave,
this note I sing:[1]

This chapter comprises the final sections from Shirley's story of her early life. It covers her experiences at university in Dunedin, her musical studies and involvement in the Student Christian Movement. The content is interspersed with material from an APW interview, 19 November 2002, along with a variety of other sources. John Murray's family background is explained.

I was 16 in October 1947 when I went to Dunedin to compete in a French-speaking contest, representing SGHS. It was there I met (and vanquished) one of the other competitors, John Murray from King's High, with his friend, Colin Newbury.

> According to a report in the *Otago Daily Times* on 7 October 1947, Colin Newbury won the competition, while the judges could not separate Shirley Cockroft and two other female students (Elizabeth Deaker from SGHS, and Mary Greig). They were given honourable mentions and John came third.

This is where the somewhat competitive element in our relationship had its origins. John thought he was going to win but didn't. Colin

Newbury turned out to be the best man at our wedding. John and Colin were out to impress and took Elizabeth Deaker and me for a walk in the afternoon after the results were announced. A correspondence of some intensity began after I went home. [Shirley and John never dated anyone else, though Shirley had her share of admirers.]

> In an APW interview, Shirley admits she was not a great sportsperson, though she did her best at netball. She once went to Dunedin with the netball team, which gave her another chance to meet up with John.[2]

Saying goodbye to Invercargill was not difficult, except for my dear parents, and especially my father, who saw that a new life was beginning for me, away from the home scene for good. Mum was, as ever, more philosophic and, I think, pleased I would do better than she had been able to. I went off by train, along with a group of friends whom I knew well, and the excitement was enormous.

So was the apprehension. What if I did not pass the exams and lost my bursary? I spent the whole of my first year worrying this might happen and was astonished to get three A passes and a B for the four arts subjects I took – English, Latin, French and Music. The only hitch was that St Margaret's [residential college] did not give my friend Lindsey Harrington a place and she had to stay on a waitlist till the very last moment, at which point they relented. So began our student life, and all the lifelong friends I made there.

> Shirley also had cousins at St Margaret's, but it was the small group of friends that came with her from SGHS who meant the most to her. They included Lindsey, Faith Skene, Pamela Norris and Elizabeth Deaker.

We were also close friends of the year ahead of us. It was a great change for us. We loved the independence, the sheer fun, the naughtiness, the new life opening up. It was all so different from everything I knew. We had rules, curfews at night, girls only.

> According to Shirley and John's son Alastair Murray, Lindsey and Shirley shared a room at St Margaret's. Lindsey would often return home late, somewhat the worse for wear, and throw stones

at their window to wake Shirley up. "Shirley would let her in, then help her throw up so they could both get some sleep. They were heartfelt mates, even though leading rather different lifestyles," he said.

Two important groups I joined were the Student Christian Movement [SCM], recommended by Robert Thornley (this was the group to join, he said, not the Evangelical Union), and the university choir, A Capella. SCM provided an entrée to ideas and people who have influenced me ever since – I owe a tremendous amount to the SCM. While I was totally ignorant of theology, I learned some concepts by osmosis, especially since the divinity students from Knox College constituted our social circle, as well as opinionated and (to my eyes) other sophisticated arts faculty students. I had several 'expressions of interest' from various ones but was generally considered to be John Murray's girlfriend. One particular and brilliant friend was Don Anderson, born with cerebral palsy, who later went to Oxford and returned to teach at Massey University.

The choir introduced me to Bach's *Magnificat* and Fauré's *Requiem*, as well as Handel and Purcell. More importantly, it contained many of my lifelong friends, such as Charles Naylor,[3] and also medical student Nigel Eastgate, the choir's accompanist for some of the time, who eventually married Lindsey. Nigel introduced me to Benjamin Britten, calligraphic writing and medical students' jokes. [Shirley was Lindsey's bridesmaid at her wedding to Nigel on 6 February 1954. Sadly, Lindsey died of ovarian cancer in 1979, aged 49.]

I loved dancing — there were college and graduation balls, and all the fun of dressing up for such. Few of us ever drank anything alcoholic because we couldn't afford it, and the daring female types who did were few. Male students took to home brew or beer of some sort. It was thought incredibly sophisticated to drink wine, and there was not a great choice of wine, anyway. New Zealand had yet to discover its reputation for producing quality wines.

I carried on with my music lessons at the Dominican convent, where I was taught by Mother Bonaventure, a large and lovely person, who kept me up to scratch. I greatly enjoyed my friendship with her. She loved hearing gossip from outside the convent walls. She was like an abbess with her white knitted stockings and big motherly figure.

I had finished my ATCL teachers' diploma in Invercargill under Thelma Boyd, but Mother Bonaventure had ambitions for me, e.g. switching me to the Royal Schools system. But I got overloaded and after one good year with her, I stopped.

Fortunately, I could use the piano at St Margaret's. We had a university trio who performed in the dining room, my first experience of proper chamber music. War rationing was continuing – we would put our butter rations for the week, labelled, in a locked cupboard outside the dining room. The food was fairly horrible, but we weren't too worried.

My musical ear came down to me on both sides of my family and I am grateful for that. I have always sung alto. I almost gave away church because I got tired of going to the Methodist church in the Octagon, which seemed fairly fuddy-duddy. SCM events happened on Sundays. I even signed up to a course run by religious studies Professor Albert Moore at 8am – I think I was looking for some desirable male company. Albie was going to teach us the theology of Karl Barth. I have never related to Barth, except he said all of theology could be summed up in the words "Jesus loves me, this I know".

We didn't have much money, but we did lots. There were SCM camps – we thought we were changing the world by what we thought. I worked in the holidays, including waitressing at Invercargill's Grand Hotel. [She was working there when Queen Elizabeth II visited the city on 29 January 1954. According to Alastair Murray, Shirley was the third fruit bowl bearer during this momentous occasion.] We would get tips from non-New Zealanders – just enough to make it worthwhile. We were also allowed to do a few weeks temporary teaching at the beginning of the secondary year, before uni began – that was real money.

Chair of the classics department was Professor Guy Manten, who arrived in 1949. Dr Agathe Thornton had arrived in 1948, the year before I began university. She was a noted German scholar who had been to Cambridge. Her husband was Harry Thornton, a Scottish Presbyterian minister. She was a mentor to me. I became super ambitious and had a mild academic breakdown. She took me aside and taught me better discipline in the way I tackled languages. "Do your language vocab in the morning when you are fresh," she would say. "Don't worry about it in the afternoon."

Agathe was an incredible role model. She held down a full-time job and had two small children. She was the first at the university to overturn the rule that married women with children could not be employed. I would sometimes babysit for her. She was a wonderful teacher. She had crimped, flyaway red hair, now snowy white. I still see the red hair.

Agathe had got a shock when she went to a parish in Scotland with her husband, and discovered what it was like to be treated as a manse wife, amongst what sounded like grey, granite attitudes. She never ceased to be a scholar.

The SCM group, sometimes referred to as the Society for Christian Marriage, was highly politicised and we were keen to do some form of evangelism. A charismatic drama lecturer from England, a Quaker, began producing plays for the SCM. One was *The House by the Stable* by Charles Williams, a sort of morality play. [See photo p97.] We all lined up for auditions. John Murray took one of the leading parts, along with Paul Oestreicher, Boyd Glassey,[4] Louise Petherbridge and Owen Robinson.[5]

Our first performance was in Dunedin's St Paul's Cathedral, then we toured the play as far as Wellington, staying in church halls on the way. We only had one car among us. We also performed it at the SCM conference in Wellington, where such luminaries as [Methodist minister and Christian pacifist] Ormond Burton addressed us. Taking part in plays really helped us meld as a group and most of us are still close friends.

> It was at the 1954 SCM conference that Paul Oestreicher, who later became an Anglican priest and peace activist, remembers kissing Shirley under the mistletoe at Scots College in Wellington on New Year's Eve. "I have never forgotten that kiss, even though she was already John's," he said. "It was my last year at university. This moment of connection has stayed with me my whole life."

> Another production the group got involved in was a one-act play, *The Director Comes to Dinner,* performed by members of the University French Club in 1950. The *Otago Daily Times* reported on 5 April that the play was "presented in a bright and lively

manner", with four performers including John Murray, Colin Newbury and Shirley Cockroft.

For the first couple of years at uni, I was a staunch Methodist. But I could see that my faith lay with the Presbyterian Church, which was dominant anyway. We were in a whirlwind of changing denominational allegiances. I could see you didn't have to stay loyal to a denomination. This was not connected to what you believed.

John was my exclusive friend, but we were so busy with groups of friends. John lived at home in a large brick house at Forbury Corner at St Clair and I lived in a hostel. I felt sorry for him to be still living at home, missing out on the essence of student life. We always knew we would get together at some stage officially. In Dunedin, we walked and biked mostly. John would sometimes borrow his mother's little Austin.

In my final year, I moved to Huntly, the old house turned into flats where senior St Margaret's members could go. I flatted there with Lindsey and Pamela. John and I got engaged in February 1952. After he had graduated with an MA in Latin, first class honours, he did some part-time tutoring in the classics department. Besides me, there was only one other person in the class. John left for Cambridge, England, in August that year.

But near the end of 1952, when I was working madly, doing my honours year in Latin and French, John's parents offered to have me at Forbury Corner, which not only saved me money but was a quiet place to work. That was an experience in itself and all part of taking on the name and family of Murray.

John Murray's background

John Stewart Murray was born in 1929 to a Scottish family living in Dunedin. He was proud of his Scottish ancestry, which flowed from both his maternal and paternal lines. His father, Dr Stewart Murray, was a GP, and his mother, Muriel Mercer, a nurse. He was the youngest of four children, preceded by three sisters, Rae, Noreen and Marjorie.

He was surrounded by doctors, nurses, and sisters who became teachers. Shirley would one day say about her husband that it was only natural he, too, would go into a life of service.

The first Mercer immigrant landed in Dunedin in 1848 on the *Philip Laing*, one of the first two ships to arrive in Otago. The New Zealand connection on his paternal side came 37 years later.

John's grandfather, the Rev Charles Murray, had come from a tenant farming family in Aberdeenshire, as explained in a family history written by John's nephew, Roderick Stewart Edmond, a professor of English at the University of Kent in Canterbury.[6] Charles Murray attended Aberdeen University and studied theology at the Free Church College in Aberdeen before coming to Dunedin in 1885. He was ordained there before leaving New Zealand to become a missionary to the New Hebrides, now Vanuatu. He replaced his brother, the Rev William Murray, who had served and died there.

When this mission failed and following the death of his first wife, Flora Cheyne, Charles returned to New Zealand, taking up ministry positions in several North Island rural parishes. He later built a thriving parish in Sydenham, Christchurch. He was known for his strong anti-liquor abolitionist and pacifist views, opposing New Zealand involvement in World War I, and clashing with many in the Presbyterian hierarchy over his anti-war campaigning.

John's father, Charles Stewart Murray, was born in 1894 to Charles' second wife Grace Boag, who was from a well-known Canterbury farming family. Following training at the Otago Medical School, Charles became a GP, then joined the Army Medical Corps, serving in Fiji during World War II. After marrying Muriel in 1918, he worked in the North Island settlements of Rotorua and Maungapōhatu during the 1919 'flu epidemic. Charles senior died in 1925 at the age of 66.

In 1928, Charles Stewart built a house at Forbury Corner in South Dunedin, where the family lived and from where he ran his doctor's practice, with Muriel helping with the administration. The Stewarts had a family pew at St Andrew's Presbyterian Church in central Dunedin, though Charles would often choose to visit his patients rather than attend Sunday worship. He retired in the mid-1950s, and the house and practice were sold.

John attended St Clair School before becoming a foundation pupil at the new Macandrew Intermediate. At King's High School, he met and became lifelong friends with Hugh Templeton (later to become a cabinet minister in the National Government of Robert Muldoon) and Colin Newbury. The trio became known as 'the three musketeers' by the school's masters.

Hugh recalls John's leadership qualities and creative way of bringing people together. These were clear even as a teenager, with a young Murray organising an end-of-year concert at the school where boys 'took the mickey' out of the masters.

Another King's High School pupil and university friend, Paul Oestreicher, remembers John and Shirley's budding relationship well. "Like so many of my friends, I promptly fell in love with Shirley – everyone did," he said. "Everybody envied John. She was clearly John's girlfriend and that was that. Shirley was irresistible, her enthusiasm, her simplicity. She was magnetic. She did not have to try hard, as it was in her nature to be outgoing, beautiful, friendly. She was easy to get on with."

In a 2006 interview, John said that early on he had never wanted to be a minister. It was only during his final university honours year that he had felt 'the call' to ministry.[7]

According to John and Shirley's son David, John's father was not keen when John announced he was going to be a minister, as he knew only too well the reality of growing up with a minister father.

After John and Hugh had completed their university master's studies, they travelled to Britain together on the *SS Rangitane*, arriving in Southampton in late summer. Hugh had won a Rhodes Scholarship to study history at Oxford, while John had won a Lewis and Gibson Scholarship from the University of Cambridge to do theological training at Westminster College. "We were part of a whole group going to Cambridge, including future Presbyterian Church leaders like Phil Spencer and Ken Orange. We indulged in deck golf and English marmalade. It was the best holiday in the world," said Hugh.

Between gaining my MA [Second Class Honours in Latin and French] and saving up desperately to go to England, I discovered the restrictions of my government bursary. An engagement ring was not enough to qualify for leaving New Zealand without fulfilling the four years of teaching – I had to be legally married. So, I had to work to earn enough to pay that debt off, and the only way round this was to take a job as a boarding school mistress. Luckily, I found such a job in Dunedin, at St Hilda's Anglican School for Girls.

My interview was short and definitive: I was to take all senior French and Latin classes, and a few of the fourth form. I at once became Head of Department in two subjects! The very English headmistress left me to my own (untrained) devices, and I found myself enjoying teaching very much. What I found less enjoyable was looking after the 30 or so boarders (aged 5-17) during the weekends and taking evening chapel services from *The Book of Common Prayer*. But it was all further education for what was to follow when I eventually got on the boat to travel to England.

Every month, after my debt to the Education Department was deducted, I had £1 13s 4d left over. That was just enough to scrape by on but allowed no saving whatsoever. I lived in a shabby old part of the college wooden buildings, where it was bitterly cold and mice were seen to run across the bedside table. Still, I liked the friends I made there among the other staff and we were all hard up in one way or another. I kept in touch with my other student friends left in Dunedin and went on a regular basis to Forbury Corner for Saturday tea.

A testimonial by the English headmistress, E.H.K. Mitchell, written after Shirley had worked there for four terms, describes her as someone with "a strong character, high ideals, a quiet and dignified manner and a good personality. We shall be very sorry indeed to lose so promising a mistress."

Notes

1   Verse 1, 'This Thread I Weave', written in 1987, was never conceived as a hymn. The poem was first published in Hope's *In Every Corner Sing*, with a melody by American composer Jane Marshall. It also appears in the NZHBT's publication *Faith Forever Singing*.

2   APW interview with Sheila Irwin, 19 November 2002.

3   These three friends – Charles Naylor, Boyd Glassey and Owen Robinson – all became prominent ministers in the New Zealand Presbyterian Church.

4   See note 3.

5   See note 3.

6   Edmond, R.S. (2013) *Migrations: Journeys in Time and Place*. Wellington: Bridget Williams Books, pp9-12, 179-206.

7   From interviews with Ann Barrie for the St Andrew's on The Terrace oral history project, September-November 2006.

4 – First years together

When we lift our pack and go,
when we seek another country,
moving far from all we know,
when we long to journey free –
Refrain:
God is in the other place,
God is in another's face,
in the faith we travel by,
God is in the other place.[1]

This chapter is compiled from interviews with Sheila Irwin for the APW, 19 November 2002, and an interview with Margaret Pannett for the St Andrew's on The Terrace oral history project, 7 November 2006. John and Shirley's wedding in England, experiences in Bossey, Switzerland, and the couple's eventual return to New Zealand are covered.

I got married in Cambridge, England, on 21 July 1954. My parents accepted that my life was going to be unpredictable, but my father was cut up about it. He had been practising his wedding speech for years. Mother was more philosophical.

I travelled by ship, the *SS Rangitoto*, from Wellington. My dear friend Faith Skene came with me to be my bridesmaid and to do her 'OE'. I took my wedding dress with me and borrowed things from friends who had already got married. Faith wore the same outfit she had worn at two of her sisters' weddings.

The 9 October 1954 edition of the *Southland Daily News* carried a description of the bride's and bridesmaid's dresses. Published under the heading News and Views for Women, it read: "The bride, who was given away by Mr H.W. Norris, of Invercargill, wore a gown of white broderie anglaise with a Medici collar and bracelet length sleeves featured on the fitting bodice … she carried a bouquet of pink and cream roses.

"Her attendant, Miss Fay [sic] Skene … wore a frock of net in pink and mauve tonings and an Elizabethan-style headdress of the same material and carried a bouquet of matching colours."

John put a notice on the Westminster College noticeboard a week before the wedding, inviting anyone who was still around on Wednesday at 12pm (the summer holidays had started) to come along to the college chapel. Amazingly, 26 New Zealanders turned up, including some from Oxford, plus the odd Scot. That was terrific for us.

It was a real do-it-yourself wedding, with guests coming early to make the sandwiches in the college kitchen. Our special friend Don Anderson gave the toast to the bride and groom, Hugh Templeton and his twin Ian were there, and Colin Newbury [studying history at Westminster College on a travelling scholarship] was our best man. John's Aunt Flora from Scotland attended. I was given away by the father of one of my close friends [Pamela] from St Margaret's, Mr Norris. I was 23.

Hugh, who had finished his studies at Oxford University, had joined External Affairs and was working in London. He remembers John and Shirley kneeling in Westminster Chapel.

Alastair Murray believes his father got lucky marrying Shirley and he knew it. "He was slightly in awe of her intellect and thoughtfulness. There was no ideological difference between Mum and Dad – they saw the world from the same perspective and really complemented each other."

Birth control was an issue, as John was still studying, so before I left New Zealand, I went to my doctor in Invercargill and had a rubber diaphragm inserted. I had another check in Cambridge on the National

Health Service. Nobody seemed to talk about contraception in those days, though I talked to my student friends about it a lot. These were pre-contraceptive pill days. The issue was all fairly theoretical for most of us.

We spent another year and a bit in Cambridge, with John incredibly busy completing his theological studies in Cambridge. I got a little job in a private dame school, teaching nine to ten-year-old boys, children of the dons. They taught me so much. I felt so lucky to get the job, which the local Presbyterian church in Cambridge, St Columba's, helped me get. It was badly paid, but interesting work. It was an exciting year, meeting John's friends.

After John had completed his BA in theology (he also gained a licence to be a preacher through the Theological College of the Presbyterian Church of England), he took up a scholarship he had won to study for a diploma at the Ecumenical Institute at Bossey, near Geneva. [This was part of the World Council of Churches and attached to the University of Geneva.] He chose to do this rather than be an apprentice minister in Scotland.

We travelled to Bossey (for the winter graduate course) on a Vespa scooter, one of the first to be made in England. Our aim was to see a bit of Europe on the way. Getting a visa to get into Vienna, still occupied by the Russians, was stressful. But by the time we got there, the Russians had left.

> Before heading to Europe, the couple stayed with Hugh in London, sleeping on the floor of his Richmond apartment. Hugh was impressed at how brave they were to travel all that way on a scooter.

> The couple travelled 5000 miles, visiting France, Germany, Holland and Austria. It may have been on this trip that John and Shirley first visited the Taizé community, an ecumenical monastic fraternity in Burgundy, France. This community, along with Iona in Scotland, which the couple most likely visited earlier in 1955, remained for them both powerful symbols of the gospel at work in the world, and as examples of effective ecumenism.

John described their journey by scooter as "a free and easy life during a long summer in Europe".[2] Their trip became the stuff of legend among the Murray family.

Again, they had no money while John studied at the institute for just over four months. He lived in, with free board, while Shirley found a job as a housemaid "to a rather strange Anglo-Swiss family" in a village outside Geneva, looking after three pampered children and doing the housework. She also did some teaching.

Housework proved not to be my forte. I never wanted to do wire-scrubbing of parquet floors again! Being winter, it was also very cold. I remember the sheets going stiff as cardboard when I hung them out on the line.

We began to see that we needed to come home in order to settle John's ministry, rather than take up offers to minister in either Scotland or England. John wanted to launch himself into a parish.

When John and Shirley returned to Cambridge in February 1956, a letter from the interim moderator (leader) of St David's Presbyterian Church in Taihape, the Rev Collin Sherriff, was waiting for them. Collin urged John to accept the call to be the parish's next minister. The parish had already tried 13 other preachers for the role, before resigning themselves to calling John. Some regarded him as "too young, too educated" but at least willing and available.

We travelled back to New Zealand on the *SS Southern Cross* – a wonderful six-week holiday – and were met at the wharf in Wellington by Collin Sherriff. The parish had been vacant for two or more years, and many people approached had turned it down. Collin begged us to accept. We also looked at Tuatapere in Southland but Taihape, in the south-central North Island, was our choice. It was a good place to make mistakes!

We arrived to a bare house at 13 Kōkako Street – there were not many options in Taihape. But we were delighted to be self-sufficient at last. John bought me an electric blanket – he knew how much I had suffered in England and Switzerland. The house had poor heating but it had some good features.

John was busy running two services on a Sunday and other monthly services at smaller country churches. I did not go looking for work as I soon got pregnant. Most women of my generation thought we should be helpmates to our husbands, supporting their careers. I did some teaching at Taihape District High School because they were short of a history teacher. I enlisted in a correspondence course in Old Testament studies, tutored by the Rev Charles Harrison whom I had known from my student days. I did this for a couple of years. It filled an enormous gap for me.

I felt a bit lost with most of my friends living in the South Island, but one makes friends in a parish anyway. We were adopted by salt-of-the-earth people who knocked us into shape. Gradually we got a feel for the New Zealand rural situation – we had to learn this from scratch.

The Presbyterian Women's Missionary Union (PWMU) had been chugging along for many years until the parish vacancy. Members wanted me to be the president – a role where you had to think up devotions and open meetings. You then moved on to the busy bee sale and fundraising. I offered to play the organ instead, though I never saw myself as an organist. I did attend their meetings – it was part of one's duty. John and I started the fireside circle for younger people. Most groups were ways of helping people make friends. We also set up a group of singers – that was fun.

People would turn up at the manse door at any time of the day or night. I found this quite alarming in the beginning. Vagrants would often come by, hoping for free food. We then found out the mayor had a fund for such things, so we sent them around the corner. There were occasions when we were taken in by con men. One long-term visitor turned out to be a criminal. He had smooth charm and knew exactly how to take us all in. He was also a great tenor singer!

Church people travelling north or south would often stay at the manse, like the Rev Jack Somerville, John's good friend from St Andrew's in Wellington.

The heating in the house was eventually fixed and the church improved. We continued to travel on our old Vespa to start with. Finally, at great expense, we bought a car – a green Vauxhall Velox.

It cost the equivalent of a whole year's salary and felt like the most terrible mortgage of our lives.

For the first few years, we travelled round the countryside, but the dust and smell of sheep got to me in the end, especially during the hot summers. We would sometimes escape to the big cities of Whanganui and Palmerston North. Sometimes we went up to the Waimarino Parish to see our neighbours on that side, Collin and his wife Wanda. She gave me lots of practical advice about being a minister's wife – no holds barred. On the other side was the Mangaweka Parish where the Rev Bruce Bissett and his wife, Isabel, had nine children! She was a quiet academic who loved books. I was scared of her children who kept a tame possum. They lived a frugal life.

The Taihape years were happy, though slightly lonely for me. Two of our children were born at the local maternity hospital, David in 1957 and Alastair in 1961. The maternity hospital had 15 beds, many occupied by unmarried mothers, sent to the country to have their babies. I became close friends to some of them. One even left us a piece of land in her will.

As new parents, we were well supported, and inundated with bootees and bonnets. The parish made us part of their family. They were also generous with gifts of food. In the 1950s, food was still expensive. Every Sunday, a whole quart of cream and legs and shoulders of lamb would appear. And we would often be given unplucked ducks in the duck-shooting season. We did bury a few.

> Eldest son David has fond memories of the five years he lived in Taihape. From his earliest years, these memories involve music. "Mum would sit beside my bed singing me to sleep or play the piano in the Taihape lounge. She would always be playing one of her favourite pieces of music."

The parish clerk, David Gordon, and his wife were very supportive. He was the first person I ever heard admit he could not say the whole of the Nicene Creed because he did not believe certain lines. It took me a while to understand why this was so. He felt the church should be exploring new ideas. He was a great help to John. Two ministers had laid the ground before us. There were also some conservative members on the session [the elected body of church elders]. It proved difficult to get even one new idea across to these men. Numbers on the session doubled to 11 while John was there, and two women were elected. [In 1956, the Presbyterian Church's annual General Assembly had allowed women to join sessions.] It was a struggle to get there but they were well respected.

Our closest friends were some Dutch immigrants, Martin and Aura Roestenburg, who were working on a farm. They had arrived in New Zealand in 1951 and, like us, were strangers in this place.

St David's became quite active in the community, running singing groups, an art exhibition around Christmas time, and other cultural events. In 1958, John asked Martin, who was an artist, to create a Christmas stable. This was built on the back of a wagon and displayed by the clock tower in the middle of town. It lasted for a number of Christmases.

Hugh Templeton looks back fondly to his wedding to Natasha Tver on 22 August 1959 at St David's. He had met Natasha, a Russian refugee, in Wellington in 1957. "Natasha had just returned from London where she had been studying drama," he recalled. "We decided rather quickly we would get married. With John being my oldest, dearest friend, having him marry us almost felt preordained.

"We had a very small wedding, just John and Shirley, and my twin brother Ian and sister-in-law Hannah. We spent the weekend with John and Shirley, then they married us and sent us away laughing. I still have the Anglican *Book of Common Prayer* that John inscribed and gave me as a little gift."

Twenty-five years later, Hugh would serve as John's session clerk at St Andrew's on The Terrace in Wellington, holding the position for ten years from 1984. "John was a hard man to say no to!" Hugh said.

A long-time member of St Andrew's on The Terrace, Pam Ormsby, remembers visiting the Murrays in Taihape in 1959, when she was on the executive of the Citizens' All Black Tour Association (CABTA). She was also a member of the Presbyterian Public Questions Committee. Formed in September 1959, CABTA aimed to combat racial discrimination in the selection of the rugby team to tour South Africa in 1960.

"There was good support in metropolitan areas for this cause to have Māori players included," Ormsby said, "but support was not so good in the country. Our minister, the Rev Jack Somerville, suggested I got hold of young Murray up in Taihape, which I did, bringing copies of the national petition – No Maoris – No Tour! – with me.

"I arrived on the bus from Wellington. Shirley met me at the bus stop, gave me lunch, then took me back to the bus to continue going north. They had a hell of a job trying to win support in Taihape, as it was such a conservative little town. But that did not stop John. He promoted the petition at St David's and through articles in the local newspaper. There was an Anglican priest at Raetihi, not too far away, who, like John, was also a supporter."

The petition attracted around 160,000 signatures, "a record number for its day, though ultimately the Rugby Union and the Government ignored it. A lily-white team was chosen instead," said Pam. "Those who marched against the tour in 1959-60 were still marching in 1981."

John said: "Supporting CABTA and the petition certainly did not gain me great popularity at that time." [3]

Support for women to be elected to the session and commitment to anti-racism in sporting contacts with South Africa were just some of the issues John and Shirley were espousing. Protest action against social injustice of many kinds was to mark John's ministry and find expression in Shirley's hymns in the decades to come.

Notes

1 Verse 1, 'When We Lift Our Pack and Go' ('Song for Travellers'), written in 1988, with settings by Ian Render and Jenny McLeod. Published in Hope's *In Every Corner Sing* in 1992 and in *Alleluia Aotearoa* in 1993.

2 From interviews with Ann Barrie for the St Andrew's on The Terrace oral history project, September-November 2006.

3 See note 2.

Part II – Finding Her Voice

5 – Tumult of the '60s

We must leave home to feel the wind of the Spirit,
we must leave home to find our faith and to stir it!

Taking the risky road that Jesus has travelled,
Seeing the knotted threads of doctrine unravelled.[1]

The Murrays spent six years in Taihape, somewhat less time than a minister was expected to stay in a first parish. In the late 1950s, John was invited to become ecumenical chaplain at Victoria University, Wellington. He turned the offer down reluctantly.

A year and a half later, he was invited again, and this time accepted. The opportunity to work in an ecumenical position was attractive to both John and Shirley, despite the fact there was no assured income or even a house to move into. It was with some trepidation that Shirley left behind the security of the St David's manse.

> When we were leaving in January 1962, one of the woman elders said to me, "Well, we knocked you into shape, didn't we? When you first came here, you had a plum in your mouth and now you don't." That was some commendation, I guess.

> So the new year saw the beginning of a somewhat strange switch in ministry. For the first seven or eight months, we lived in the previous Prime Minister's [Sir Walter Nash] house in Harbour View Road, Northland, which the new owner had lent us. It had chandeliers and huge reception areas, and was totally unsuitable for a small family. We lived in it with what sticks of furniture we had. The students loved to come up to visit out of curiosity.

I became the provider of a huge amount of food and drink. It was an interesting time. One advantage was we had tons of babysitters. At that time, students from Malaysia, Indonesia and other Asian countries were arriving to study in Wellington. I was terrified living in the city, plus I had two small children. Over time, I grew to love Wellington.

John was the first ecumenical chaplain at the university. He had to establish the job with the help of a motivated but rather disorganised committee. The job had very little structure, and no support from the university or the wider church. John did not even have a room from which to operate, and I certainly got no support from the university or church either. We had a lot of insecurities to start with, as the job was rather precarious.

I was allowed to go house hunting and eventually an old house in Grove Road, Kelburn, was bought to be the chaplain's house. It cost £6500 and was shabby but comfortable. Our youngest son, Rob, was born in 1963. David went to Kelburn School, the younger ones to pre-school.[2]

By 1960, television had arrived in New Zealand. David remembers his mother buying with her own money the first television set the family had ever owned. He also remembers his parents buying an LP of the Beatles' *Sgt. Pepper's Lonely Hearts Club Band*.

Many years after Rob's birth, Alastair, then a teenager, recalls a funny conversation he had with his mother concerning the birth of her youngest son. "Mum and I were chatting about family matters and talking about Don, her ribald old uncle. He liked to kid around and had a real smoker's wheeze. She recalled that Uncle Don had sent her a telegram just after Rob's birth, congratulating her on 'her front row'. Did I understand what that was all about, she asked. I burst out laughing and had to explain that having a third son completed the set needed to fill up the front row in a rugby team. She had been wondering about that since 1963."

Rob was baptised at the Kelburn Presbyterian Church which we had started attending. But it was quite a struggle to get there on occasions, as John would have the car, taking a service elsewhere, sometimes at St Andrew's [on Wellington's The Terrace] when the minister, the Rev Jack Somerville, was away. I felt rather excluded and eventually stopped going. I don't think anybody noticed my absence. I began to read a lot more instead.

It was more satisfying meeting up with my old friends from the SCM who were then working in Wellington. I became part of the executive of the local SCM branch.

It was an exciting time to be in Wellington, especially among students – a great influx arrived at the university during the 1960s. Young people were full of unrest and excitement, what with the Beatles visiting New Zealand in 1964, the availability of drugs like LSD and various political causes like the Vietnam War and the anti-nuclear movement. All these things stirred up the students, outside their normal worries like money and study.

John suspected the university Vice-Chancellor had hoped the newly appointed ecumenical chaplain would keep the students quiet. "But I learnt the art of protesting from them," he said. "It was a creative time. Although I was chaplain for six years, the university authorities never officially recognised me."[3]

As we lived close to the university, our house was a great visiting place for anybody feeling disturbed or idle. [John's nephew Rod Edmond, later professor of literature at Canterbury University in Kent, England, lived with the family for two years, in a sleep-out on the property. Other students used this accommodation on occasions.] Eventually John got a room on the university campus, which he shared with the Roman Catholic chaplain, Father Matthias.

I found it a strenuous time because students are hard to get rid of after doing babysitting! We/I spent time listening to their ideas. I had to learn the art of disappearing. One student offered to take our three children for two nights – the only holiday we had had without children. I was so grateful. We went as far as Waikanae, a coastal settlement north of Wellington.

John was not always there as he was also warden of the Presbyterian Church's Stuart Williamson Hostel on The Terrace. [John also started a series of reading parties for students at Wallis House, an ecumenical retreat centre in Lower Hutt, just north of Wellington.

Study material included the work of theologians Paul Tillich and Teilhard de Chardin.] And he was involved, as most ministers are, in doing other things for presbytery committees. He was very interested in public questions, chairing the Presbyterian Church's Public Questions Committee for a short time between 1966-67. They were entertaining years, we made great friends, but the chaplain's job was quite unstructured.

The university's religious studies department wasn't properly established. We were also moving towards the so-called heresy trial of Lloyd Geering, Presbyterian minister and principal of the Theological Hall in Dunedin.

At the beginning of the 1967 academic year, John had asked Geering to preach a sermon at the inaugural student service in the Wesley Methodist Church. The year before, Geering had published a series of articles in the Presbyterian Church's monthly publication, *The Outlook*, in which he drew a distinction between the death of Jesus as a human being and his 'resurrection' as an act of faith.

At Wesley Church, Geering preached on the theme that 'man has no immortal soul', a concept considered to be synonymous with 'life after death'. News of his controversial views soon hit the headlines. Some have described the events arising from this sermon as a defining moment for many in the church. It certainly brought theology into the public arena in a way it had never been before.

It was an exciting but horrific time. I was on the fringe of anything theological, but I was stunned at the reaction to this sermon. Students were excited by Geering's words. The clergy, in contrast, were not supportive, though some thought as he did. And so began a long sequence of events we could never have guessed at.

Geering was charged with 'doctrinal error' and 'disturbing the peace and unity of the Presbyterian Church', by Auckland conservative minister Robert Blaikie and leader of the Layman's Association Robert Wardlaw. The case against him was presented at the General Assembly in Christchurch in 1967. Television and radio were there to record the charges being laid and during the later debates. Geering again suggested the bones of Jesus might lie elsewhere in Palestine and that the resurrection had been wrongfully interpreted by churches as a resuscitation of the body of Jesus. After a two-hour hearing, he was found not to have committed doctrinal error and the case was dismissed.

Following the Assembly, Geering's opponents continued to debate the issues. This led the church to eventually adopt a set of doctrines, including statements about the resurrection and eternal life. A further complaint against Geering was brought to the 1970 Assembly. This followed statements he had made during a television interview in Australia – statements that were consistent with what he had said in 1967. This time, the church decided to dissociate itself from Geering's public position, in effect reversing its 1967 decision. Some wanted to see him removed from his position of principal at the Theological Hall in Dunedin.

> It took me a while to understand the gravity and the sense of what Lloyd was saying. It was exciting because it was so different. It was beyond me, but I so appreciate all the teaching Lloyd has done over the years.

Shirley revealed further thoughts about Lloyd in an email to Canadian hymn writer Ron Klusmeier in 2014:

> Lloyd speaks with clarity and a deep scholarship. He's now 96 and has always had a rather dry speaking voice, but he is a wonderfully kind and intelligent human being. He's an integral part of the Westar Institute [US Progressive Christian research centre] and was early in promoting the Jesus Seminar [studying the historical Jesus].

> His own life story is a testament to overcoming griefs that would fell most people. He lost his first wife, Nancy, to tuberculosis when they had two very young children, and later his long-time partner Elaine, who supported him through the heresy business. His public promotion by John, who asked him to be resident theologian at St Andrew's [in 1983], gave him a 'secular pulpit' as well as a church one. Though neither of us can go as far as he does theologically, he lives his beliefs with great cheerfulness and a positive attitude. He and his third wife, Shirley, even joined the St Andrew's singers

on occasions! His retirement from lecturing there was received by a packed church full of non-church goers, with the most tremendous ovation. You can see that I'm a fan as well as a friend.[4]

Four years later, in September 2018, Shirley again emailed Ron Klusmeier about Lloyd, who had turned 100 earlier that year:

He is still producing books. He is slightly deafer but has, in no other way, stopped in his tracks and writes more cogently than before. I'm not sure that I go all the way with him – in fact, not – but I greatly respect his thinking … I'm not so certain about anything! Life, death, the whole darn thing.

In 1971, Geering was appointed Chair of the newly established Religious Studies Department at Victoria University of Wellington, retiring in 1984. In retirement, he became an honorary associate minister of St Andrew's on The Terrace and continued giving public lectures at the church under the umbrella of the St Andrew's Trust for the Study of Religion and Society. This trust was originally created to support his continuing influence. He authored more than 20 books and became a sought-after lecturer and presenter throughout the country and on radio and television.

In *Presbyterians in Aotearoa 1840-1990*, the author of the period 1961-1990, Jim Veitch, concluded: "After the debates, Lloyd Geering became the best-known Presbyterian minister in New Zealand, and was more popular outside the Church than within it."[5]

Aged 106 in 2024, he is considered New Zealand's most highly decorated academic, appointed Commander of the Order of the British Empire in 1988, then Principal Companion of the New Zealand Order of Merit in 2001. He was re-designated Knight Grand Companion in 2009. He and his wives – Elaine, who died in 2001, and Shirley, who died in 2021 – remained close friends of John and Shirley their whole lives.

Notes

1   Refrain and verse 1 of 'We Must Leave Home' ('Hymn for a Progressive Christian Community'), written in 2013 as a 'stir up' to discussion for a gathering of Progressive Christians. Published in Hope's *A Place at the Table*, 1993.

2   Unless otherwise stated, the quotes from Shirley in this chapter are taken from an interview with Margaret Pannett for the St Andrew's on The Terrace oral history project, 7 November 2006, and another with Sheila Irwin for the APW, 22 November 2002.

3   From interviews with Ann Barrie for the St Andrew's on The Terrace oral history project, September-November 2006.

4   Email to Ron Klusmeier, 6 September 2014.

5   McEldowney, D. (Ed.) (1990) *Presbyterians in Aotearoa 1840-1990*. Wellington: Presbyterian Church of New Zealand, p155.

6 – Parish demands

Every day I will take your word,
answer your compassion's claim,

celebrate every sign of hope,
every deed done in your name;

help me see you are always there,
and your light can shine through me,

every day in your Spirit,
I'll find the love and energy![1]

In 1967, Shirley and John and the children, then aged ten, six and four, moved to Murray Place in Merivale, Christchurch, to take up a ministry position at Knox Presbyterian Church, Bealey Avenue. Murray Place would be their home for the next eight years.

> I think John was motivated by several factors. The house in Wellington had to be re-piled, which meant the family would have to move to a temporary and very cold manse in Johnsonville, our three boys got chickenpox, I got a terrible 'flu and John began to think a change of scene was what was needed. His mother also lived in Christchurch and was getting older. [John's father had died in 1964.]
>
> Knox Church was large and flourishing, and very demanding for one person. It really needed a team.[2]

According to John, the parish had around 700 members, a congregation of up to 500 people and a session of 50. The church had benefitted from the liberal ministry of the Rev Malcolm (known as Mac) Wilson and was forward-thinking and liberal in its theology. For John, this was perfect as it extended his experience. He also found it good to be back in parish life again. However, with such a large parish, he could find himself running weddings or funerals nearly every week![3]

> We arrived at Knox at a time of enormous energy and outreach. There were many forward-thinking people in Knox and a strong tradition of good preachers. There were also plenty of leading women in the congregation and I was not expected to be one.
>
> One disadvantage for John was the number of rest homes to visit – about 30. This was hugely demanding and meant he could be busy all week. A wonderful deaconess, Alice Swan, tried to do some of the pastoral care. She was John's right-hand person. But she couldn't do everything either. A second minister, Jack Strang, was appointed in 1969.

The years in Christchurch were some of the busiest for John and Shirley. Reflecting on the challenges facing Shirley as a minister's wife and mother, son David said: "Christchurch was a conventional manse. I think she did a great job, being a mother and minister's wife, and she did her best to balance all the demands on her time.

"There was a bit of yin and yang between Mum and Dad – Dad was outgoing and sociable while Mum was more introverted. She had a lot of hosting to do – parishioners and church colleagues like the Revs Charles Naylor and Jack Somerville. But it was challenging to share your parents with parishioners and so many others. Mum and Dad's friends also came to stay, e.g. Lindsey Eastgate, Mum's good friend from Invercargill, and her husband Nigel. They'd all known each other from university days. Lindsey was outgoing and quite different from Mum."

Youngest son Rob remembers lots of people coming through the manse, many of whom the boys didn't know, nor why they were there. "We always assumed they were there because of some pastoral need. I recall one hot Christmas in Christchurch when Dad invited 'the spinsters of the parish' (my phrase, and not very PC I'm afraid) for a sherry after the Christmas Day service – and they sat, and sat, and sat as the traditional Christmas lunch got frazzled in the oven.

"Dad very much kept his own clock. A favourite saying of his was that he had 'tons of time', even when he clearly didn't. That didn't always go down well. Dad appeared to put ministry before family. This is not a criticism, more an observation on his priorities."

David recalls lots of singing round the piano when the family had time to relax together – the Murray family piano was always with them. "Dad was a good singer, a bass baritone, though he could not really play the piano. Music was a uniting factor for us all – we boys all had music lessons. Al was musical, Rob and I not so much. Dad liked singing opera; he also liked the great tenors. Mum loved listening to Kiri Te Kanawa and Bach, not so much Beethoven, one of Dad's favourites."

Music united the family, but for the sons, the attraction of attending church and Sunday school began to pall during these years. "I went to Sunday school, but was never a believer," said David. "Dad did not push religion on us. I also went to Bible class and youth group on Friday nights, and sometimes went to church and sat with Mum. When I was a teenager, they stopped making me go to church. And when the time came for confirmation, I said I didn't want that.

"But their values moulded me. We were a liberal left-leaning family. I was an oddball at high school in Christchurch, a very conservative city. I can remember going on anti-war protests, another tough thing to do. My (paternal) grandmother – we called her 'Bobo' – was usually a National Party voter and would have given Dad regular feedback on what was happening. She sat in the back row of Knox Church and sometimes I sat with her."

> Friendship was a hugely important part of what people were hungry for and were prepared to give. There were lots of activities like the friendship circle for young couples, and parish camps at Woodend, which the boys liked. I am not a lover of church camps, however, as I like my comfort! There was the women's guild, and a good proportion of women elders on session. I remember Judith Hay, wife of Christchurch mayor Hamish Hay, objecting to the new version of the Lord's Prayer.

We did lots of entertaining at the manse. Some visitors were wonderful, some were bludgers. The previous minister, Mac Wilson, and his wife Elinor were great supporters. Elinor was a marvellous model for me of someone who had never been tied down by convention. They had a huge, rambunctious family, and were generous and lively, as was the parish itself.

Elinor, then retired, was practical and gave me great support. She told me not to worry about the state of the manse. One of our guests was the General Secretary from the World Council of Churches, Philip Potter, a tall West Indian. The boys had a great time bowling cricket balls with him down our backyard.

Alastair recalls his mother attempting to join them in playing backyard cricket. "Mum was born a left-hander and, as was the culture of the day, she was made to use her right hand as the predominant. It didn't help her with sports, however, as she never really knew which hand was the right one. Back in the early '70s, on a warm summer's day, Rob and I begged her to come and have a bat in a game of backyard cricket. She strode to the crease, picked up the bat right-handed, missed entirely and was bowled. She promptly marched off, but before she got far, we begged her to have another go. She strode back, picked up the bat left-handed but with the exact same result."

Other prominent guests included the South African activist and journalist Dennis Brutus, Rhodesian-born political activist Judith Todd and president of the World Council of Churches Bishop Alphaeus Zulu. John had become the first chair of the National Council of Churches' Human Rights Commission during these years, as well as founder and first chair of the Citizens Association for Racial Equality (CARE). With John being so busy, what Shirley really wanted was a job of her own.

I managed to get a part-time librarian's job in a primary school in Papanui. This got me out of feeling everything in my life revolved around church. I also sang with the Royal Christchurch Musical Society. What with all the activities we were involved in, we needed babysitters every night of the week. But I was also expected to cater for the babysitters and, in the end, I found the struggle too much. My musical life outside the home was, therefore, brief.

Alastair and David Murray remember their mother being able to purchase her first car once she had her own income, a green Morris Minor 1000 Traveller, with a distinctive outside wooden frame. "She was proud of that little car – it gave her independence. I remember revarnishing the woodwork for her at one point," said David.

"She also enjoyed the independence that having her own money gave her," said Alastair. "We had our school uniforms, enough to eat and a bicycle – all a boy really needed. We seemed to have the same as everyone else.

"In the 1960s, the family got a holiday home at Leithfield Beach, north of Christchurch, thanks to a small inheritance from an aunt. We had lots of holidays there. I remember packing up and heading north, singing crazy songs together, like The Quartermaster's Store, along the way. It seemed a real adventure, though Leithfield Beach is only 45 minutes' drive from Christchurch. In 1973 Mum's mother died. I remember she heard about that while we were on holiday at the beach."

David recalls fun times at the beach house too and a lot of card-playing. "Mum was from a great card-playing family. I guess there was not too much to do in Invercargill in wintertime. Mum and Dad were both competitive. They also played Scrabble together. Eventually I gave up card-playing to do other things. Rob and Al are better card players than me."

Elinor supported us again when John got some study leave to go to Washington DC in the United States in 1974. She thought I should go with him and gave me $100 to help with the fares. She also offered to look after the kids. I was very touched by that.

I had one or two skirmishes with hymn writing while we were in Christchurch. I had always tinkered around with poetry and loved funny songs, like [American singer-songwriter] Tom Lehrer's. The seeds were perhaps sown while we were in this parish. John became frustrated as he searched for hymns to suit different gospel passages. I began to wonder why we did not sing New Zealand carols and tried a few mawkish attempts of my own. I would never sing them now, though.

In 1974, John helped initiate a television hymn-writing competition, called Sing a New Song, with John one of the judges. It was produced by broadcaster John Terris and resulted in six television shows featuring the winning entries. Methodist hymn writer Colin Gibson, encouraged by John and Shirley to enter, came second with his hymn 'Singing Love'.

> While we were in Christchurch, John had begun talking to like-minded people like Guy Jansen, Roy Tankersley and Wallace Woodley about the need for New Zealand to have its own collection of hymns rather than relying on hymns from overseas. This was the genesis of the New Zealand Hymnbook Trust, founded in 1979, which sought to promote hymns that said something to New Zealanders in New Zealanders' language. It was a brave thing to do.[4]

> My hymn-writing efforts really came to a head when we moved back to Wellington and John took on the joint position of minister of St Andrew's and master of Everton Hall.

So, the Murray family packed up again. The only thing that did not go with them, however, was the green Morrie station wagon. It was not considered strong enough to cope with the Wellington hills.

Notes

1   Verse 3, 'Every Day I Will Offer You', written for a Presbyterian women's conference held in Wellington in 1991. Published in *Alleluia Aotearoa* with music by Colin Gibson. Ron Klusmeier has also composed a tune for this hymn.

2   Unless otherwise stated, the quotes from Shirley in this chapter are taken from an interview with Margaret Pannett for the St Andrew's on The Terrace oral history project, 7 November 2006, and another with Sheila Irwin for the APW, 22 November 2002.

3   From interviews with Ann Barrie for the St Andrew's on The Terrace oral history project, September-November 2006.

4   See chapters 9 and 10 for a history of the New Zealand Hymnbook Trust.

7 – A centre for radical action

Where we are torn and pulled apart by hate
because our race, our skin is not the same,
while we are judged unequal by the state
and victims made because we own our name,
humanity reduced to little worth,
dishonoured is your living face on earth.[1]

John and Shirley were thrilled to move back to the capital city in 1975, with John taking up his new dual role of minister at St Andrew's and master of Victoria University's student hostel, Everton Hall.

> St Andrew's had come to such a low ebb, in fact it was at the point of closing. This meant there was not enough money to support a full-time minister. Session clerk Bert Orange persuaded John that he might be able to do something about it. If we helped launch the new Presbyterian/Methodist student residence, Everton Hall, he could be minister of St Andrew's and there would be some kind of financial to-ing and fro-ing.

> This turned out to be quite crazy because St Andrew's ended up paying Everton Hall for the privilege of having John run it and our living right next door.[2]

St Andrew's was the first Presbyterian Church in New Zealand and therefore hugely significant. In his 2016 history *The Story of St Andrew's on the Terrace 1975-93*, John wrote: "What confronted me when I arrived in Wellington was a church that was dark, dingy, dirty and more-or-less derelict. The congregation was dwindling, making the church an obvious target for those who wanted to buy it and demolish the building for their own commercial purposes."[3]

John agreed to become its minister, as long as his focus could be on ministry to the city, with ministry to the parish coming second. His first priority was to open the church up each day, and to find and support activities that would attract the city's inhabitants and workers. In 1975, church attendance had sunk to a low ebb and the session numbered only seven.

Within his first few weeks at the church, one of John's first actions was to dispense with the services of a long-established choir, "which consisted of no more than ten people, mainly sopranos including one elderly woman who held her music book upside down, a loud tenor and a couple of basses whose voices were clearly past their best. They thought they ran the place."[4] Once the choir had gone, John felt he could begin his ministry.

The Murrays lived at 27 Talavera Terrace, adjacent to Everton Hall, for the next three years. This had once been the residence of the Vice-Chancellor of Victoria University and was, Shirley said, a grand but shabby building.

> Three years living there was quite long enough. St Andrew's slowly started to pick up and the hall too. For those first years, I had the title 'mistress of Everton Hall'. I was a kind of house manager and had to make lunches for committees. With 125 students in residence, the work became far too demanding.
>
> Working at the hall was hugely enjoyable and stressful. Students were living in a flatting type of arrangement, so I had parents ringing up all the time wanting to check on the morals of the place. At this time, there were many Asian students, including Colombo Plan students who had the money to come to New Zealand.
>
> The question that has always bothered me is why St Andrew's was paying Everton Hall for us to be there when we were working 24 hours a day for the Hall. St Andrew's could not afford to do this. [John later said that he felt St Andrew's was treated badly in this arrangement. "This was one of my sour moments in my ministry."[5]]

St Andrew's finally got established and was able to pay John full-time. The church bought a manse for us at 11 Talavera Terrace. This proved to be a good home despite the lack of parking. It became our life for 17 years. Ministering in an inner-city church was stimulating and demanding, and I was glad to be free of the stuff that had taken up my time in our suburban parish in Christchurch. I relished being back in Wellington and began to love it again.

Soon after they arrived in Wellington, John asked Shirley to write something about The Terrace and she wrote 'Jesus Christ is Lord of all The Terrace'. "If you ask Shirley about that hymn now, she will deny she ever wrote it. I saw it as an expression of hope and determination that we were not going out of business," said John.

"The city around us was expanding and people were thinking they could buy St Andrew's and knock it down. I wanted to relate the church to the community. There were banks on one side and Parliament on the other. New buildings were going up and inner-city people were moving out to the suburbs. I was involved in a social gospel, related to the affairs of the world around us."[6]

An early initiative at St Andrew's was free lunchtime concerts for city workers. The New Zealand Symphony Orchestra used to have its offices beside the church, so an easy relationship between the two organisations developed. The church's reputation as a centre of musical excellence continued to grow over the decades.

In 1976, on the last Sunday of each February, St Andrew's began honouring its history with a service on the Petone foreshore, on the other side of the harbour from Wellington. These services were conducted at the Iona Cross, erected on the foreshore in 1940 to mark the arrival, 100 years previously, of the first minister of the 'Scotch Church' in New Zealand, the Rev Andrew Macfarlane, and his flock. This annual event and commemoration was open to all in the Wellington Presbytery (a regional governing body of the national church) and continued for many years. An occasional commemoration has been held in more recent times.

In 1978, Shirley initiated an Amnesty International group at St Andrew's for city workers to come to on their way home. Once a month, members of the congregation would sit down with Shirley to write letters for Amnesty. Later, she became Amnesty's national religious affairs co-ordinator. In this role, she put together worship material for churches and connected with other faiths when the opportunity arose.

John became convener of the Joint Presbyterian and Methodist Public Questions Committee in 1975. In 1978, he was appointed national coordinator of the movement seeking a repeal of the Contraceptive, Sterilisation and Abortion Act, and more humanity in how women were being treated.

The following year, 1979, St Andrew's on The Terrace, as it was now called, marked, with a week-long festival, 100 years since it moved from its site on Lambton Quay to The Terrace. It also developed A Declaration of Intent, which set out the aims and aspirations of the church and its people.

John claimed that his ministry at St Andrew's relieved Shirley of a lot of the expected duties of a minister's wife. "Shirley was finding her own life in a very real way. Her hymn-writing only really began in 1975, and I owed it to her to give her the space and not to bring the parish to the manse. We had done that in Taihape and to some extent in Christchurch. An appreciation of women's rights was becoming stronger."[7]

John may have been wanting to lift the burden of ministerial wifely duties from Shirley, but by her own account, she seemed to have remained remarkably busy.

> St Andrew's developed a totally different way of understanding how ministry happens. We had parties at the manse and study groups, partly because I hated the guild room at St Andrew's and the smell of old carpet. We also had heaps of visitors, many of them clergy overnighting on their way to meetings. Sometimes I felt I was running a boarding house!

> When we first went to St Andrew's, Governor-General Sir Keith Holyoake had his own special pew. Former National Party leader Sir Jack Marshall, and our good friend Hugh Templeton, elected as MP for Karori in 1975, were also in that circle. Jack Marshall disagreed with what John was preaching on South Africa and war and peace generally, so he left St Andrew's.

Those who felt uncomfortable with the direction John was taking the church would often change their allegiance to St John's, one and a half kilometres south of St Andrew's on Willis Street. These departures were commonly referred to as The Terrace Waltz.

John felt he had prophetic things to say. He had great support from some people and a lot of dissension from others, so it was not easy to hold this variegated congregation together.

In Christchurch, Monday was always our day off, but in Wellington John worked Monday to Friday to match city workers' hours. He tried to take a half day on Friday and all of Saturday off, if there were no weddings. There were not so many weddings during that time, and certainly nowhere near as many as there had been at Knox Church in Christchurch.

We used to come out to Raumati [on the coast north of Wellington] where we had acquired an unpretentious little bach at 154 Rosetta Road. So, we managed to get 24 hours off. That was about the most we ever got, and even that was often interrupted by phone calls. Even on holiday, which ministers see as their quality time, you can be pursued. The Glen Innis homestead, a holiday home for Presbyterian ministers a few hours north of Wellington, was a haven for us.

It's hard not to resent the pulls on John's time from people in and outside the church. I once got so inflamed about this, I wrote an article for the Presbyterian monthly publication, *The Outlook,* about the church being one's husband's mistress and being a demanding mistress too. I got that off my chest. Often it was hard not to feel you were being edged out because everyone else was more needy than you.

When John and Shirley moved back to Wellington, their sons were 18, 13 and 11. The eldest, David, had left school and started at Christchurch Teachers College. He moved with the family to Wellington and studied at Victoria University. David lived for a year at 27 Talavera Terrace, before leaving home and increasingly becoming involved in left-wing politics.

The younger two continued attending Bible class, but eventually drifted away. "Dad said that when we were 16, we could make our own decisions," said Alastair. "That was progressive of him. He could have insisted we remain involved while we were living at home. None of us was interested in the church, and the habit just faded away. Dad and Mum were disappointed in this, but a massive migration out of the churches had begun to happen. Moral codes were beginning to change, and churches began to lose their roles. People were getting their information elsewhere."

Long-time friend and collaborator Ron Klusmeier believes that both John and Shirley were disappointed that none of their sons kept any church connections. "Shirley worried that their sons' view of the church had been poisoned by what they saw as the church hurting their parents. I think Shirley felt the church had hurt both her and John, yet she was also proud of what John had achieved within the church."

As regards life in the manse, Alastair recalls his father being away all day, then home for half an hour, by which time the phone would ring. "His dinner would get cold, then he would go off to a meeting. Mum did seven-eighths of the parenting. Dad worked a lot in his study, especially late into the night on a Saturday when he was preparing his sermon. Mum was his support staff.

"Dad learnt the tricks of being the male in the room, how to capture people with oratory. He was a good studier of people. But he was not narcissistic and did not lord it over people when he won a battle or an argument. Mind you, he lost a lot of battles too. Dad was always busy doing 17 other things, saving the world and getting the New Zealand Hymnbook Trust underway."

With her eldest son no longer living at home, Shirley began to long for another job. She gained her first in 1978 at Parson's Bookshop in the central city, a job she was overqualified for. "She kept quiet about her university degrees," said Alastair.

"Mum did not do the stereotypes as a woman. When I was 17, I was filling in a form which asked about my parents' occupations. I asked them so I wouldn't get it wrong. Dad described himself as a minister of religion. I turned to Mum – 'Are you a housewife or a homemaker?' 'Neither of those,' she said, 'you can call me a household executive.' She was quick with words, intellectually bright, and good at giving a finger to the establishment."

Grandson Alex Grady describes his grandmother, whom he called Grandshe, as a "very busy minister's wife and mother of three rambunctious boys. I think she found all of that pretty challenging. There had always been an open-door policy at the manse, but Shirley loved having time to herself. Big events and having endless visitors sapped her energy a bit and put her out of her comfort zone. She drew more energy from quiet times, writing and reading. She had all these creative gifts. After the three boys had left home by the early 1980s, she had the opportunity to blossom as a hymn writer."

Alastair fully appreciates that being in an all-male household was strenuous for his mother at times. "When she got really fed up, she would stand at the window at Talavera Terrace and look over at Oriental Bay. She would threaten to leave us and get a wee apartment over there. She even told us she was saving up her runaway money to do so.

"Mum wrote hymns when we were not around. We had mostly left home in the '80s. She had lots of time when Dad was not home. We didn't realise how important her writing was."

John, "a big presence who filled the available space", according to friend and Anglican priest Dr George Armstrong, could be a polarising figure, even within his own congregation.

"Everybody loved Shirley," said Presbyterian minister Mervyn Aitken and his wife Lesley, "but not everybody loved John. Most people respected and admired John, but they didn't necessarily love him the same way they loved Shirley. That was probably just because of her personality, and her compassionate approach to people. She had that warmth.

"John had a huge energy for what he was doing and some Saturday nights he would be in his study the whole night, writing his sermon for the Sunday service, then go straight down to church. Shirley was probably a good foil to John. They were hugely supportive of each other, had great mutual respect and an excellent relationship."

Shirley may not have always agreed with John and his actions but she always admired his courage and appreciated his talents.

John has given me a lot to learn from and I always backed him on the big issues. The offshoots of some of his causes have been harder to take, e.g. the difficult people who become part of the cause and who think the manse is an easy touch. As a manse, you are open to phone calls at any time of the day or night.

From the 1980s, Shirley and John and their church were becoming increasingly politically active, with St Andrew's recognised within the wider city as a centre for radical action.

In 1983, St Andrew's on The Terrace became a peace church and, in 1984, declared via signage on the front of the church that its buildings and property were nuclear-weapons-free zones. This was backed up by annual peace pilgrimages on Good Friday to Wellington's Cenotaph war memorial.

Good friend the Very Rev Pamela Tankersley remembers St Andrew's involvement in the anti-nuclear issues of the 1980s. "At one point we had St Andrew's protesters outside the church, while in the hall police were taking a break during their protection of a United States delegation meeting with members of the then Foreign Affairs Department. The church was caught in a dichotomy between the roles of radical action and providing pastoral care to those who needed it. St Andrew's recognised that the police were not the enemy; they simply had a job to do. This is how St Andrew's took the Gospel seriously."

John was also outspoken on homosexual law reform and helped start GalaXies, monthly services for gay and lesbian church members and friends.

St Andrew's, the Murrays and the Springbok Tour

But it was the protests against the South African Rugby Tour (better known as the Springbok Tour) of New Zealand in 1981 that really galvanised St Andrew's and the Murray family.

For 56 days between July and September that year, near civil war raged throughout the country, as deeply held pro-tour and anti-tour views split families and communities. It was the largest civil disturbance the country had seen for decades. More than 150,000 people took part in more than 200 demonstrations in 28 centres, with police formed into specially trained riot squads and issued with visored riot helmets and long batons to control demonstrators.

Previous proposed Springbok tours to New Zealand had been cancelled – one in 1967 and another in 1973. But in 1981, then Prime Minister and leader of the National Party, Robert Muldoon, chose to ignore UN and Commonwealth leaders' opinions and resolutions. These called for sporting boycotts as a way to put pressure on the South African government's apartheid system. With an election looming in November 1981, Muldoon set out to capture the provincial heartland of New Zealand where support for the proposed tour was high.

Shirley stood shoulder to shoulder with her family's and church's involvement in many of the Wellington protests.

> Our common belief as a family was that the tour was wrong – this was our common religion – but it was an exhausting and traumatic time. Week after week, we gave our all to the protests.

> In 1981, I had got a job as a clerk/researcher in the Labour Party research unit at Parliament. I was a bit of a guinea pig really, job sharing with a younger woman who worked the mornings while I worked afternoons. In itself, that was a breakthrough and worked well for us. It was good to have an income again, but the pay was abysmal, and it never went up during the seven years I worked there. I got the lowest salary in the unit but had the highest qualifications.

> When I joined, Robert Muldoon's National Party was still in power. But 1981 was a highly exciting year with the threatened Springbok Tour. I was asked to sort out papers about Muldoon's attitude towards South Africa. This meant a crash course in politics.

> I did a lot of foot work, delivering papers to various MPs. This was before electronic mail and there are lots of corridors in Parliament. Electronic mail came in about 1988, when I left the unit.

> St Andrew's got heavily involved in protest action against the tour and I was proud our church became a place where people wanted to hold their forums or meetings about matters to do with human rights. St Andrew's might have been shabby, but it was proving to be a place with life in it.

I joined many of the St Andrew's protests, e.g. sitting down on roads and facing the lines of baton-wielding police. It was a great bonding experience, though not always a pleasant one. Things got quite violent when a tour supporter scattered excrement on the St Andrew's communion table.

Then there were the threatening phone calls. One of our sons, answering the phone at our home, heard the caller say his father would be killed if he did not do something or other. Another person pro-tour and against our protests made a malicious call to the fire service, resulting in a fire engine being sent to our house in Talavera Terrace.

The worst experience was being with John in Riddiford Street, Newtown [29 August, second test], when the police batons came down around us. John tried to rescue a woman who was badly battered. I had a bucket of white paint poured over my duffle coat from a balcony above me. The violence on this occasion was one of the worst of the tour. There was TV footage of John dragging a woman out from under a policeman's baton – it played for a while on TV.

Our eldest son, David, who led a group of marchers, was singled out by Muldoon because of his communist beliefs. He was arrested, held in a police cell overnight, then taken to court and vilified in the *NZ Truth* weekly newspaper. Our other two sons also got embroiled in the protests, pulling down barbed wire near Athletic Park in Newtown.

John was invited to join a protest group that intended to mount a passive prayer protest in the parliamentary gallery on 7 September, three days before the third and final test in Auckland. When the Speaker, Sir Richard Harrison, rose to read out the parliamentary prayer, the nearly 100 protesters rose too, joining with him in saying the words. As the public is not allowed to speak from the gallery, this caused great consternation. The protesters then turned their backs to the Speaker, which was considered an act of 'contempt'.

John remembers Muldoon turning 'from pink to red to white' with anger. He marched up to the Speaker to order him to call the Sergeant at Arms to evict the group. "A few of us, those who could be identified, were banned from the precincts of Parliament for one year from that date. I will never forget the viciousness of Muldoon," John said.[8]

Parishioner Pam Ormsby was also part of the passive protest. "As no one told the group what exactly constituted the precincts, we did not know where not to go, so the ban was ignored and fell flat."[9]

Ormsby, who died in 2023, was immensely proud of the African National Congress centennial award she received in 2012 for her contribution to the international campaign against apartheid.

Notes

1   Verse 2, 'O God, We Bear the Imprint of Your Face', Shirley's first attempt to write a hymn about racism. She and her family learnt something of the cost of racism during the 1981 Springbok Tour of New Zealand.

2   Unless otherwise stated, the quotes from Shirley are taken from an interview with Sheila Irwin for the APW, 22 November 2002, and another with Margaret Pannett for the St Andrew's on The Terrace oral history project, 7 November 2006.

3   Murray, J.S. (2016) *The Story of St Andrew's on The Terrace 1975-93: The Ministry of the Very Rev John Stewart Murray.* Wellington: St Andrew's on The Terrace.

4   See note 3.

5   See note 3.

6   Video interview with Canadian hymn writer Ron Klusmeier, Raumati Beach, 2014.

7   From interviews with Ann Barrie for the St Andrew's on The Terrace oral history project, September-November 2006.

8   See note 7.

9   Ormsby, P. (2012) How New Zealand helped to end apartheid. Paper delivered at the ANC centenary conference, Wellington, 18-19 August.

8 – Claiming space for hymn writing

How shall we see you
if not in people
knit to your nature, focused in sight –
angels and artists,
teachers and healers,
heart-and-soul people, children of light.[1]

In 1982, John and Shirley spent six months overseas. For John, this time included a three-month pulpit exchange with the Rev Dr Douglas Lapp, minister of the Metropolitan United Church in Toronto, and three months' study leave. John's aim was to discover more about ministry to inner cities, particularly chaplaincy to office workers.

Being in Canada meant Shirley could attend the conference of the Hymn Society of America (later renamed the Hymn Society in the United States and Canada) in Ottawa. There she heard English hymn writer Fred Kaan and met the Rev Dr John Ambrose (see chapter 11). For a brief time, she also worked as a volunteer in the office of Amnesty International and put together a small booklet of hymns and prayers concerning prisoners of conscience. John and Shirley remained best of friends with Doug Lapp and his wife Ethel for many years afterwards.

Leaving Canada in September that year, the couple travelled to London with several European stopovers on the way. In Italy, they attended the 15th International Council of Amnesty International in Rimini, revisited the Christian community in Taizé, France, then travelled on to Amsterdam. Next on their itinerary was Cambridge,

UK, the first time they had been back in 30 years. On their way home, they visited son David in Manila, the Philippines, where he was doing post-graduate research. They returned to Wellington in October 1982.

In 1987, Shirley published a privately printed collection called *In Every Corner Sing*. This contained 28 hymns, designed to fit familiar or established tunes. In her foreword to the book, Shirley writes of "having to stock some corners of the Christian household with new themes. For me, human rights and racism, women and peace-making all need singing about, and words to sing are hard to find.

"Some corners need refurbishing, since the word styles of the past do not always express the theological emphasis we now value ... I take it for granted that inclusive language is the mode in which Christian people must express belief."

In an interview with Ron Klusmeier, John said the collection "gave people something to sing and were not just listening to me ranting on.

"Initially we used old hymn tunes, so as not to be too difficult. One of the hymns from this collection, 'Loving Spirit', still moves me greatly – it was so deeply personal. Not everything Shirley wrote had a political edge. These hymns spoke in and through what I wanted the Gospel to say. I was just lucky to have married the right woman, one who was going to produce such extraordinary hymns. Our congregation will remember Shirley's hymns long after they have forgotten all my sermons."[2]

The couple's close friend Kevin Clements, emeritus professor of the National Centre for Peace and Conflict Studies at the University of Otago, sees John as Shirley's advocate and promoter. "Shirley was always modest about her hymns – John was the one with the public profile and the connections with parliamentarians. But Shirley was modestly building up an international reputation which was equal, if not more important than John's."

Shirley lived a life round the edges of John for a long time, said Clements. "Her poetry was a way of asserting her own space. I think she had some anxiety about being a dutiful parson's wife. This wasn't the destiny she wanted for herself. The women's movement, at its peak in the 1970s and '80s, and the peace and environmental movements were all backdrops to her hymns. She was trying to make sense of them. The patriarchy of the church helped her discover herself as a woman. She was cynical about that."

Another motivation for her hymn writing, he said, was to contextualise theology, "to try to develop an indigenous national identity".

The Rev Mervyn Aitken is grateful to Shirley for enabling him to stay in the church.

> She came at a time when we were searching for new words to sing. She did it magnificently. She helped us feel we were singing our deepest thoughts. I give thanks for her theological strength; she produced something for the new world, for the new directions in which the church was going. I loved her for that. Ministers at that time were struggling to find things that congregations could sing. Once they got the tune right and the words were right, they were away.

> Shirley took people with her. Her words helped us to move from God up there to God in us, and to God in the world around us. Rather than saying you can get there if you believe in God, she was saying you can get there if you believe in yourself.

> She didn't think the church itself was the greatest creation, but, on the other hand, the church gave her a vehicle for her poetry, for her creativity. I think she wrote for her own spirituality, more than for the church – it's there in all her hymns.

Shirley later reflected on her decision to use familiar tunes for her first collection of hymns, which she had done to help them gain acceptance. "It was the most retrograde thing I ever did. I'm sorry I began in that mode, but I couldn't see another way around it."[3]

In 1988, Shirley began working one day a week as a researcher on National Radio's *Hymns For Sunday Morning*. This involved sorting through old vinyl records, trying to create a varied programme each week, and preparing scripts for the announcer to deliver. She explains further:

> I had to have variety and a feeling for all the sorts of traditions, so everyone felt catered for. This wasn't possible with the library

of records available. Many were so old, e.g. recordings by the Glasgow Phoenix Choir, which had been disbanded years earlier. [It has since been restarted.] CDs were not common in 1988, so there weren't many lively, contemporary things at all.

I had to bundle up the records and walk from one building, through a rabbit warren, and down to the old Broadcasting House to deliver this cumbersome load into the right hands. The day disappeared just like that. It was an interesting experience, but I had had enough of it after a year.[4]

This was to be Shirley's last part-time job. Increasingly she saw her life and a future devoted to hymn writing, though she still struggled to carve out the time needed to pursue these skills.

John becomes Moderator

In 1990, after 15 years at St Andrew's, John became Moderator (formal head) of the Presbyterian Church of New Zealand. This was the year that both St Andrew's and the national church celebrated their 150th anniversaries. The sesquicentennial service on 25 February was broadcast live on national television, fronted by John both outside and inside the church. Knox College Professor of Church History, Peter Matheson, was the preacher on this occasion and there was a recorded message from the Governor-General, Archbishop Sir Paul Reeves.

The 150th anniversary service took place the day after the opening of Te Kākano o te Aroha, the Wellington Māori Pastorate's church marae (communal or sacred space) in Moera, Lower Hutt. John, who described the new marae as a "seminal achievement", had been a leading light in its establishment, gaining backing from all churches in the region.

Shirley had composed a special hymn for 1990 and for the anniversary service. 'Great God of All Time', sung to a well-known tune by C.H.H. Parry, honours the church's origins in New Zealand and its bicultural journey.

In a voice-over during the singing of this grand hymn, Shirley said: "Singing is important to me and singing about what I believe is most important of all. I want to sing about peace, caring for the earth and each other, what it means to be a woman and my own ups and downs in believing too. Singing faith joins me to the community of hope. I want to write about that hope by singing new meaning into the Christian story."

Shirley recognised that the church had already begun crumbling, but it "had enough spirit still to make this a really good occasion".[5]

John's itinerary was organised by Pam Ormsby, later dubbed by Shirley as "the Moderator's Minder". John wanted to visit every presbytery in the country during his 18-month stint as Moderator. One presbytery of the 25, Taranaki, refused to have him visit. John admitted his appointment was not a popular one and was more in honour of the 150th anniversary of St Andrew's than of him.[6]

"I tend to polarise people," he said. "A large part of the church is still afraid of becoming involved in social and political issues."[7]

John often made contact with local mayors on his travels and spoke to church gatherings of the need for prophetic leadership. Shirley, however, did not look forward to being a moderator's "lady".

I am not a public person and don't enjoy publicity. But it was also great to get an overview of the church during 1990.

The moderator's lady used to be given a wardrobe allowance, but I was told to buy just the one good suit. It proved impossible for me to go everywhere, so I stayed home. Over the years, the church has taught me how to be happy on my own, so I did not object. And I have never been one to join committees.

I did join John on a number of his visits, however. One I will never forget was a 'friendly visit' to Te Puke, where I really sensed the church's growing conservatism and fundamentalism. On a blackboard inside the church, someone had written some awful things like 'John Murray approves of abortion, no death penalty, satanism'. The preacher during the Sunday service accused John of not being a biblical preacher, and of approving of gays and lesbians. It was all very embarrassing, and some members of the congregation began to weep. TV3 was waiting at the church door with a camera as we left the church. It was all so vitriolic, I burst into tears too.

But in other, smaller places I saw many more positive things of people doing the gospel. We just wanted to go and listen.[8]

Close friend and St Andrew's on The Terrace member Rosemary Lawrence remembers how hurt Shirley was when she saw John ousted from some meetings during his tours as moderator. "John went with his open heart. Unlike previous moderators, he wanted to visit every presbytery in the country. Shirley was hurt when she saw John lambasted because of his radical views. They were such a great team and really complemented each other."

Looking back on 1990, John wrote of his impressions of the church in a Christmas letter to friends: "What is the church like? Speaking generally, passive, inward-looking, more concerned with doctrine than gospel, mostly negative towards diversity and pluralism in belief, culture, gender, sexual orientation and so on. A church based more on a theology of exclusion than on the inclusive Christ. There are many excellent exceptions but, on the whole, we need a basic mind shift from 'either … or' to 'both … and'. I dare to believe this is what the world needs too!"

This letter, like many others around this period, contains details about Shirley's successes in hymn writing and publication. In this same letter, John noted: "One of the best things on my moderatorial visits is an evening of Singing in Worship, which Shirley and I do together. A sort of 'road show!'"

Hopes for ecumenism

Preparing for the 1991 World Council of Churches (WCC) Assembly in Canberra, Australia, filled Shirley and John with much more positivity, however, giving them hope that ecumenism was a very real possibility. (The WCC was founded in 1948 and has 352 member churches. It meets in Assembly every seven or eight years. The 1991 Assembly was its seventh.)

> After our experience in the SCM and John's study at the Bossey Ecumenical Institute in Geneva, ecumenism remained significant for us. I didn't want to be thought of as a Methodist or a Presbyterian but as someone who follows Jesus and is a Christian.

Ecumenism lay behind the establishment of the New Zealand Hymnbook Trust too. John was always committed to the WCC and so I began writing hymns for them.

Two years before the WCC Assembly in Canberra in 1991, people from around the world attended a workshop in Melbourne to discuss the content and themes of the Assembly. John and I both contributed to this. This is when I met Swedish hymn writer Per Harling and my work was introduced to Asian church leaders and theologians.[9]

Shirley wrote two hymns for the 1991 WCC Assembly – 'Spirit of Love' ('Weaver Spirit'), written for one of the sub-themes, and 'From the Waiting Comes the Sign', a meditation. Her 1986 hymn, 'Loving Spirit', was sung to a setting by I-to Loh during one of the communion liturgies.

A few years later, she was invited to write the theme song for the WCC's ninth Assembly, to be held in Brazil in 2006. Her hymn 'God, In Your Grace' reflects the overall assembly theme of 'God, in your grace, transform the world'.

It was the ecumenical aspirations of the WCC that most appealed to the Murrays. However, even in 2006, Shirley could see the ecumenical dream had disappeared from New Zealand. "It has now been replaced by interfaith aspirations."[10]

The Presbyterian Church's General Assembly was held in Invercargill in November 1991 – nine months after the WCC Assembly – and presided over by new Moderator the Very Rev Duncan Jamieson. Debate and decisions around the place of people of homosexual orientation in church leadership positions dominated the agenda. Notice of motion number 4, which included a clause affirming "that those who continue in sexual acts in any context outside of heterosexual marriage are not appropriate persons to be in the leadership of this church" was carried. Out of the 418 voting members, 91, including the Very Rev John Murray, recorded their dissent to the decision.

An amendment, brought by the convener of the Book of Order and Judicial Committee, Bruce Corkill, added "that this expression of opinion be referred to the Special Committee without prejudice to any subsequent Assembly in this matter, and without prejudice to the status of any member of this church until further resolutions of the Assembly". In effect, those in ministry and who had been open about their homosexuality were able to retain their present positions, at least for the time being.

One change, promoted by John, did pass at this Assembly, however, and that was the church changing its name to the Presbyterian Church of Aotearoa New Zealand. This was to acknowledge the church's special relationship with Māori.

Some weeks after the Assembly, Shirley wrote a letter to Colin Gibson in which she said she was "feeling ashamed to the core about all the Presbyterian Church has done". She described John being "so angry and overcome at what they were doing (some of them unwittingly) that he burst into sobs. John and I had a restorative 'tangi' [cry] when the session ended.

"One small victory was around resolutions brought by the Joint Public Questions Committee. [These urged the Government to enact the Human Rights Amendment Bill in its entirety, adding several previously prohibited grounds of discrimination.] These included 'sexual orientation' and passed without a murmur. May the Methodist Conference do better."

In 1991, St Andrew's on The Terrace placed a second plaque on the outside of its building declaring itself to be an inclusive community, welcoming all people of every creed, race, class and sexual orientation. The congregation's stance against the 1991 Assembly decision was clear.

The national church has revisited the homosexual rights issue multiple times over the following three decades, but continues to hold conservative views on inclusivity in church leadership.

Retirement

On 4 July 1993, John and Shirley retired from St Andrew's on The Terrace, after serving the congregation for more than 18 years, almost half of John's entire ministry.

In April 1992, Shirley had written to George H. Shorney, chair of Hope Publishing Company in the United States, with whom she had developed a close friendship and publishing relationship: "Our home situation is about to change, since this very day, John has announced to our congregation that he's going to retire from next July. Since he is not a 'retiring' type of person, I don't know what his next set of ideas will be, but this leaves us much more free than the tie of parish life.

"We shall be moving, in mid-July, to a house of our own, along the coast [168 Rosetta Road, Raumati], about a 40-minute drive from Wellington. This, in itself, is an enormous thrill, since we have always lived in manses … Please promote my hymns – we've now got a mortgage!"

Shirley also expressed her feelings in a handwritten letter to Colin Gibson, dated 26 May 1993: "I haven't settled to doing much, since John and I are going through that strange period before leaving St Andrew's on 4 July, when everyone knows we're going, but it's still business as usual … There's hardly time to shift house or hold a garage sale – which we must do to save our sanity."

Tributes flowed during the final service and farewell for John and Shirley. In his written tribute, Lloyd Geering said: "If it had not been for John and Shirley Murray, St Andrew's on The Terrace may well have had to face closure by now. John has shown a rare flair for the kind of viable future which may be possible for an inner-city parish. Shirley has shown quite unusual skill in composing hymns for a rapidly changing world.

"The two of them have constituted a team which will be exceedingly difficult, and probably impossible, to replace. And to boot, each of them has been the kind of person to whom all sorts of people can readily relate. St Andrew's has been exceedingly well served by their leadership."

Colin's heartfelt tribute to Shirley was published in the July 1993 *St Andrew's News*:

> I guess that by now the congregation of St Andrew's on The Terrace knows that it has seen the flowering of a quite extraordinary talent, and the selfless gift of that talent, not just to St Andrew's, but to the worldwide Christian church.

Shirley Murray's hymns are sung wherever Christians rejoice in the liberating spirit of Christ, wherever they wish to address issues of peace and justice and equality. Their images speak of tenderness, compassion, aroha; they express a challenge to adventurous faith and personal commitment to social action. They have the vitality, freshness and warmth of the personality of their author, and that's why I react with excitement and pleasure when I open one more letter in a correspondence that goes back now for many years, to draw out its precious enclosure of another beautifully crafted hymn text.

Keep writing, Shirley, and in every corner we shall continue to sing your words.

In terms of energy, Shirley recognised it was time for John and her to leave St Andrew's. "I was only too happy to leave behind the demanding side of ministry work. We now had much more time to devote to the New Zealand Hymnbook Trust."[11]

Shirley was never one to let too much solemnity get in the way of the chance to have a bit of fun. She penned a song called 'It's My Place', based on Tom Lehrer's 'She's My Girl'. This was sung during festivities in the hall after the farewell service and published in the July 1993 *St Andrew's News*.

Fish gotta swim, birds gotta fly,
I gotta love one parish till I die:
a concrete-coated lump, it may be just a dump
but to me – it's my place …

On Sunday we all straggle in through the door
and we're lucky if we've all got there by ten thirty-four
the sermons are hot stuff, though the messages are tough
but it's my place, old St Andrew's.

the church that's all-inclusive,
the church that's non-abusive,
the church that's Sabbath-warming,
the church that's habit-forming,
the church that's got the goods,
well that's the church
that heaven meant for me.

You may turn up and find that there are Moslems and Jews,
and Buddhists have been known to occupy the pews,
the concerts are superb, though the lectures may disturb,
but it's my place, old St Andrew's.

the church that's truly liberal,
the church that's really Biblical,
the church that's sane and cerebral
(the fundies think we're terrible)
the church that's got a heart,
that's got a part
for even types like me.

So though
the kids all make a racket when you try to pray
and the sound system burps in a most disgusting way,
the minister's in drag - but the truth is in the bag,
so, oh well, what the hell,
it's my place, old St Andrew's.

Notes

1 Verse 4 from 'How Shall We Find You?' written in 1995 and published in *Every Day in Your Spirit* in 1996 as a response to questions raised by Professor Lloyd Geering. Shirley tries to express the confusion of searching for God through intellectual arguments, scholarly writing or even church tradition.

2 Video interview with Canadian hymn writer Ron Klusmeier, Raumati Beach, 2014.

3 Bell, G. (2014) In conversation with … John and Shirley Erena Murray. *Sine Nomine*, Newsletter for the Southern Ontario Chapter of the Hymn Society of the US and Canada. Winter edition.

4 Interview with Margaret Pannett for the St Andrew's on The Terrace oral history project, 7 November 2006.

5 See note 3.

6 From interviews with Ann Barrie for the St Andrew's on The Terrace oral history project, September-November 2006.

7 Morris, M. (1991) Still surprised he was chosen as Moderator. *Hawkes Bay Herald-Tribune*, 2 May.

8 APW interview with Sheila Irwin 22 November 2002.

9 See note 6.

10 See note 6.

11 See note 4.

Shirley and her brother Bruce, c1935

Shirley and Bruce in Invercargill, c1941

On the running board of Uncle Jack's Chevrolet with friends, c1940.
From left: Jill Preddy, Shirley, Anne Preddy, Bruce and Peter Preddy
(The Mollison family photo album)

Shirley, aged 15 or 16, on her way somewhere special

Head prefect Shirley, principal Muriel May (centre) and first assistant Christine Cumming (right) leading the Great Trek from the old school to the new, 1948 (Photo: Janet Pack, SGHS Archives)

A tender moment between Shirley (left), Colin Newbury and Lindsey Harrington. Shirley and Lindsey were often mistaken for twins.

Shirley does the ironing in St Paul's Cathedral, Dunedin, before a performance of *The House by the Stable*, 1951.

Close friends, from left: Lindsey Harrington, Shirley, Winifred Slater and Pamela Norris

Shirley and friends sporting their University of Otago blazers, October 1952.
From left: Winifred Slater, Pamela Norris, unknown, Shirley, Lindsey Harrington,
Shirley Coster, unknown and Paddy Smart

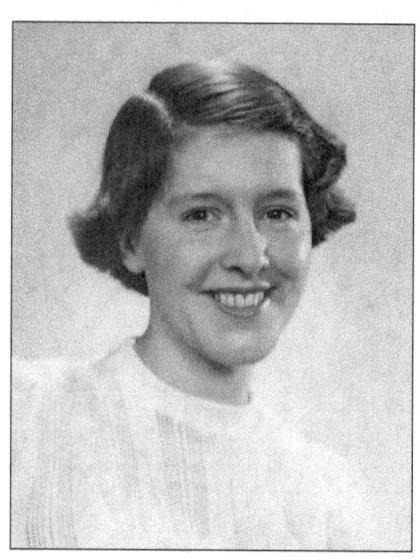

Shirley, 1952

Graduation day, 1953

John and Shirley on their wedding day, 21 July 1954

The wedding party.
From left: Faith Skene, Colin Newbury, John and Shirley,
Bill Norris, Principal of Westminster College,
the Rev Roy Drummond Whitehorn, and Aunt Flora Murray

John and Shirley sitting by the River Cam, Cambridge, with an American friend (foreground), July 1955

John and Shirley in Scotland on their newly purchased Vespa scooter, August 1955

John and Shirley's first home on their return to New Zealand
– St David's Presbyterian Church manse, Taihape

John and Shirley with baby David Stewart, born January 1957

Celebrating the marriage of Hugh and Natasha Templeton,
outside St David's Church, Taihape, 22 August 1959

Shirley in Wellington
with (from left) Alastair,
baby Rob and David,
1963

Shirley, holding Rob's hand, visiting
Lindsey Eastgate (née Harrington)
in Dunedin, c1966

John and Shirley with their growing family, Christchurch 1971.
From left, Rob 8, Alastair 10 and David 14

Part III
– Publishing in New Zealand and Abroad

9 – Birthing New Zealand hymns, 1979-1993

Take my gifts and let me love you,
God who first of all loved me,
gave me light and food and shelter,
gave me life and set me free.
Now because Your love has touched me,
I have love to give away,
now the bread of love is rising,
loaves of love to multiply.[1]

John Murray recounts how the New Zealand Hymnbook Trust was born and its publishing achievements up until 1993. Headed 'Broodings of a Sixties Dreamer', the information was first published in the summer 1999 edition of *Music in the Air*, then reprinted in Colin Gibson's *Knowing the Song*, Appendix 3.[2] Additional information provided by the author.

When I realised that it was taking me as long, or longer, to choose the hymns as to prepare the sermon each Sunday, I knew something had to be done. Where was I – and surely a multitude of ministers – to find words to sing that would be relevant to the late '60s, let alone the next millennium?

What we all needed were new hymns, in new words, for a world of social protest, theological revolution, ecumenical encounter and bicultural community, and in a language both inclusive and indigenous.

It was in the early '70s, while minister of Knox Church, Christchurch, that I got together with a small group of musicians and put the question – where can we find a new hymn book? At Knox, some of us had already put together a *Worship Book*, now over 25 years old, having passed through several editions and revisions. You remember the Medical Mission Sisters, Taizé songs, Fred Kaan, Sydney Carter, Geoffrey Ainger and others? But these were all, gladly, borrowed from outside our country. What of our own?

As I remember, four of us gathered: Guy Jansen, Roy Tankersley, Wallace Woodley, each of eminent ability in church music, and myself. We had a few meetings to explore the possibility of a new hymn book, and then I was off to Wellington, to St Andrew's. I was soon followed to Wellington by Guy Jansen.[3]

The idea of a new hymn book lay restless in me. I put a proposal to the Joint Commission on Church Union for their backing. Surely they would see this idea as a God-given way of promoting ecumenical worship, and so the goal of church union itself? They thanked me, wished me well, and moved on to the next item of business.

The breakthrough came when Geoff Chapman of Collins Liturgical Publications contacted me during a visit to Wellington. I had already been in touch with the Australian hymn book committee, who were putting together a comprehensive ecumenical hymn book to serve their progress towards church union.

Could New Zealand 'piggy-back' on the *Australian Hymn Book*, and maybe add a supplement of its own? Chapman suggested.

Our supplement to *With One Voice*

And so, in 1979, the New Zealand Hymnbook Trust was born, set up by Guy Jansen, Roy Tankersley [who became John's organist and musical director at St Andrew's] and me. Alan Woodley, the Methodist Connexional Secretary, began to prepare a constitution. Five churches – Anglican, Baptist, Associated Churches of Christ, Methodist and Presbyterian – willingly, but offering no funding, became the foundation members of the Trust as an incorporated body. Their national chief executives, Jenny Cotterell (replacing her husband), Stan Edgar, D'Arcy Woolf, Alan Woodley and Bill Best, were the trustees.

About this time, we set up our first editorial committee, comprising Jillian Bray, Rob Elder, Tony Georgantis, Colin Gibson, Jock Hosking, Guy Jansen, Shona Murray, Lester Reid, Roger Williams, and D'Arcy Woolf, with myself as chairman. We were all nominated by our churches. Professor Colin Gibson acted as words editor and Guy Jansen as music editor.

> Shirley recalled these early days in a 2002 interview:
>
> I have never taken lessons in hymn writing but have learnt a lot by osmosis. I first saw hymn writing in action when watching Colin Gibson and John Murray on the floor sorting out pages for the supplement to *With One Voice*. I watched Colin, especially, looking through these hymns, altering phrases because much of the language seemed non-inclusive or irrelevant. I learnt a great deal from watching how Colin worked.[4]

Preparing 'our supplement' as an addendum to the *Australian Hymn Book* was the only way to get started. We decided on three principles of selection: to be contemporary, ecumenical and 'multicultural'. Though we wanted to emphasise New Zealand writers and composers, this did not eventuate – except for Colin Gibson's 'He Came Singing Love' and 'Where the Road Runs Out', Helen Clyde's 'And Did You See Him, Little Star?' and Shirley's 'Come Now, Lord Jesus'.

> Shirley often reminisced about the excitement of seeing her very first hymn officially published:
>
> In the early 1980s, I will never forget the thrill of seeing one of my hymns published in a real, bound hymn book, *With One Voice*. It was an Advent carol, 'Come Now, Lord Jesus' – apparently the editors were rather short of carols. I have always scribbled and written silly things and poems and love limericks. I had already written a number of attempts to familiar tunes for our own congregation.
>
> 'Come Now, Lord Jesus' was not set to a familiar tune. It was inspired by a concert I went to of the King's Singers in Wellington. One Zulu tune – LALA MNTWANA, which means "Sleep now, child" – tugged at my heart strings. It is about a mother standing

on the railway station farewelling her guy who is going off to work in the mines. She is holding their baby and wondering whether he will ever return. The original melody was arranged by Shona Murray.[5] [There have been other settings since.]

However, a real breakthrough came with the inclusion of 20 hymns in Māori and Pacific Island languages. These were not contemporary, but well-known and often-sung hymns in those churches, and so, for the first time, Pākehā worshippers could share in multicultural services.

Sing Praise, a Catholic hymn book edited by Father Charles Cooper, was published with some Māori hymns about this time, but for use only in the Catholic Church.

The question of translation into English was solved by providing a 'literal' and non-singable translation, interlined with the original words. Tawhao Tioke, Setu Masina, Lagi Sipeli and Jim Kiriau helped me prepare these English translations.

As for the English-language hymns included, they were quite a hotch-potch. They were certainly not all contemporary, and some we called 'gap-fillers', hymns we felt should have been included, but were left out by the Australian hymn book committee.

When *With One Voice with New Zealand Supplement* was released in New Zealand in 1982, Collins Liturgical made a 'killing'. Tens of thousands of copies were sold because most of our churches were using hymn books dating from the 1920s, and were longing for something 'modern'.

Nowadays *With One Voice*, though about 20 per cent of its hymns were written in the 20th century, seems out-of-date. But, at the time, and for the next decade, it opened up a whole new range of songs and became very acceptable.

All this brought to the editorial committee a tremendous sense of achievement, a great load of exhaustion and very little money! Out of the hundreds of thousands of dollars from New Zealand sales of *With One Voice*, the Trust 'earned' only between $5000 and $6000.

We had bridged the gap between the old denominational British hymnals and a modern ecumenical hymn book. But we wanted to do more. We wanted to produce a really authentic New Zealand collection.

John added more in a 2014 interview:

We decided we wanted a book by New Zealanders, for New Zealanders. 'Praise, My Soul, the King of Heaven' is a great hymn but it belongs a few centuries ago. I wanted to move on from *Church Hymnary, 2nd edition*, which dates back to 1927, and to try to break into a new world of thought and a new context for the Gospel.

I knew we had some talent there. We decided every new set of words (except for wedding and funeral hymns) should have a new tune. We worried this might put people off. Our aims were to be ecumenical (not all churches wanted us, of course), contemporary (language imagery would belong to our own time and place), and of the identity of New Zealand. We wanted something for ourselves – not from the northern world.[6]

The dream comes true

So was born, in 1993, after a long gestation over two decades since those first meetings, *Alleluia Aotearoa*.

Some changes were necessary in order to proceed. A new board, with a broader range of talent (and not just denominational nominations), was chosen: Jillian Bray, Colin Gibson, Guy Jansen, Douglas Mews Sr, Shirley Murray, Cecily Sheehy, for a short while William Southgate, later to be replaced by Ian Render, and myself. This proved to be an excellent, talented and ecumenical team. As work progressed, we enjoyed working with each other and did so to great effect. And we were independent of the churches!

New Zealand had been becoming a 'nest of hymning birds', known worldwide for songs and choruses by such people as Dave and Dale Garratt, Brent Chambers and Richard Gillard, and more recently, by authors and composers such as Colin Gibson, Shirley Murray and Douglas Mews Sr. Now we felt was the time to publish 'our own book' in every sense.

At the beginning we had little money. However, thanks to the generosity of the Methodist Church of New Zealand/Te Hāhi Weteriana o Aotearoa, and its grant of $15,000 through the Prince Albert College Fund, the future of our work was secured. Other smaller donations and loans, including $5000 from the Alfred and Isobel and Marian Reed Trust, made the dream possible.

We called for contributors through church papers and a steady stream of offerings was received, several hundred in fact. As we met to consider and sing all of these – a mammoth task of great labour and, sometimes, moments of discovery – we found that many were so wedded to past styles of theology and music that they eliminated themselves.

Shirley explained more about the Trust's standards for selecting hymns in a 2002 interview:

I was executive secretary for the editorial committee for some years, so I saw the material as it came in. Many of the submissions were appalling, some mediocre. The worst thing was they were imitative. We had set up rules that said if we were going to sing New Zealand hymns, then they should be in contemporary language, no more King James' version stuff. They must be indigenous to the degree there would be nothing in them that would offend us as New Zealanders but would promote us being New Zealanders. They must also be ecumenical – they should not cater for only one bias.

The Trust stood by its standards and has collected something quite precious. Even if they are no longer sung, they have stated where we were – they sing theology. Hymns are described as the folk song of the church, but they are also our theology. It saddens me if we are still singing hymns like 'Onward Christian Soldiers' and there are parts in 'Once in Royal David's City', for example, that make me wilt. The line in the fourth verse – 'his children crowned, all in white shall wait around' – is really a reference to the poor little babies who died before growing up. Lots of things need to be changed to make hymns relevant for today.[7]

Then we would find what we considered to be writers and composers of real talent and promise, such as, to mention only a few, Marnie Barrell, David Dell, Nigel Eastgate, Radha Wardrop, John Weir and Gerard Crotty. All our editors produced excellent material in words and music as well. The title of our book, *Alleluia Aotearoa*, links the traditional sung cry of the faith with the indigenous name for our own country in which we express our praise to God!

> Church of Scotland minister and hymn writer John Bell admired the new publication. "I was impressed that in New Zealand, a smallish country, Shirley should – with others – have encouraged a groundswell in writing texts for public worship. This had never been a phenomenon in Scotland," he told the author in November 2021.

The process of compiling a hymn book, even a comparatively small one of only 163 songs [61 of them, more than one third, written by Shirley], is always more exhilarating and tedious than is expected. *Alleluia Aotearoa* was no exception.

The book was spiral-bound and arranged alphabetically rather than in traditional sections. We also included a number of 'fillers', i.e. The Lord's Prayer in seven New Zealand languages and a couple of poems by no less a writer than Joy Cowley.

In 1992, we contracted with Radio New Zealand to record 22 of the songs. This proved to be a wonderful 'appetiser' for our waiting market.

Archbishop Sir Paul Reeves, who had listened to the songs of *Alleluia Aotearoa* on his Walkman while traversing the streets of New York, wrote the foreword: "The issue for those who compose sacred songs, hymns (call them what you will), is to match the energy and vibrancy of the world and give us something real to sing. *Alleluia Aotearoa* does that … For years we have lacked a good hymn book … the banal has tended to triumph over the worthwhile. There is no reason why this should continue. I commend *Alleluia Aotearoa* as a very significant contribution."

And the churches now think this too. Already, five years after publication, *Alleluia Aotearoa* is well into its second reprint and continues to sell steadily. It sells well in Australia too and may be heard even in the USA, Canada and Britain. With this publication, the Trust became in every way independent and able to make its own future.

Notes

1 Verse 1, 'Take My Gifts', written in 1988 in response to a church stewardship programme, is now sung in church services of every kind. The tune by Colin Gibson, TALAVERA TERRACE, named after the street where the Murray family was living, is emphatic and exuberant.

2 Gibson, 2021, pp407-411.

3 Musical director and educator Guy Jansen founded the New Zealand Youth Choir in 1979 and the New Zealand Secondary Students' Choir in 1986. He died in 2019.

4 APW interview with Sheila Irwin, 22 November 2002.

5 Video and audio interview with Ron Klusmeier at Raumati Beach, August 2014.

6 See note 5.

7 See note 4.

10 – Restless for more, 1994-2014

Carol our Christmas, an upside-down Christmas:
snow is not falling and trees are not bare.
Carol the summer, and welcome the Christ Child,
warm in our sunshine and sweetness of air.[1]

John Murray describes the work of the New Zealand Hymnbook Trust from 1994 to 2002. From 2003, the story is continued by **John Thornley**, who became co-manager of the Trust with his wife Gillian in 2003. John and Gillian Thornley retired from the role in 2014.[2] Additional information provided by the author.

The editorial committee was still restless. The restlessness was centred on the celebration of our main annual festival in which church and community join forces – Christmas!

This has been the easiest and the hardest time of the year for clergy to choose appropriate carols. Easiest because everyone wants to sing again 'Silent Night', 'Once in Royal David's City' and 'O Holy Night'; but you can't sing 'In the Bleak Mid-Winter' and celebrate Christ's birth in our summertime. A handful of New Zealand carols had been printed in *Alleluia Aotearoa*, including that first of all New Zealand carols, 'Te Harinui', by Willow Mackay, from way back in the '50s. But surely we could expand to something more!

Shirley Murray's words and Colin Gibson's music to 'Carol Our Christmas' ('Upside Down Christmas') in *Alleluia Aotearoa* had caught on and were being sung more and more. So, taking these opening words, the Trust gave birth to a new book in 1996. It has 52 authentic New Zealand carols for us to sing in our churches, our schools, our end-of-the-year parties and concerts. [17 of these 52 carols – a third of the book – are by Shirley.]

In an interview in 2004, Shirley said:

Whenever I write a carol, hope and peace are the two enduring themes. Peace is such a bland word, it needs teasing out. Peace is inextricably linked to human rights and justice. There's a trinity there: peace, justice and hope, and in that order.[3]

And a decade later, she continued:

Carols are one of my favourite areas of work, because they are so challenging, not just because I am a southern hemisphere person when Christmas comes. They are the most theologically challenging part of the story for me. Incarnation is much more important than arguing about resurrection; being embodied is more important than talking about where we go hereafter. Carols have always posed a lot of questions. How do you relate to what might be called the gaiety and festivity of what Christmas is meant to be and how do you say something about the child in the manger?

One of my first attempts at writing anything involved stealing an idea from a beautiful Ghanaian tune, I think, 'Kneels at the Feet of His Friends'. I turned it into a mawkish New Zealand one about 'Dancing in the Sun'. Of course, it didn't work. But I wanted to turn around the seasons and the ideas.

I have written about 20 carols and every Christmas, I struggle again to deal with humanity and God and this amazing baby. Carols have kept hustling me, annoying me, making me work on them. The last one I wrote is called 'The Christmas Child is a Troublesome Child' or 'Troublesome Carol' [first published in Hope's *A Place at the Table,* 2013]. This is about the childhood of Jesus, which was surely like any other kid's.

Jesus became very annoying to the system. When you remember that, carols cease to be throw-away, jolly songs, and start to dig at you, to make you worry and wonder what God is saying through this. I sometimes introduce imagery from my own country but generally I write songs that will apply to almost anybody wanting to talk about the Jesus person, not just the Jesus baby.

'Star-Child' and 'Peace Child' are well known. Every year I wonder whether I will find another angle on what it means to be fully human, to suffer like a human, to be Mary or Joseph. We need to take the people from the story and translate them to where we are.[4]

The Trust's editorial team was the same, with the addition of former editor Shona Murray, but alas, without the jovial and learned presence of Professor Douglas Mews, who had died in 1993.

As Shirley explained in 2002:

The editorial team had become a tightly knit group of friends who knew how each other worked. Different styles of hymns were now emerging, with some difficult for congregations to take on. The board realised some might be more performance pieces than sung in the traditional way.[5]

Again, we called for contributions, many of which, as before, simply imitated traditional carols, with a sprig of pōhutukawa or the chime of a bellbird added. But there were 'finds', including work by Bill Bennett, Jocelyn and Christopher Marshall, Jackie Wise and Mark Wilson, as well as by the editors themselves.

And, to 'fill the gaps', we chose six poems by Joy Cowley, Shirley Murray, Peter Cape and Eileen Duggan.

Carol Our Christmas is the first ever book of New Zealand carols for all churches and for all who want to sing Christmas here in a southern sunny summer season. In 1997, the editors released a cassette and CD of 24 recorded carols. [See photo p201.]

Joy Cowley, in her introduction to *Carol Our Christmas*, wrote: "For this country and its people, the prevailing symbol of the Christmas season is not snow but light. The star that heralds the Christ child in our midst is the sun, and even the sound of its name is symbolic blessing ... In this volume of New Zealand carols ... not only do the words and the music here reflect Christmas in Aotearoa, they offer us a wide experience of music and rejoicing."

Our three books have changed the voice of singing in our churches. A New Zealand hymnody, contemporary, ecumenical, indigenous, is now a unique fact and something to be proud of.

In 1997, one of the editors, Shirley Murray, was invited to speak at a world ecumenical conference on music and liturgy in Asia. She recalls how proud she was to represent the only country of the many attending that had produced three uniquely indigenous books of worship, *Alleluia Aotearoa, Carol Our Christmas*, and *A New Zealand Prayer Book* of the Anglican Church, first published in 1989.

A further partnership with TV One's *Praise Be* programme led, in 1999, to publication of a video *Songs of Praise from Aotearoa*, with 24 hymns and carols from the *Praise Be* library.

Faith Forever Singing

In 1999, the Trust set aside $10,000 as an Endowment Fund in honour of our own writer/composer, Professor Colin Gibson, for students wanting to write or research hymns in New Zealand. With the new millennium approaching, it also set about planning a new project, *Songs 2000*, providing new hymns and songs for congregational singing – 'small songs', refrains, responses – all to help us sing our faith and hope in a new and very different century.

This became *Faith Forever Singing*, published in 2000. Editors for this book were Jillian Bray, Msgr Charles Cooper, the Rev Craig Forbes, Colin Gibson, Shirley Murray, Shona Murray, Ian Render, Sister Cecily Sheehy, with John Murray as chair. Of the 80 hymns published, 38 are written by Shirley.

In his foreword to the book, Governor-General Sir Michael Hardie Boys, said: "A new collection such as this, written by our own contemporaries here in New Zealand, in the language and the music of today, can give us stimulatingly fresh insights, and an antipodean perspective with which we can readily identify … The hymns in this volume … are extraordinarily diverse in their content and in the sources that they draw upon."

In 2002, the Trust published a booklet of 27 hymns, entitled *He Came Singing Peace: Songs to Overcome Violence*. These were drawn from the previously published collections, *Alleluia Aotearoa, Faith*

Forever Singing and *Carol Our Christmas.* The collection, most of which was written by Shirley, was published to help New Zealand churches, and perhaps schools too, connect to and take part in the World Council of Churches' Decade to Overcome Violence, 2001-2010. In his preface to the book, John Murray wrote: "The Trust offers you this booklet so that, together, our songs of hope and peace will drown out all the songs of hate, revenge and violence, helping to change the thinking of people everywhere."

New co-managers

In 2003, management of the NZHBT transferred from John Murray to Gillian and John Thornley as co-managers. John and Shirley Murray, Sister Cecily Sheehy, Jillian Bray, Guy Jansen and Ian Render stepped down from the Trust. Colin continued as a Trust member, joined by newcomers Roy Tankersley from Palmerston North, Sarah Mitchell from Dunedin, and Barry Brinson and Marnie Barrell from Christchurch.

Colin Gibson shared a tribute to John and Shirley's work on the Trust at a Hymnfest held at Wesley Methodist Church, Palmerston North, on 5 October 2003:

You have brought into being a body of hymnology and religious song that acknowledges the past but has freed us for the future, which is the distinctive voice and expression of Christian faith in these islands. It can stand proudly with the best contemporary work produced in other Christian cultures overseas.

Shirley, you brought clear bright language and thought, memorable images, drawn from our common life, a deep sensitivity to the sufferings of the oppressed and persecuted, and a passion for justice, equality and freedom. You created texts which refuse to simply recycle old clichés, which demand and provoke fresh thought – in this you are a true daughter of John Wesley – and poetry which moves, encourages and persuades us to care about issues and about people. You enabled us to speak – no, to sing – in the language of our times, freed from ancient gender and cultural biases; truly inclusive language, forming modern texts for modern people, contemporary hymns for New Zealanders. And we love you for it.[6]

Colin praised John for his formidable powers of organisation and persuasion as manager of the Trust:

…your fearless challenge to indifference and lassitude in the church, your total commitment to enlightened theology, and your tireless energy for the task in hand.[7]

In the following years, ecumenically-organised hymn singing occasions continued to promote and spread the knowledge of New Zealand hymns, songs and carols. Several workshops were held during 2003–2004, marking the tenth anniversary of the publication of *Alleluia Aotearoa*. Colin Gibson ran workshops in Auckland/Northland in 2012 and 'downunder' Kiwi carol singalongs became a feature in Palmerston North.

During 2004 two new 'singalong' CDs were recorded. *Singing Love* featured Colin Gibson playing 27 of his hymns from *Alleluia Aotearoa* and *Faith Forever Singing*. *Singing Faith* covered 18 of Shirley's hymns played by Roy Tankersley.

Hope is our Song

The Trust's fourth book, *Hope is our Song*, was launched at the National Hymn Conference held at Wesley Broadway Church, Palmerston North, over Labour Weekend in October 2009. (See photo p204.)

The title of the new collection of 158 hymns (46 by Shirley) was found in the last verse of Shirley's text 'Nothing, Nothing in All Creation', following a suggestion by editorial board member Marnie Barrell.

The new collection included 'Hymn for Anzac Day' ('Himene mō te rā o Anzac'), Shirley's text and Colin's music (see chapter 28). In her foreword to the book, the Rt Hon Helen Clark, then administrator of the United Nations Development Programme, said: "This hymn will make a significant contribution to the expression of our nation's identity on Anzac Day." She anticipated it would be widely sung in memorial services in New Zealand and overseas in the years to come.

"We should all be proud of the poets and composers who have contributed to this volume of New Zealand hymns. They have given us words and melodies to reinforce our understanding of our place in the world, our relationship with our beautiful land, and our responses to contemporary social issues."

The 2009 conference was attended by about 80 people, including seven from overseas: Jim and Jean Strathdee from California; Susan Jacobs from South India; Clive Pearson, Michael Earl and Ann Perrin, all from the United Theological College of the Uniting Church in Australia; and Deborah Carlton-Loftis, newly elected executive director of the Hymn Society in the United States and Canada. During the conference, Carlton-Loftis presented Shirley with a plaque marking her becoming a Fellow of the Hymn Society in the United States and Canada. Shirley was the first woman and first person outside the US to become a Fellow.

Jim and Jean Strathdee's keynote presentation, The Power of Song in Transformational Faith Communities in USA, Canada, Central America and India, reflected their far-reaching ministry in music. At the Saturday night worship in the Cathedral of the Holy Spirit, Jim led the singing of the Shirley Murray text 'Look in Wonder', singing the tune he had composed for Shirley's words.

The Auckland chamber choir, Viva Voce, conducted by John Rosser and accompanied by Michael Bell of St Matthew-in-the-City, recorded 27 songs from the new book. Released in late 2010, the CD received positive reviews from church and choral publications, and is a valuable resource in helping spread new songs through church and community groups.

John and Gillian Thornley co-managed the NZHBT until October 2014. Other appointments followed, with James Mist, the then Waiapu Cathedral director of music, working with Philip Garside Publishing Ltd to transfer the printing of the Trust's music books to a print-on-demand basis. These and the Trust's CDs are also now available in digital PDF and MP3 formats online.

In 2014, John Murray spoke of the legacy of the Trust, which in four books had published almost 500 hymns and carols by New Zealanders, for New Zealanders:

We have made an impact, but there have also been great upheavals in New Zealand. Those who go to church number only between ten and 15 per cent of the population. Only half the population claim Christianity as their religion. That figure used to be 80 to 90 per cent.[8]

John also spoke of the split in theology and practice, between traditionalism and evangelicalism:

The Trust moved more towards liberal or progressive Christianity but it is a confused issue. We live in a multi-faith world. However, the church by and large has avoided this reality. I would call the work of the Trust part of a new reformation of the church.[9]

Notes

1   Verse 1, 'Upside Down Christmas', written in 1986, "is a carol for our part of the world down under", says Shirley in her notes to the hymns in *In Every Corner Sing*, 1992. Colin Gibson's tune, REVERSI, refers to a popular board game of the time which involves turning over counters to reveal different colours.

2   Gibson, 2021, pp411-418.

3   Thornley, J. (2004) Hymns of Shirley Erena Murray: Part One. *Music in the Air*, winter edition.

4   Video interview with Ron Klusmeier, Raumati Beach, August 2014.

5   APW interview with Sheila Irwin, 22 November 2002.

6   Gibson, C. (2004) "Thank you, Shirley and John". *Music in the Air*, Summer edition.

7   See note 6.

8   See note 4.

9   See note 4.

11 – Embraced in America

Creation sings! And we are in the music,
the movement of God's energy and art,
a liturgy that links our life to angels,
a litany that rises from the heart.[1]

Getting to know the hymns of British hymn writer the Rev Dr Brian Wren marked a turning point for Shirley. Meeting him in New Zealand in 1988 led to many doors opening overseas, and eventually to her long relationship with Hope Publishing Company in the United States. Her hymns were first introduced to the United States, however, in *The Presbyterian Hymnal* in 1990, with five appearing in that collection.

But it was Hope Publishing Company, a family-based Christian firm dating back to 1892, that really promoted her work. In the 1970s, '80s and '90s, Hope's partners became aware that new hymn writers were emerging in many countries around the world, including the United Kingdom, Australia and New Zealand, and they were keen to establish an international body of new hymns. They were also able to offer these new hymn writers a more reliable income stream than they had been accustomed to in their own countries.

Shirley explains more in an interview with Canadian hymn writer Ron Klusmeier:

> I discovered Brian Wren in 1977 when *The Australian Hymn Book* came out. It featured just one of his hymns – 'I Come with Joy to Meet My Lord'. [It was later published in *With One Voice with New Zealand Supplement.*] From the moment I saw the clarity

with which he writes and the simplicity, I remember thinking I would like to be like that.

I was gently introduced to more of his stuff by the Rev Dr John Ambrose [of the United Church of Canada] at a conference in Ottawa in 1982. John Ambrose was taking us through one of Brian's texts which begins (altered later) 'This we can do for justice and for peace'. It wasn't just the theme that attracted me – it was to do with the clarity, simplicity and something undefinable – how he could put hard theological things into acceptable and exciting ways. I then began looking at what he was producing – many little hymn books with Hope Publishers. They were accessible and I liked the theology I was reading. I related to it because Brian's tradition of the United Reformed Church is very much what I feel at home with. But it was more than that.

In 1988 he ran hymn-writing workshops in New Zealand and Australia, and we met up in person. A few years later, in 1992, I met him at a workshop in Nashville [the General Assembly of the United Methodist Church] at which Brian taught us how to write good liturgical prayers. That's a discipline that is very helpful to a hymn writer. This was most productive for me. He has always been adventurous with his vocabulary, but also with his imagery. This makes him slightly outrageous but sometimes he is expressing exactly what no one else is able to express in that way, e.g. 'Bring Many Names, Beautiful and Good', a hymn that explores names for God.

I believe his book, *Praying Twice*, should be basic to every theological college. It offers a wonderful overview of what hymns are, what they can do, who their composers are and how they deal with the topics they choose to. I owe Brian a great deal – he has been my mentor, somebody who could craft good words with simple meaning, but which go to the heart of an issue or a person. His hymns are both personal and political. He does not stay with conventional wisdom and that is hugely appealing.[2]

Like Shirley, Brian was a wordsmith, not a composer. And both had a flair for writing in verse. Brian's wife, the Rev Susan Heafield, interviewed along with her husband in 2022, said Brian wrote about

400 hymns, a similar output to Shirley's. "I think Brian and Shirley got on so well because they were words people," said Susan. "They also worked with some of the same composers. Thanks to Brian, George Shorney [then president of Hope] created a great relationship with Shirley."

In January 1991, Shorney proposed (in a memo dated 17 January) that Hope "represent all of Shirley Murray's hymns here in the United States and Canada. This includes those already written as well as any future hymns she might author." The fee suggested was US$1500, with ten per cent royalties paid annually. Shirley would, in time, become one of Hope's most popular hymn writers, with her collections becoming best-sellers.

From the mid-1970s onwards, Hope had acquired the North American rights for works of leading hymn writers and composers of the British hymnic explosion. They included the work of Fred Kaan, Brian Wren, Joy Patterson, Erik Routley and Fred Pratt Green. Both Shirley and Colin Gibson, who also went on to have two single author Hope publications, retained copyright for any of their work published in New Zealand and the Asia Pacific region. Sydney Carter, composer of the much-loved hymn 'Lord of the Dance', also signed a contract with Hope in the early 1990s.

One of Shorney's aims with these hymn collections and supplements was to introduce new hymns from established and emerging writers and composers.

Hope aimed to release a first publication of Shirley's work before the annual meeting of the Hymn Society in the United States and Canada in July 1992. Hope also proposed that Shirley and John come to the US, at its expense, two weeks before the conference to visit the company's office in Chicago and to help celebrate the centenary of Hope's founding. (See photos p192.) John was invited to preach at First Church, Wheaton, Chicago, and also in Washington DC, where the Hymn Society conference was held.

In Every Corner Sing was Hope's first publication of Shirley's work, recapturing the title she had used for her first, words-only collection published in New Zealand in 1987. The new book contained 84 hymns – 'the complete body of her hymnic works to date' – in contrast to her earlier collection of 28.

In their foreword to the book, the publishers (in effect, George) paid tribute to Brian Wren for calling their attention to Shirley's hymns. "He believed her to be a hymn writer of the first rank, and that she deserved to be introduced to the world outside Australasia. Further investigation proved him correct in both respects."

In Every Corner Sing, described as providing "a long look into the loving heart of Shirley Erena Murray", includes musical settings for most of the hymns. Among them are settings by New Zealand composers, Colin Gibson in the majority, and some new tunes, particularly by American composers. All her work published by Hope included her middle name Erena. This name was not included in any NZHBT publication until 2008 when the 'Hymn for Anzac Day/Hīmene Mō te Rā o Anzac' hymn sheet was published.

The annual conference of the Hymn Society in the United States and Canada was held at Washington's National Presbyterian Church from 5-7 July. Its theme was Your Songs and Mine: Ethnic and Cultural Diversity in our Hymns. Colin and his wife Jeanette also attended that year, as did John Bell of the Iona Community in Scotland. As well as discussing her work and the newly published book, Shirley and Colin introduced those present to a broad range of New Zealand authors and composers, including Douglas Mews, Jillian Bray, Ian Render, Jenny McLeod, Peter Godfrey and Nigel Eastgate. George Shorney said Shirley was "received like a breath of fresh air" at the conference.[3]

In a workshop, Shirley explained that it was only in the last decade that home-grown hymns had been accepted in New Zealand churches, which previously had sung imports. The country was learning to view itself as a Pacific nation and not as a European land moved south, she said.[4]

That year, George introduced Shirley to the prolific American hymn composer, arranger and editor Carlton R. ('Sam') Young. This would mark the beginning of many years of musical collaboration and a great friendship (see chapter 25). That year, George stepped down as Hope president, assuming the role of chairman instead.

In March 1993, Shirley floated the idea to George of a collection of hymns/songs on women's concerns. Outlining the idea to Colin Gibson in a handwritten letter dated 26 May, Shirley said:

I've become aware of a need for this material in women's groups and also for consciousness-raising (I hesitate to use that tired term) in ordinary congregations, more, perhaps in North America and Australia than here. George replied enthusiastically and has already sent a bundle of books for my perusal (Ruth Duck's collection and Sylvia Dunstan's among them).

I took care to explain that these were not to be exclusively by women, but to reflect women in the biblical tradition, the 'invisibility' factor, images of God and issues of justice. So far, I have found more male hymn writers than female addressing these themes. What would you choose from your work? So I'm to be a 'consultant editor' and research material from this side of the globe. Do you have any texts you could suggest? I'm especially interested in Australia and the UK. Do you know the work of Anna Briggs? ('Lullaby Now' is in *New Song*.)

Brian Wren's work is a good resource, though I fear he sometimes overworks imagery to do with the female physiology. I'm extremely tired of wombs and breasts and birthing. I think a couple of Marnie's [Marnie Barrell] from *Alleluia Aotearoa* would qualify. I'm tossing in for your scrutiny two recent attempts of mine, neither with settings so far.

Writing to George in April that year, Shirley had also suggested that another dimension of such a collection might be that of feminine imagery for God, citing hymn writers like John Bell and Fred Kaan who had been exploring such ideas.

By November, George was suggesting someone in North America should drive the project, with Shirley remaining as a resource person and consultant. She was happy with this refocus, agreeing that "having to circulate primary material round my end of proceedings" had been a slow method of working.

However, despite George's initial support and enthusiasm for the idea, it came to nothing. In April 1994, George wrote to Shirley: "You will be disappointed to learn that we have moved the project on women's concerns to a back burner. Last fall, a group of well-intending females held a conference on re-imagining. It ended up with a lot of goddess Sophia stuff and it has practically paralysed the mainline church. When and if this blows over, we may be able to take another look at the project."

There is no record of Shirley's response to this decision.

Shirley's next collection with Hope, published in 1996, was *Every Day in Your Spirit: New Hymns written between 1992 and 1996*. Shirley dedicated the book of 41 hymns to her grandchildren, Alexander, Elizabeth and Fergus.

Publication followed several years of correspondence between Shirley and George, as they discussed what new hymns should be included and what music should accompany them. The intention was that Shirley should introduce both books at the Hymn Society conference in Oberlin, Ohio, that summer, and during her two-week Routley lectureship in hymnology for the Presbyterian Association of Musicians summer school at Montreat, North Carolina. Again, Hope covered all Shirley and John's expenses from New Zealand to these events. "You are very generous in your support of our traipsings," Shirley wrote to George in March 1996.

Shirley received her advance copies of *Every Day in Your Spirit* at the end of May 1996, a few weeks before her departure for the States. It included the hymn 'We are the Singers', which Shirley wrote for the Montreat Conference. The four verses include six different biblical images, one for each day of the week's worship. The tune in this collection is by Jane Marshall. Shirley faxed George on 30 May:

> I have *Every Day* in my hand and what a dazzling effect! It's a brilliant cover and I love it. I feel it exudes energy and the delineating of the design script in fine black has helped the strong colours stand out ...

> I'm sure I detect your own hand in the back cover blurb. It's a fine vote of confidence in my continuing survival. I think the quality and variety of music in this book is outstanding. So I am surprised to find no list of composers. Was this intentional?

> Of course it's like the new baby and I keep examining it for fingers and toes ... I hope you feel happy with the production. Thank you always for your faith in my work – something I value greatly. And now to spread the good news around, with much enthusiasm – Shirley.

At the Hymn Society conference, Shirley and John not only discussed the new book, but again introduced members to other New Zealand hymns. True to her ecumenical spirit, Shirley also introduced them to the work of Pastor Per Harling from Sweden and Professor I-to Loh from Taiwan, both of whom she had met at the World Council of Churches' Assembly in 1991.

> Attending these Hymn Society conferences was a good experience and Hope certainly encouraged me to meet other composers and writers. But I was also aware that rather a lot of sanctimonious rubbish had been published, which our hymn book editors in New Zealand would have rejected. Poems without poetry and doggerel without theology are not what we need.[5]

In June of that year, Shirley spent two weeks as the Routley lecturer in hymnology at the Presbyterian Association of Musicians' summer school in Montreat, North Carolina. This annual conference is named after the English congregational churchman, theologian and hymnologist Erik Routley, who was named a Fellow of the Hymn Society in the United States and Canada posthumously in 1985.

In a video interview with Sam Young and George Shorney in July 1996, Shirley described being the Routley lecturer as "a great experience". This interview was one of a series in which leading hymn writers from Hope's stable discussed their work and the art of hymn writing. The video production, however, was never completed.

But in her interview for the St Andrew's oral history project, she confessed that having to deliver daily lectures when she did not see herself as a lecturer had been "quite a trial".

Some of her classes, the largest of which was 40, the smallest 20, introduced budding hymn writers to her own work; others were more hands-on, focusing on the craft of hymn writing and how to incorporate new concepts like lasers and computers into hymns. Shirley admitted struggling to do this successfully herself:

> How can we express faith through our computerised lives? I can't break this barrier either.
>
> I did find a great deal of enthusiasm or over-enthusiasm for going back to old language. That surprised me, even though they saw

themselves as leading contemporary lives. But there was also a great eagerness to express new ideas, if they had them. There were some funny efforts and some commendable efforts. The world needs more text writers – there are heaps of composers already.[6]

Faith Makes the Song: New Hymns written between 1997 and 2002 appeared in 2003. Shirley dedicated this book of 50 works to granddaughters Isabella, Anna and Rachel. Settings are a mixture of New Zealand, American and Swedish contributions, including six by Jenny McLeod.

In the book's foreword, George Shorney described his company's relationship with Shirley in more detail. This was sparked by introductions from Brian Wren, he said, and fostered by then Hope editor, Carlton 'Sam' Young, "who urged us to take a very careful look at this talented hymn writer". It was during his 1991 visit to New Zealand that Hope's executive editor, Jack Shrader, convinced Shirley to join Hope's hymn-writing team.

"Thus, her career as an internationally recognised hymn writer began," wrote George. In Hope's opinion, "Shirley now clearly ranks among the best in her chosen field ... with some of her best work yet to come!"

Brian Wren wrote the foreword for Shirley's next publication with Hope, the 2008 collection *Touch the Earth Lightly: New Hymns written between 2003 and 2008*. Shirley dedicated this book of 60 hymns to her husband John, "without whom these hymns might never have been written, and to mark a lifelong passion for singing the faith, with my love and gratitude".

Brian praised Shirley's gifts as a poetic hymn writer. "The hymns are public poems, for the church to say and sing. They take God in Christ seriously, trust in the working of God's spirit, and are acutely aware of the urgent claims of peace, social justice and reverence for God's creation on planet Earth. The author knows and explores the power of English speech rhythms and poetic meter in a way that stimulates composers to lift her words with fine tunes. Where others can get wordy (myself included), Shirley Murray is pithy. Where others get stale, she is fresh and refreshing. Where others are dense, she is economical. Saying and hearing her work, I keep finding lines, words and phrases that make me say, 'Darn it! Why didn't I think of something like that?' And then 'Wow! I'm glad she did!'"

Brian pointed to several examples of Shirley's powerful use of language, first among them the Advent carol, 'Bring in Your New World':

> Bring in your new world, child of the east,
>> dangerous leader,
>> born to be pleader,
>> prophet and priest,
>
> come with your judgment, voice for the poor,
>> born to collision,
>> God's righteous vision
>> here at our door.

Shirley's fifth publication with Hope was *A Place at the Table: New Hymns Written Between 2009 and 2013*. This time, her dedication was to George H. Shorney "who, never having met me before, greeted me with an instant hug. In happy memory of his large vision, encouragement, friendship and marvellous generosity of spirit, with love."

She also thanked Hope Publishing Company for "accepting my work without question and giving my New Zealand voice a chance to be heard over the years from 1992 until now" and paid tribute to her "worldwide circle of composer friends, all of whom have a particular place in my heart for the interest and delight they provide me, and especially for their friendship, as well as their music".

In her introduction to the book of 47 hymns, Shirley described the collection "as a kind of spiritual autobiography of the years since writing *Touch the Earth Lightly*, published four years previously. Her themes continued "to centre on peace, partnered with justice, as these relate to our own faith journey". She admitted to finding her life "further away from the church and closer to what Jesus is actually pointing to". At the same time, she embraced the concept of "an interfaith and interactive world" in which making connection with people of different beliefs and viewpoints has become "imperative for our human survival".

Shirley's sixth and final collection of hymn texts published by Hope was *Life into Life: New and Collected Hymns*. This appeared in 2019, only months before her death. Shirley had hoped it would have been published earlier, fearing it could become her obituary if publication was delayed too long.

Despite suffering a stroke in early 2018, which affected her speech and writing ability, she continued to email her many close friends, and was grateful for this technology.

Corresponding with Ron Klusmeier in late 2018, Shirley expressed some ambivalence about the book: "It's a bit of a rag-tag collection and I don't feel very happy with its contents ... I've got to admit that energies are low and I don't feel like writing – rather re-reading and wondering where my theology has altered!"[7]

In May 2019, Shirley again emailed Ron about the book: "Hope ... are putting all the bits and pieces I've left in some sort of order. I trust something will emerge that's not too embarrassing."

That month, Shirley assigned the copyright to all her works to Hope Publishing Company worldwide.

In their foreword to the book, the publishers wrote: "Shirley's hymns have been published in over 30 major denominational hymnals across North America, and many more in Europe, Australia, New Zealand and Asia. She has truly become one of the most influential international hymn text writers of our time. It has been our pleasure and good fortune to work with her over the past three decades."

The first section of the new book (70 works in total) contains 34 new texts by Shirley, written from 2014 to 2019. Section two focuses on previously published texts paired with new tunes written since first publication. A 'green' section comprises Shirley's hand-picked hymns about environmental stewardship, while a fourth section is made up of her all-time favourite texts grouped together for the first time.

Brian Wren added some further comments in an introduction to the book: "Read or sing through this book and you will meet the remarkable gifts of Shirley Murray, who combines simplicity with profundity, respect for scripture founded on a willingness to look beyond its literal meaning, theology in poetry, and language that can bring us to tears or move us to say 'Ah-ha', and 'Wow!'"

Hope Publishing Company remains deeply committed to promoting Shirley's hymns, ensuring their availability and viability. In a tribute for this biography, Hope's associate editor of hymnody, Carl Daw, said the company will sometimes make editorial adjustments in order to reflect Shirley's vision with integrity in changed circumstances. It recently made an authorised revision of her hymn 'For Everyone Born', for example, "providing alternative language for passages that worked against her intention to be inclusive and affirming". As part of its stewardship of her texts, Hope intends continuing such work "so that a widening circle of readers and singers may continue to be challenged and inspired by Shirley's clear and prophetic voice". [For the revised text of 'For Everyone Born', see Chapter 29]

According to Hope vice president Scott Shorney (George's son), the company has no plans to alter any other texts of Shirley's, nor does it normally allow others to make alterations. However, it recently allowed the Church of Scotland to make slight word changes to five of Shirley's hymns. These will be included in its upcoming Supplement to its *Church Hymnary: Fourth Edition* (commonly known as *CH4*). In correspondence with the author, Shorney stated that the original versions of Shirley's work would always be available.

Notes

1   Verse 1 of 'Creation Sings!' was written in 2000 for the American Association of Musicians to celebrate the gift of music. Shirley draws on rich musical terminology as a metaphor for the energy and art of God.

2   Video interview with Ron Klusmeier, Raumati Beach, August 2014.

3   Shorney, G.H. (2002) Foreword. *Faith Makes the Song.* Hope Publishing Company.

4   McKinley, D. (1992) The 1992 Annual Conference of The Hymn Society. *The Hymn*, vol 43, no 4, 10, October.

5   Interview with Margaret Pannett for the St Andrew's on The Terrace oral history project, 7 November 2006.

6   Video interview with Sam Young and George Shorney, July 1996.

7   Email to Ron Klusmeier, 10 November 2018.

12 – The art of hymn writing I

Loving Spirit, loving Spirit,
you have chosen me to be;
you have drawn me to your wonder,
you have set your sign on me.[1]

In July 1996, president of Hope Publishing Company George Shorney and editor Carlton ('Sam') Young interviewed Shirley on video as part of their series on the new hymn writers who were part of Hope's stable. Although a completed production was never realised, the interviews remain of great archival value. What follows are Shirley's answers to ten questions put to her during this interview.

Three people encouraged me most to become a hymn writer. Myself (I was so frustrated with the hymns that already existed), John (he was always looking for hymns for his sermons and could find very little) and Colin Gibson whom I didn't know until the mid-'70s. Colin is thought of as Mr Methodist Musician of the New Zealand church. He is a professor of English, a humorist, good with children and good with both music and words, which is rare, I think.

Brian Wren has always been a great encourager, supporter and mentor.

What is my personal favourite hymn? Isn't that like saying which one of your children you love best? But I keep going back to 'Loving Spirit' because it was the first one that introduced me to another world of hymns. It was the first of my hymns sung in an international setting, at a World Council of Churches' Assembly. It is also the only hymn of mine that has been translated into Braille. That touches me.

I have been both an editor and been edited. John Wesley said you are stirring up a nest of hornets if you touch an author's work. "Either let them stand for better or worse or add the true reading in the margin or at the bottom of the page that we may no longer be accountable either for the nonsense or the doggerel of other men." That's it for me.

As an editor, I have a rather cautious policy in re-editing what I call the classics. Then there are those that fall between the classics and contemporary hymns. So I have a very slow approach to changing such things as [John Bunyan's] 'Who Would True Valour See' as it is set in its poetical form. But if a hymn has no lasting value, this doesn't really matter. Classics should stand. That's my modest opinion about this.

I am not that attached to the great classic hymn writers like Isaac Watts and Charles Wesley – perhaps I sang too many of their hymns in my youth. I did steal the line 'In every corner sing' from the 17th century English poet and clergyman George Herbert. I also treasure the hymn 'My Song is Love Unknown' by the Puritan minister Samuel Crossman, written in 1664.

I have had some problems with hymn book committees wanting to edit some of my hymns, e.g. one committee wanted to change 'Loving Spirit' to 'Holy Spirit'. Some committees have problems with words of colour, particularly the word black.

These days, I rarely have a tune in mind. People will offer them to me, and I like people who are prepared to play around with metres, rather than using the old safe ones all the time. I have a good musical memory. I am not a great singer but I do remember tunes. Tunes are what I thrive on. I have only had one of my tunes published and that was for 'Alleluia Aotearoa', the opening hymn in *Alleluia Aotearoa*.

I owe the Presbyterian tradition a lot but never felt the Presbyterian Church was the boundary of where I am. I grew up as a Methodist. Labels have never meant much to me because I feel part of a much wider faith community. Faith community and the word Christian are more important to me than any denominationalism.

You ask about my thoughts on feminism. Gender has no importance in a hymn writer, but there is an historic imbalance in that there are so few hymns that ever mention women or make them visible, therefore I have tended to explore that particular area.

I've been writing hymns for 40 years. I have learned to be more careful than I was in the beginning. My technique has improved. I am leaner and more economic in the way I use words. I love using compact metres and I have learned how to use longer metres more intelligently. I have not come to the end of the learning process.

Themes are exciting. There is so much more to keep writing about. At the beginning, I would never have thought of writing a hymn about AIDS. Unemployment I am not frightened to write about – my family has experienced that. Health and healing are other areas that have come towards me, especially to do with the health system of our country – it has been failing those in need. My interest lies with justice and injustice and who gets the care and from where. There is much more work to do.

I did not find much satisfaction in traditional sacramental hymns, e.g. for communion and baptism, so have written two or three. I also think new hymns are needed for the church year, e.g. Holy Week, for political prisoners, for the issue of peace which was the heart of the Gospel for Jesus. I am not so good at writing hymns for children.

I rarely write anything quickly anymore. In the beginning I thought I was rather smart. Now I realise what I wrote was not well polished or thoughtful enough. One thing I have been struggling with a lot is the theme of old age or growing older.

People often come to me with a request for an occasional hymn, e.g. for women's suffrage or sport. [In 1994, Shirley wrote a hymn 'Celebrate, All Human Beauty', sung to Beethoven's Ode to Joy, for a service in Wellington marking the end of the World Triathlon Championships held in the city.] These hymns do not take so long to write.

Divisions in the church

The church has changed enormously over the past 40 years. The Presbyterian Church is the second largest non-Catholic denomination in New Zealand, second only to the Anglicans. Its heyday was in the 1960s, but in the '70s it became nervous about its theology. We had a 'heresy trial' [concerning the statements made by the Rev Dr Lloyd Geering, see chapter 5] which rocked our church and divided us sharply. Congregations realised the clergy had not been open about what they were thinking and reading, and a lack of trust developed.

We now have distinct fundamentalist and more radical groups. As a result, the church is shrinking. I find this sad. I feel I am living through a slow death. Then I realise I am part of a much wider faith community than the Presbyterian Church and that this should not worry me. Perhaps we are waiting for something else to grow or develop.

In the United States, I sense still a strong core of traditional belief which is carrying people into the next decade or two. I find that theologically puzzling. Most people seem to be staying with 19th century ideas. I would like to be carried into the next millennium – where are the words that will do that? The church has not splintered in the way it might have but the melting pot of ideas is perhaps moving us to multi-faith concerns rather than denominational Christian concerns.

Working with New Zealand composers

We have many musicians in New Zealand of many different styles who are continuing to create a musical explosion. The New Zealand Hymnbook Trust has done a lot to introduce new hymns to our churches. In the 1960s and '70s, New Zealand was responsible for about 80 per cent of the charismatic choruses being written worldwide over that time – this is quite astonishing.

I work a lot with Jillian Bray who is from the Gospel Chapel tradition. Her compositions are mostly informal and flexible, and the hymns she writes are beautiful. Ian Render, an Anglican vicar, has composed tunes for my texts, as has Cecily Sheehy, a Roman Catholic nun who specialises in writing for children and family groups. The late Dr Douglas Mews, who was an editor for the Hymnbook Trust for a time, was also Roman Catholic, as well as a superb organist and musician. Colin Gibson is our best-known musician and composer. Our theology may differ, but I admire his talent for introducing new hymns to congregations and for his skills as a craftsperson.

Although some of the older hymns have influenced and inspired me, I owe most to contemporary people, particularly to Brian Wren who encouraged and taught me, and is a marvellous poet and hymn writer. The Scottish minister and hymn writer John Bell is a friend and has influenced me a great deal. He has made me look at Celtic hymns and the connections you can make with popular tunes. His theology of work and worship is very fine.

As a hymn writer, you need a friend or somebody who will be honest with you to tell you when you go off the track – not just an encourager. My husband John does that for me – he can be a severe critic.

Hymn writers have to be poets, otherwise their words would be banal. On the other hand, poetry is private and hymn writing is public.

I love poetry and parody and wit in poetry. T.S. Eliot and his mysticism influenced me greatly in my student days. The American poet Wallace Stevens influences me. He says God and the imagination are one. I am still playing with that theological puzzle. I love that line. And I love the poet Robert Frost, of course, while Ogden Nash is my all-time favourite.

Nash once wrote a metrical exercise that I sometimes use in my hymn-writing classes because it breaks the rules:

> I didn't go to church today
> I trust the Lord to understand
> The surf was swirling blue and white
> The children swirling in the sand.
> He knows, he knows how brief my stay,
> How brief this spell of summer weather,
> He knows, when I am said and done,
> We'll have plenty of time together.

I also dabble in writing poetry. I always get drawn back into metrical poetry because of the poetry I admire. I do not write much free-flowing poetry.

Delight in precision

There are irrational reasons why we love hymns. Most people think it's mostly about the music. For me, it must stay visually fresh, with a meaning that gives lots of levels of satisfaction. It has to have a precise sort of form – I delight in precision. It should be able to say what it has to say in quite a short span – four verses are usually plenty – and it must lead to an emotionally satisfying feeling. Hymns are about heart as well as gut and head. That sums it up for me.

I dislike sloppiness in words and woolliness, e.g. words like foundation, creation – abstract words that tell you very little. I love tightly-knit lines. I respond to work that is spare and simple. Brian Wren once gave me the three monastic vows: simplicity, clarity and strict obedience to the hymn form, which you can't get away from – this art has a certain and delightful restraint.

Metaphors are important to me, of course. In the carol 'Star-Child', I use the phrase 'heaven's lightning rod' to refer to the electric quality that comes from the action of the spirit on our human qualities. I have used simple relational metaphors, e.g. God as mother, father, friend and lover in the hymn 'Loving Spirit'. I understand new dimensions of motherhood as I grow older and become a mother, then a grandmother. Good hymns should grow deeper for people as time goes on.

I like to use Māori language in hymns, though I am not a Māori speaker. My husband John is. I use some words, about six to eight, that I feel safe to use, e.g. tapu [sacred], mana [prestige, influence], aroha, the last having a much broader meaning than the English word love. In New Zealand, we are trying hard to co-exist as a bicultural country. At the same time, we are also becoming multicultural.

All our theology in New Zealand is upside down. We don't have springtime at Easter. Instead, we think of burning leaves and planting bulbs for the spring. We can't talk about robins and reindeer and snow at Christmas time, which is why I wrote 'Upside Down Christmas'. This explores the images that make sense to us in summertime.

What we sing we believe and what we believe, we ought to sing. It's the best way to convey theology and the most enjoyable way to express it. Protestants have always done this. Hymn writers have a responsibility to stretch people's horizons and to pull them into new theology that is memorable. Sermons will be forgotten, but hymns are memorable. They are the place for new ideas, new metaphors, new politics, for all our faith expressions to be held.

When do you stop working on a hymn? You must do plenty of pruning and endless retuning. Write down the theme you want to address and when you have addressed it, stop. The same applies to sermons, some of which can be long and straggly and should have been stopped long before the end. Every verse of a hymn should expand on the theme.

If all my hymns disappeared bar one, I would hope it would be one with peace at its heart, as active peacemaking is terribly important to me. This is at the heart of what Jesus came for. I have written peace carols and peace hymns. I value peacemakers.

Note

1 Verse 1, 'Loving Spirit', written in 1986, as a simple reflection into metaphors of God. Published in *Alleluia Aotearoa* in 1993 with settings by David Dell and Colin Gibson. It was sung to a setting by I-to Loh during a liturgy at the World Council of Churches' Assembly at Canberra in 1991.

13 – The art of hymn writing II

Something beautiful for God,
in my seeing,
in my being,

something beautiful for God
let the Spirit make of me.[1]

Shirley the poet is the epithet most commonly used by the interviewees for this book. Retired Anglican priest George Armstrong admits that, at one time, he dismissed her hymns as being 'a bit lightweight'.

"Reading her hymns today has given me a new respect for her calibre, and for her radical ideas – not so much political as poetical. I have always believed in poetry rather than theology, though I didn't really understand that till about ten years ago."

Armstrong points to two hymns that impress him greatly – 'When at this Table I Receive a Blessing' and 'A Single Grain of Wheat'. "The former is a personal hymn of approach to communion, an honest hymn that opens up the table to the needs of the world around us. It enables people to be deeply engaged in this part of the liturgy if they want to be.

"'A Single Grain of Wheat' is magnificent, rich with metaphors of death, decay and new life. It was published in her last collection with Hope, *Life into Life*, with music by Lim Swee Hong (see chapter 24).

"I read these hymns again and wondered why I had never appreciated them before. Shirley's poems remind me of [German poet Dietrich] Bonhoeffer's. His poems are some of the finest I have ever read. Shirley understood what was happening in New Zealand and in the world at a deep level. She also had the great ability to think in metaphors."

Shirley's final interview with Sheila Irwin in 2002 focuses exclusively on the art of hymn writing and what drew Shirley to this particular art form. She explained that the incentives that had started her off writing hymns 25 years previously remained the same. "There is nothing extant that expresses what I want to sing about; there is also so much to sing about. Both these things are real prods to get me going."[2]

This chapter comprises the material from this interview, as well as extracts from recordings Shirley made four years later for the St Andrew's oral history project, a video interview made in 2014 by Ron Klusmeier, and the chapter written by Shirley for Janet Wootton's book *This is Our Song: Women's Hymn-writing*.[3]

In Wootton's book, Shirley goes deeper into her motivations for becoming a hymn writer. She wanted to sing hymns that resonated with the world she lived in, and she wanted to discover and use imagery that evoked the New Zealand environment. She also wanted to express something of New Zealand as a bicultural nation and of Māori culture. Above all, she wanted to get away from the sentimentalism of the old 18th and 19th century hymns, away from poorly crafted language and "incomprehensible biblical jargon".[4] And she sought to "write myself into faith".[5]

At the same time, Shirley, prompted by John seeking hymns that expressed or reinforced what he was trying to say in his sermons, realised how many urgent themes needed addressing: peacemaking, racism, refugees, care of the earth, healing. New interpretations of the sacraments and seasons of the church year were also needed. But her abiding theme is peace, "in all its many manifestations".[6]

> There are three components to a hymn: the words come first, then the tune and thirdly, the faith of the people singing it. It was so wonderful being part of the St Andrew's on The Terrace congregation who were willing to try out my hymns. Maybe they had them foisted upon them, but when they tried them out, they were very fair to me. I got a lot of encouragement.

First of all, I wrote hymns to familiar tunes, then very quickly I began to see, and here I agree with Colin Gibson, that if you are going to use contemporary words with contemporary imagery, they don't marry well with 19th century hymn tunes.

I don't write music because it is such a refined skill. Hymn music has to respect so many rules and you have to have an inspiration for it. Words are where I stop. Very few people can write both good texts and good music. Tunes are immensely important, but congregations are generally lazy about adopting new tunes.

Everyone finds time for the things they really want to do. Writing hymns is quite a portable skill, but it does require patches of quiet time without interruption. It could be the time spent walking down the beach. Life being what it is, I am often surprised I ever wrote anything, especially in those busy years between 1980 and 1990.

In the beginning, I was writing out of a vacuum. Amnesty International has no religious bias but did have a religious affairs officer, who was me. My task was to draw together people of all faiths, if possible, to do what they could for specific prisoners who were in prison because of their faith. There was absolutely nothing to sing, we had nothing in common to sing. One of my first hymns on this topic – 'God of Freedom, God of Justice' – was taken up by Amnesty International in English-speaking countries. This encouraged me because I realised there was a vacuum here and I could fill it.[7]

Shirley's earlier attempt to write a song for human rights was 'Sing a Song for Peace and Justice', which was sung at a Human Rights Day at Old St Paul's, Wellington. She later described this as "a superficial song".

At the time of the 1981 Springbok rugby tour, I could find no hymn that addressed the subject of racism. Perhaps I did not know John Oxenham's 1908 hymn 'In Christ There is No East Nor West', but I felt you had to hit the subject harder, and to express it in terms that people today would find truth in. So my first hymn about racism was 'O God, We Bear the Imprint of Your Face'.[8]

Shirley's own involvement in the 1981 Springbok Tour, including the arrest of her son David and public denunciation of husband John, who had led a protest in Parliament, were further prompts for this hymn (see chapter 7).

> In 1992, a pastor in Los Angeles wrote to me during the race riots in the city that year. He told me he had found that hymn and was so grateful. That was encouraging. Although I am not always pleased with all my work, when something hits the spot, it is terribly gratifying and encouraging.
>
> Inspiration for a hymn can come quickly or take days of mulling on a particular topic. Something begins to tickle your ideas. Sometimes it might be prompted by something I read in the newspaper, e.g. a good headline. And titles of books are good – I might run my eye down a list of book titles. These are often skilfully chosen and might make me think of a phrase. 'Living proof' is the phrase I am playing around with at the moment – about the incarnation, though it is hard to get rhymes for proof. A multitude of things will feed into that – I listen to the radio a lot. Other people's lives and my own experience are all mixed up in the hymns I write.[9]
>
> I love catching a little phrase or a little idea from anywhere, out of the blue. 'Touch the Earth Lightly' was stolen from a poster, in turn borrowed from an Australian Aboriginal saying. I sometimes see things in someone else's writing. The best composers did this too. I have stolen a phrase like: 'There is no way to peace: peace is the way', a quote from a pacifist clergyman in the United States, A.J. Muste. I first saw this on a Peace Movement poster and used it as my punch line to my 1985 hymn 'O Christ Who by a Cross Made Peace Your Sign: A Hymn for Peace'. That sort of stealing is ok.
>
> I often scribble things down, then lose the bit of paper. But I love catching an idea from the great thinkers like Dietrich Bonhoeffer or Teilhard de Chardin and then turning it around. Maybe I am a cheat. I try to extend what I borrow but retain the essence of what the writer was writing about.

To be successful, you must use the ordinary words that people know and use, then you must lift them so they are beautiful as well as functional. I have not come to the end of learning here.

In order to write anything – a tune or a text – you have to have listened to 1000 tunes and read 1000 texts. When they come together well, it is an amazing feeling. But the craft is tough. I have to learn not to let ideas run away with me. The heartbeat of a hymn is a good metre that catches the ideas you are trying to put together. Metres can keep you in a straight jacket. This can be loosened up but I did not know how to do it in my early attempts.

I like perfect rhymes; I don't like half rhymes. English is full of temptations to put things like born and storm together. I don't like tired rhymes, e.g. love and dove and above. We all love the sound of a good rhyme. Rhymes are a challenge and a necessity for me. The ear that is attuned to the traditional hymn waits for the rhyme at the end of the line from the previous line.

Repetition is one of the tricks or mechanics of writing any song. A lot of lyrics have repetition to make their point. Hymn writing as an art and craft form is quite different from poetry.

It has taken me years to really feel comfortable with this craft. I have a great deal of respect for people who can use unusual words and somehow integrate them so they flow in a hymn. I have tried this myself with awkward words like crutches, stigmas, bullet, drugs, soup-kitchen, laser – they will sit well if the line is able to carry them along.[10]

I appreciate and relate to precise and clean language, as opposed to flowery and fudgy. I am, in knitting parlance, a plain rather than purl sort of writer. I like language with crunch and bite that gives a jolt of reality. I like using short syllables, but also words mellifluous enough to be poetic and singable – above all singable.[11]

In New Zealand, we can introduce words and concepts that are distinctively ours but there is a huge danger in throwing in things like a pūkeko in a punga tree in order to make it sound like a New Zealand hymn. I am wary of doing this. The first time I tried writing a serious hymn with a couple of Māori words in it, I tested it out with my friend the Rev Ron Matthews to see whether he thought it would work. He said, go ahead, after all words like aroha and mana are two pretty common words. I would hate to have used those words wrongly. There are also ways of thinking about our country in the images we choose. Think of Colin Gibson's hymn 'These Hills Where the Hawk Flies Lonely'.

Hymns also have to work outside New Zealand, in the way the Gospel has to. In terms of global Christianity, there is a local flavour but, in the end, the deep truths are applicable to us all.

My hymn writing coincided with a wave of enthusiasm for women's rights, so I was keen to see that inclusive language was used so women were there, not invisible.[12]

Women's rights are close to my heart and I am especially proud that both my grandmothers signed the Women's Suffrage Petition presented to Parliament in 1893. When I worked for the Labour Party as a researcher in the 1980s, I could observe ongoing efforts the women MPs were making to help women achieve equality.

Sometimes I have written quite stroppy hymns, e.g. 'Where God Enlightens, Bless the Light' [published in the 1996 Hope publication *Every Day in Your Spirit* but first written in 1989 to continue the Easter theme of the Ecumenical Decade of the Churches in Solidarity with Women – 1988-1998]. It's about the ordination and rights of women to be priests and prophets. It might be a little stroppy, but I think it still needs to be sung. Women both here and in other countries have not been given their full place in the church.[13]

When this hymn was first published, a traditional spiritual hymn tune for 'Go Down Moses', was suggested to accompany it. However, Shirley later heard that some African Americans were insulted that this tune was being used. Canadian hymn writer Ron Klusmeier subsequently wrote a new tune – "a good ending to the story", Shirley said.[14]

During the same Ecumenical Decade, Shirley wrote 'Of Women, and of Women's Hopes We Sing'. The hymn was published in her first Hope publication, *In Every Corner Sing*, with a tune by Jane Marshall. In 1993, the centennial of Women's Suffrage in New Zealand, it was sung widely. Again, she received a complaint – this time from men who said they could not sing it.[15] Shirley admits:

Having already nailed my colours to the mast of inclusiveness, and tailoring language to suit an ideology of gender balance, that could be a contradiction in itself. … Early on in my hymn writing, I learned that the politics of inclusiveness are subtle, language is an inherently dangerous tool and it is wise to heed the needs of the *whole* congregation, when new and possibly jolting ideas are involved.[16]

As a hymn writer I feel the need to introduce ideas about women and other vulnerable sections of society, e.g. children and old people, into hymns. There are very few hymns about old people or growing old. I like lines that draw me in as an older person – that gave rise to the third verse for 'For Everyone Born, a Place at the Table'. Everyone has the right to be there.[17]

And to cheer herself up as an older person, Shirley also wrote 'Let My Spirit Always Sing, Though My Heart Be Wintering'. This hymn on growing older, with a 'beautiful' tune by the US hymn writer Rusty Edwards, has been sung on the United Nations International Day of Older Persons in New Zealand. "I have always wanted a hymn to sing on growing older which is positive and not regretful," said Shirley in the Hope publication *Every Day in Your Spirit*.

I recraft my work tremendously. As soon as your hymn becomes a public item, you will discover lines or words you wish you had not put in. A hymn (unlike a poem) is going to become part of a community of people and repeated, you hope, more than once. This means that even the tiniest preposition has to be right.

I write heaps of versions before I am really satisfied. Someone once said: 'Never think you have created the world's greatest hymn. Let it cool and the longer you let it cool, you will discover more and more changes you would like to make in it.' This is quite true. Once the words have cooled, I can see what needs to be attended to.

You do your best with every word in the text. You need to make sure it is saying what you started out to say and that it's kept its register – i.e. it's kept to one important theme without wandering too far, and you have concluded it. It is like a tiny sermon, though I hate to say that because often sermons are very boring!

Hymns can be a teaching device, though this was more so in the past. But because there are whole generations of kids and young people who don't even know the Bible stories, it is rather difficult to know how much biblical allusion to make. Colin Gibson sometimes writes to teach stories to people of all ages. His hymn 'Twelve Disciples Jesus Had' runs down the list of the disciples, like a mnemonic.

Hymns for special events

I began writing hymns for funerals, weddings or other special events quite early in the piece. The people at St Andrew's, when John and I first arrived, had little choice in the hymns they sang. It's amazing that you can use Psalm 23 for both a wedding and a funeral. What about something more joyful and more focused on two people in love and getting married? So, in 1988, I wrote 'Come to a Wedding' for my son Rob and daughter-in-law Christine's wedding and that encouraged them. [See chapter 15.]

I have now written about three wedding hymns but I am better at funerals because when you have had someone live a rich and full life, then there must be something to sing that is sheer thanksgiving. I have written at least two hymns on these themes.

I have written hymns on sudden deaths. One, written for the death of a younger child, 'Little One, Born to Bring Us Such Love', was hard to write because I had someone in mind who helped focus it for me. It was an attempt to bring some comfort in a situation of utter grief.

I have written one about being told you have a terminal illness – 'When Our Lives Know Sudden Shadow'– written in 1995 for a friend who died from AIDS. This was taken up by the World Council of Churches during the peak of the AIDS pandemic, and has been used for other times of sudden tragedy.

Then there is my own reality of cancer. I was diagnosed with breast cancer in 2000 and had a year of being ill. I was having to collate what I had written in previous years. In the year I was sick, I wrote a number of hymns – but none about sickness; they were mostly about life. Perhaps I was clinging to life or realising, in a fresh kind of way, how precious life is.

I feel I have been given a marvellous reprieve and I am not that especially good at thinking about, or writing about sickness. I wish there were more and better ones for people to sing. I only knew one when I was growing up, the 19th century English hymn 'At Even, Ere the Sun Was Set, the Sick, O Lord, Around Thee Lay'. Healing miracles need to be reinterpreted through eyes that know science.[18]

Two or three hymns I wrote in 2000 were green hymns, i.e. hymns about care of the earth. Eco-theology is where we should be at now. My hymn 'Touch the Earth Lightly', written in 1991, has now been published in many hymn collections internationally.[19]

In 2006, Shirley wrote 'Look in Wonder', as a response to the documentary *An Inconvenient Truth*. Fronted by former United States Vice President Al Gore, the film was a wake-up call to the world community to recognise and respond to the dangers of global warming. The hymn was first published in her 2008 Hope collection *Touch the Earth Lightly*, and later in *Hope is our Song*.

Recently, I have been exploring some of Lloyd Geering's lectures on wisdom, i.e. the similarities between the person of Jesus and wisdom literature. [The Greek philosophical concept of] Sophia and what Jesus personified are closely linked. 'Wisdom Be Our Guide', written in 2007, is loosely related to the Apocryphal book, *The Wisdom of Solomon*. Its chorus is about how ordinary people, with God's help, can turn the world around.

Working with composers

I am proud of New Zealand composers – our musicians are world class, but text writers are not so common. Many of my texts have been set by New Zealand composers, including Colin Gibson, Jillian Bray, Ian Render and Douglas Mews. But when my work got known outside New Zealand, I began to make links with composers of many sorts – this has been one of the great thrills of my life. People began to send me tunes they had written for my words. They could see the familiar tune perhaps did not do my words justice but also they might relate to that particular text.

Now I work with composers from all round the world, from Sweden to Taiwan, to Brazil to North America. People just keep sending me tunes, and this keeps me so busy, I find it hard to sit and critique all of them, and I have never found a way of saying I can't be bothered with this tune. There is always some merit somewhere.

Charles Wesley wrote more than 5000 hymns. He even wrote a hymn on a child cutting his tooth. But it is not in numbers that one counts good hymns. Most of us have a handful of favourite hymns we will always love.[20]

What is different in our life now that did not exist for earlier hymn writers? And what will be relevant for the next generation? The big one is science and technology that is changing how we see the world and how we think. I am still working on this in my tiny way. [Shirley uses metaphors like cursors and codes in her 2008 hymn 'In What Strange Land' – see chapter 14.] Hymn texts are starting to emerge but I need composers who lift them and match the idea that we are moving into a different place as we evolve.[21]

What about the future?

I now sense a church that is slightly insecure and becoming more conservative by the day instead of embracing the things that really make sense of the world. This is rather a wide judgement, but, to me, if something isn't real in terms of how it can be understood by anybody, then a few select people knowing certain jargon or ideas isn't good enough. Besides, the world is in such a state that it needs all our energy and understanding to work with each other.

I don't see the church tackling much outside itself. I've waited for ages to find any statement about the church's attitude towards the war in Iraq, for instance. That is why I can't sing any of the old hymns that have triumphalist overtones, e.g. 'Onward Christian Soldiers'. We need to chuck out a lot of the old hymns because they do not match what we really believe now. I hope we are now more doves than hawks.[22]

I believe the hymn of the future has to have less Christian dogma and more openness, less mention of the Cross and more mention of God as an inclusive being. I would like to see some interfaith hymns – we have tried this on the Kāpiti Coast to some extent. But is this a hopeless dream, I wonder?[23]

Teilhard de Chardin says that, in the end, an energy will arrive when all the good and all the bad and all the suffering is gathered up and made into something dynamic that will change the world. Until that happens, you have to keep gathering up the good. This idea appeals to me.[24]

Notes

1 Verse 1, 'Something Beautiful For God', a hymn of personal dedication, echoing words attributed to Mother Teresa. The hymn has been set by many composers who have responded to the simplicity and plainness of this prayer-text.

2 APW interview with Sheila Irwin, 22 November 2002.

3 Wootton, 2010, pp295-307.

4 Wootton, 2010, p301.

5 Wootton, 2010, p306.

6 Wootton, 2010, p301.

7 See note 2.

8 See note 2.

9 See note 2.

10 Video and audio interview with Ron Klusmeier at Raumati Beach, August 2014.

11 Wootton, 210, p297.

12 See note 2.

13 Interview with Margaret Pannett for the St Andrew's on the Terrace oral history project, 7 November 2006.

14 See note 10.

15 See note 13.

16 Wootton, 2010, p295.

17 See note 2.

18 See note 2.

19 See note 13.

20 See note 2.

21 See note 13.

22 See note 2.

23 See note 13.

24 See note 10.

14 – Introducing new hymns

Come and find the quiet centre
In the crowded life we lead,
Find the room for hope to enter,
Find the frame where we are freed:

Clear the chaos and the clutter,
Clear our eyes, that we can see
All the things that really matter,
Be at peace, and simply be.[1]

Shirley saw hymns as the folk song of the church and the people's voice. She believed that when the last word of the most rhetorical or astute sermon was forgotten, people would remember, 'Jesus Loves Me, This I Know…'

In an article published in 2004, Shirley set out some clear guidelines on how congregations and church leaders should approach the learning of new hymns.[2] "If we're still singing 'Abide With Me', and equating change with decay, there's something rotten in the state of our theology," she wrote.

"So, in the drama which is liturgy – words, music, dance, silence, body language – hymns are our best way of gathering the people into a sense of community. As Scottish hymn writer John Bell says: 'Within the worship of the church, they shape what we think, what we believe, and what, ultimately, we do, as those who follow Jesus Christ.'"

Shirley's knowledge of what creates or destroys meaningful worship where hymns are involved developed from "a lifetime of pew-sitting and hymn-singing". With some passion, she drew up a list of suggestions of dos and don'ts regarding hymn-singing, choosing and teaching:

- Train the clergy/worship leaders properly! Make sure they study and sing from a whole variety of hymn books and have the chance to discern what is really speaking to contemporary people.

- Don't leave the choosing of hymns to random ideas or last-minute selection (or the organist, God bless him/her) without this training. It is like reading only the Bible and only one version of the Bible.

- Use your theological training to connect hymns with the lectionary or theme for the day – not as accompaniment or decoration in the service, but as content. This is doing theology.

- Teach the integration and usefulness of hymns, not only as sung, but read aloud to enhance the preaching, prayers, responses, liturgical dance, offerings, all movement through the liturgy. There are infinite treasures here to help the beauty and sense of worship, but you have to know how/where to find them.

- No music is better than bad music.

- Silence and meditation are more effective than poor singing, especially if your resources are slight.

- A well-read hymn can enhance occasions such as weddings or funerals, even if it cannot be sung.

- If hymns are new, and your congregation can't yet sing them, work round this by having the words well-read, by a competent voice. Or use voice over a quiet rendering of the music, if you can trust your accompanist (see later), or have the people learn just the refrain until they are confident. Of course, this is a chance to teach or familiarise people with something fresh or different. Take time before formal worship begins for the congregation to learn the new tune, getting them to read the words first. Trying to learn a new tune in the middle of worship is not a good idea.

- Consider reading through the words of a hymn sensitively, and guide people through what is being said, perhaps with short ideas for meditating and pausing between verses. Use more than one voice, or several voices to come from different places, allowing varied colourations. A hymn can be used as the text of the sermon, ending with the hymn being sung.[3]

- Money! Priorities! Budgets with attitude! One of the lowest priorities given in any parish I know is allocating money for worship support, e.g. quality music accompaniment, and teaching, music/hymn resources, back-up recordings, a parish library of such for whoever plays, and a fund for the training of young musicians and readers. Over the top? It's a hugely important investment, on several levels. In terms of the value we place on the experience of worship and its impact, this is not unrealistic.

- Better the building fall down than the quality of worship be threatened by inadequate leadership (clergy or accompanists) and uninformed preparation.

- Hire or lure the best possible accompanists to your worship. Suss out their musical ethos and be sure they understand the style and content expected of them, and where the boundaries lie in choosing music/hymns.

- NB: The organist is not necessarily the best person to teach new hymns – you need someone with an ordinary, true voice, who can hold a tune-line, is competent and willing to give it a go.

- And where the worship leader is not confident about music at all, let there be a dash of humility – enough to ask someone else to lead the singing, choose the hymns and thus employ others' gifts.

A wish list from a hymn writer

The article concludes with a short wish-list from Shirley's point of view as a hymn text writer:

1. I wish worship leaders would read the whole hymn first, before selecting it, find the kernel ideas, then allocate it to its place in the service. Obvious? Not at all – some verses of some loved hymns are shockingly inappropriate for a variety of reasons, including inexplicable theology, as in 'Praise to the Holiest in the Height', insulting references to other cultures, as in 'Hills of the North, Rejoice', double entendres as in 'Majesty, Worship His Majesty', not to mention language and gender questions. Don't settle for a stance like:

Just give me that old-time theology
don't muddle my mind by hymnology,
with words like 'inclusive' or 'gender-abusive'
or questions on God and Christology.

2. I wish that indexes to hymnals were more reliable, and that worship leaders trusted their own judgement more, by knowing the contents of the books they use. A good example is the recent Australian *Together in Song*, which lists various themes, including Ministry of Women.[4]

3. I wish they would avoid the bad marriages of new words to old familiar tunes and have the courage to introduce new ones. Congregations will enjoy them!

4. But worst coming to worst, I wish that if they can't cope with the tune, they learn how to choose another (or none) with due regard to the style as well as the stresses. I have endured seeing 'Loving Spirit' set to STUTTGART, and 'Spirit of Love' to O PERFECT LOVE. One might as well sing 'Away in a Manger' to the tune for 'Onward Christian Soldiers', though I fervently hope no one will consider doing this because of the obvious mismatch and dubious theology.

Shirley concludes her article on the effective use of hymns with some words she respects and treasures:

> "The Christian community sings. It is not a choral society. Its singing is not a concert. But from inner material necessity, it sings." So wrote [20th century Swiss Protestant theologian] Karl Barth, adding: "The community that does not really sing … can at best be only a troubled community that is not sure of its cause, and of whose witness and ministry there can be no great expectation."
>
> If you don't sing it, you don't believe it!

Notes

1   Verse 1, 'Come and Find the Quiet Centre', written in 1989 for a New Zealand Presbyterian women's conference on the theme of 'Making Space'. The hymn has travelled widely and had many different settings, including SANCTUM by Jillian Bray.

2   This article was first published in March 2004 in *Candour: A Magazine for [Presbyterian] Ministers,* titled The Folksong of the Church. It was republished in *Music in the Air,* (Summer/Autumn 2009). Reprinted with permission.

3   Further suggestions on ways to learn new tunes and use hymns effectively can be found in the introduction to the New Zealand Hymnbook Trust's 2000 publication *Faith Forever Singing,* pp x and xi.

4   Australian Hymn Book Company. (1999) *Together in Song: Australian Hymn Book II.* Melbourne: Harper Collins.

Part IV – Beyond Parish Life

15 – From mother to Grandshe

We have a life that is greening and growing,
centred on Jesus, the root and the vine,
we are a place for each race and each rainbow,
household of faith with a pledge of new wine,…[1]

"A quiet achiever who enjoyed throwing the odd hand grenade" is how middle son Alastair describes his mother. "She had a wicked streak, as you can see in the words of some of her hymns."

Alastair also sees his mother as "ridiculously modest", who might well be horrified that a biography about her was being written. "On the other hand, she cared hugely about her work and she would get angry when people changed the words of any of her hymns."

Modest Shirley might have been, but youngest son Rob remembers her being quite tickled a couple of times when her name turned up in the five-minute quiz in the then *Dominion Post* (a Wellington newspaper). "Kāpiti writer Shirley Murray is best known for writing in what genre?" the question might read.

Alastair loved Shirley's sense of humour. She would often send him witticisms cut out of the paper, e.g. the brilliant thoughts of American writer and cartoonist Ashley Brilliant. "Mum loved these. 'There is nothing wrong with growing older, but where does it lead?' was one she and I enjoyed.

"She used to ring me every night, always at dinner time, even if we were living in different time zones. She was really thoughtful, the perfect mum and grandmother. Mind you, she was always on about my weight and my smoking, but she was not holier than thou about it. I could always make Mum laugh."

Rob admits he was always a little hazy about her alter ego as a hymn writer, simply because the topic was not often discussed, and he and his brothers were not churchgoers. As a result, they were rarely exposed to her music. "I came to realise she wrote hymns when she decided to donate a hymn to me and Christine for our wedding in 1988. It was called 'Come to a Wedding', sung to the Gaelic melody for 'Morning has Broken'. [The hymn is published in *AA*, with the music arranged by Jillian Bray.] It was all uphill from there. There was quite a bit of mirth surrounding this hymn.

"When my younger daughter, Isabella, was born in 1997, we told Mum we were calling her Isabella Alice Erena. Mum paused and said nothing for ten seconds. Then she said: 'That's an awful lot of vowels.' That was it. She made no other comment."

Alastair admits that all three brothers took quite some time to realise how important their mother's writing was. It came home to him on one occasion when he was picking up his daughter, Anna, from her crèche.

"I told the supervisor that Anna would be picked up by her grandparents the following day and gave her their names. When I arrived at the crèche the next day, one of the carers asked me about my mother. 'You mean your mother is Shirley Erena Murray? The hymn writer?' She was overwhelmed and clearly in awe of Shirley. This gave me quite a surprise, as I hadn't realised my mother was a real star. Mum was quite self-effacing when I told her the story. She just laughed."

In 1986, when presented with her impending status of grandmotherhood, the pressure was on for her to choose a name that her first grandchild would call her by. "Mum had always picked us up when we used the word 'she' rather than a woman's proper name," said Alastair. 'Who is *she*? The cat's mother?' she would ask.

"One evening, she made an announcement. 'I am not the cat's mother, but I am the Grand She.' Now and forever in the family, she became known as Grandshe and Dad became Grandjohn."

Son David believes John and Shirley loved being grandparents, despite their own busy lives. "Mum came up to Auckland for Fergus's homebirth in 1986, helping out for two or three weeks, teaching us the ropes. Dad joined us after the birth. She and Dad did the same when Alex was born in 1988. Mum hated flying but she made an exception on this occasion, and it was greatly appreciated."

Shirley wasn't too keen on her two grandsons taking their mother's surname of Grady, says Fergus, especially if the next grandchildren were girls, which they turned out to be. "She was worried the Murray name would die out. I also inherited the family middle name of Stewart. Fergus Stewart Murray Grady. At least the Murray clan got the first three names."

On one occasion when the boys were sick, Shirley made an emergency trip from Wellington to Auckland on the overnight bus, to help David and his wife Janelle, who were both working. Travelling by overnight bus was preferable to flying, which Shirley did her best to avoid.

Near the end of 1991, five-year-old Fergus came to live with John and Shirley for a month, so he could start school. His parents were teaching at Atiu College in the Cook Islands. John and Shirley had also visited the family there during their tenure.

"Learning by correspondence had not worked for Fergus, so we decided to send him back to Wellington to stay with his grandparents. This meant he could start the term at Clifton Terrace Primary School," said David.

Fergus remembers being at a bit of a loose end as a young kid living in the Cook Islands. "There were very few kids who spoke English. I didn't have the best vocabulary at that stage and I ran a bit wild," he said.

"My first memory of Grandshe was turning five and starting school in New Zealand. I was an energetic kid and had Grandshe running after me from day one. John and Shirley would walk me to school and Shirley would pick me up in the afternoon.

"On about the second or third day, Shirley had barely arrived home and put the kettle on when she got a call from the school. I had fallen off a slide, broken my arm and grazed my face. Shirley took full blame and for the rest of my childhood – my brother and cousins will attest to this – she spoiled me rotten, as any grandma should."

She was mortified, as this accident was so early in her new grandparenting responsibilities, David said. "She telegrammed us about the incident and we were horrified too. But Fergus soon healed and all was well."

When his parents returned from the Cooks, Fergus would still spend weekends with John and Shirley. He has fond memories of removing stamps from envelopes to add to his Grandshe's enormous stamp collection.

"There would always be lots of postcards and letters stuck on the fridge. A lot of it correspondence to do with Amnesty International. I found that interesting. I also liked helping John out with chores and tasks around the house.

"Shirley was so musical, so we would have lots of singalongs round the piano. John taught me to whistle. They were fun times. Just hanging out without my parents was quite unique."

Alex believes Shirley found a lot of joy in being a grandmother. "She would light up when we and our cousins were all together.

"I remember Christmas in Wellington, when they were still at St Andrew's, and singing Shirley's hymns. I did not understand the importance of them then. But I always looked forward to Easter and Christmas services and afterwards, going back home to Shirley and John's and singing round the piano."

Fergus and Alex have fond memories of sharing time with their grandparents on the Kāpiti Coast, at their bach and at their new home further up the road. "Until I became a teenager, I spent a lot of weekends up there. My brother and I would have turnabouts," said Fergus.

"Sometimes, we would get up early and watch FA Cup football games together. Shirley would often talk to me about sport in her later years. I guess she knew that interested me. She would usually watch the rugby too."

Fergus was aware what busy lives his grandparents led, even in retirement. "Alex and I were happy to keep ourselves amused and let them get on with what they had to do. They gave us the space and we enjoyed their company.

"John and Shirley often had friends over. John was always busy with community activities and with people. Shirley was not as social as John, but she had a lot of close friends apart from John, for example people overseas and mutual admirers."

Alex recalls fun times spent at their lovely house in Raumati. "They had a nice garden and a flat lawn that was perfect for cricket and croquet games. I played lots of indoor games with Shirley too, like tiddlywinks and monkeys in a barrel. There was always music in the house. Both of them sang. Grandjohn's bass baritone drowned out most voices in the room. Shirley had a really great voice, too. She probably had perfect pitch and a very good ear for music."

Alex remembers Shirley writing at the piano during the evenings, using a pencil. "Grandjohn would be reading and listening to the Concert Programme on the radio. I knew I couldn't watch TV because Grandshe would be working, but she would find fun things for me to do."

Shirley's cooking also made an impression on her grandsons. "She loved making me curried egg sandwiches," Alex said. "Often her meals were meat and three veg, but they were done well. Grandjohn and I would do the cleaning up. Shirley was also a keen gardener and there was always a good vege garden."

Alex wonders whether Shirley's thrifty, waste-not attitude to all things, especially food, had something to do with her living through the Depression in Invercargill. "When she moved from the house in Raumati to Sevenoaks Retirement Village, I remember laughing with my uncles when we saw that most things in her pantry had expired by several years."

When Fergus and Alex started high school, they spent less time up in Raumati because of weekend sporting commitments. But John and Shirley would frequently come down to Wellington to watch their grandsons.

"Fergus and I were into theatre and music. Grandshe and Grandjohn would come to all our performances. That was special. Creativity was infectious in their household. They had such a passion for the arts, music, theatre, film. I studied drama and English literature at Victoria University [of Wellington] before moving to Melbourne to continue my drama studies. I would talk to them about Shakespeare. Grandshe had an encyclopaedic knowledge and was so well read.

"In the last decade of her life, she would get three or four books from the library each week. I remember talking to my grandparents about films they had seen and music they loved. They were also curious about what we were doing, what we found interesting, what we were reading and learning at school. Grandshe stressed that it was not what you learnt that was important but learning how to learn. She had a real thirst for knowledge and was interested in technology too. She loved using her iPad."

Alex admired their commitment to social activism. "They always had a cause to fight for, like the White Poppies for Peace movement, Amnesty International or Grandjohn's support for euthanasia in his later years. I am grateful for these things."

Fergus appreciates that so much of Shirley's work is grounded in 'Kiwi culture'. He also believes it was his grandmother's example that helped him forge his own way in a niche industry – film-making and film distribution – that relies on royalties. "There was never any pressure on my brother or me to be anything or anyone, even though we had come from a line of ministers and doctors. I went to film school in Melbourne, Alex to drama school."

During her later years, Shirley's grandsons were often living abroad (Alex now works at Unity Technologies in Austin, Texas) but kept in touch with Shirley and John by phone and email. This made space for their younger granddaughters to spend more time with them.

Anna remembers the house swaps her family did with Shirley and John every summer and school holidays. "When we came to visit or stay with them, Grandjohn would often take us to the beach or the swimming pool or the park so Grandshe could get on with her writing. Looking back, I now appreciate why he did these things."

On 6 January 2018, nearly a year after John had died, Shirley attended Alex and Sophia's wedding in New Plymouth. This was the only wedding of a grandchild she got to attend. As she had done for Rob and Christine's wedding, she wrote a hymn for the occasion – an adaptation of her earlier 1988 hymn – even though the ceremony was non-religious. Again the words were sung to the Gaelic melody for 'Morning has Broken'. Alex remembers talking to her about what marriage meant, with emails going back and forth as the words and lyrics were developed.

A Wish: For Sophia and Alex

Here is a song and here is a blessing
this summer day, and long as you live:
  wishing you life with infinite sparkle,
  wishing you joy this promise will give!

Thanks for the love that holds us together:
parent and child, and partner and friend;
  thanks to the God whose love is our centre,
  knowing no boundaries, knowing no end.

Love is the gift and love is the giver,
love is the gold that makes your day shine,
  love forgets self to care for the other,
  love changes life from water to wine.

Marriage needs kindness, marriage takes courage,
facing each other's struggles and fears,
  heart to heart speaking, trusting the moment,
  sharing the journey, laughter and tears.

All of us round you offer our blessing:
here is our hope your marriage will prove:
  health of the body, health of the spirit,
  always together,
  always this love.

But only a few weeks after this happy family event, on 13 February, Shirley had a stroke. It was barely a year since John had died. Her few happy months of comparatively good health and freedom had come to a sudden end.

"Towards the end of her life, Sophia and I moved to the United States," said Alex. "Grandshe and I probably only saw each other once a year. I would speak to her on the phone, but talking had become difficult for her. She did a good job at learning how to speak again but she lost a lot of confidence and would get tired quite quickly. This made phone conversations difficult."

Shirley's granddaughters, Anna and Rachel, then 19 and 17, will never forget the rather unconventional Christmas dinner they shared with her in 2018. Their parents, Alastair and Lynda, were not in Wellington that week, leaving their daughters to take care of Grandshe.

"Rachel and I had forgotten that nothing much would be open on Christmas Day," said Anna. "We managed to scrounge some food from neighbours and then shopped at all the Mobil and BP petrol stations between Karori and Kāpiti, trying to buy a few extra things and getting a bit lost on the way. We bought Christmas crackers, biscuits and muffins and then made sandwiches for Grandshe. She was unimpressed but grateful at the same time. 'At least you came,' she said.

"We felt embarrassed, but it was a fun occasion. We stayed quite a while, despite our hangovers from the night before. Grandshe put on lots of the hats from the Christmas crackers, including a purple one in honour of Grandjohn. She relaxed with us and took her time in speaking. We have good memories of this day."

Fergus has happy memories of Shirley attending a preview screening of his documentary *Camino Skies* at the Shoreline Cinema in Waikanae in 2019. "That was quite special and emotional for me. She wasn't that able-bodied nor well, but she stayed for the question-and-answer session after the screening," he said.

Shirley's friend and helper, Alida van der Velde, took her to the screening. She remembers how much Shirley enjoyed the occasion, even though it had been a big effort for her to go. "She was so glad to be there for Fergus," Alida said.

Fergus was acutely aware how frustrating Shirley found it losing her easy way with words after her stroke. "Grandshe was always such an articulate person who had relied so much on words and the power of words. Having the stroke made it difficult for her. It was also hard for the family because she would get frustrated, even though we could understand pretty much everything she said."

Because neither of her grandsons grew up in the church, their appreciation of Shirley's gifts as a hymn writer came later in their lives.

"It was probably when I was in drama school that I began to appreciate what a well-recognised writer she was," said Alex. "I began reading her hymns and heard some recordings. I am grateful to have been able to talk to her about some of her hymns, especially the more controversial ones, like the 'Hymn for Anzac Day'. Her activism and hymn writing went hand in hand."

Alex loves Shirley's carols, particularly 'Upside Down Christmas', which he describes as 'a classic'. He also found her 'Lullaby for Judas' interesting. This describes Judas as a child, an innocent child who does not know what his future will bring.

"She wanted to picture the human experience in its highs and lows, humans as fallible beings, with weaknesses and strengths. She dealt with the light and the dark of human experience – she didn't gloss over things. She had the courage to confront the difficult topics. I find this particularly inspiring, and it is what makes her reputation so great."

Alex believes Shirley had a certain New Zealand reticence, but she found her voice in her hymns. She rarely talked about her own thoughts and feelings, instead choosing to express her emotions through her hymns.

"Shirley would like to be remembered as an advocate, a fighter for social justice. She liked to stir the pot a bit, to kick the hornets' nest. She felt it was important to do this and she enjoyed doing it. She was critical of the status quo, and questioned authority in church and government."

Alex is proud that his grandmother wrote unflinchingly about the things Jesus stood for. His grandfather might have been at the head of the march, but he sees Shirley as just as much an activist through her hymn writing. "Her words will stand the test of time and will be sung for many years to come."

Note

1   Verse 4 of 'We are the Singers', written in 1995 on commission from the American Presbyterian Association of Musicians for the Montreat Conference in the United States. The hymn explores various biblical images and has been set by several composers including Jillian Bray, Jenny McLeod, Jane Marshall and Ron Klusmeier.

16 – A home of their own

Go gently, go lightly,
go safe in the Spirit,
live simply, don't carry
much more than you need:
go trusting God's goodness,
go spreading God's kindness,
stay centred on Jesus
and where he will lead.[1]

In 1992, the Murrays sold their bach at 154 Rosetta Road, Raumati South, and bought a larger home just a few doors further north at 168 Rosetta Road. This became their home following their retirement from St Andrew's on The Terrace on 4 July 1993. They would live there for the next 12 years.

Shirley was delighted to move, finally, from a church manse to a home of their own and to be freed from the ties of parish life. She had clearly been looking forward to spending more time with John but she may also have wondered how John was planning to spend these retirement years. Their friends Mervyn and Lesley Aitken believe John did not know how to retire – "he was a bit like a caged lion, pacing around with nothing to do. I think Shirley found that frustrating. He was soon involved in a plethora of activities. I think she found that a bit rough because she really wanted some space together to share some interesting things."

In March 1994, John left for South Africa to spend six weeks in and around Johannesburg as a peace monitor for the World Council of Churches' programme to monitor the country's first post-apartheid general election. John saw this mission as "taking up the ministry again … This was an experience which I had longed for since a meeting at the Ecumenical Institute at Bossey, Switzerland, in 1954 with Gabriel Setiloane, a South African scholar who specialised in the structure and function of divinity – truly an archangel."[2]

Shirley found her new fax machine the only practical way of communicating with him, faxing George Shorney in April 1994:

> John seems to be relishing the experience. He shares a room with Dutch theologian Albert van den Heuvel (they probably talk all night!) and each day travels around in a small VW car, with a pale blue WCC flag held out the window. He does long distances round these townships. Greatly impressed by patience and hope of the black people. The only Afrikaners he has met seem appalled that anyone drives around there without being shot.

> John hopes to be in Pretoria after his stint of work, to see the Inauguration [of new president Nelson Mandela on 10 May] – what a moment! Returns near end of May after looking at church lay centres for peace/conflict resolution.

Retirement also marked a busy and productive period in Shirley's life. She and John continued as members of the editorial board of the NZHBT, stepping down in 2003. The Trust's four major publications between 1993 and 2009 contain 162 of Shirley's hymns (see chapters 9 and 10). Hope Publishing Company in the United States produced five collections of her work between 1992 and 2019, a total of 256 texts (see chapter 11). At the same time, Shirley's work was being picked up and published in hymn collections of many different denominations throughout the world – from Canada to Australia, Scotland to Taiwan.

Shirley and John also welcomed four more grandchildren – all girls this time – during their retirement years. Rob and Christine's daughter Elizabeth was born in 1995, Isabella in 1997; while Alastair and Lynda's daughter Anna was born in 1999, Rachel in 2001.

Back home, John continued his involvement with the World Court Project (the United Nation's International Court of Justice was established after World War II), Amnesty International (he helped set up and headed the work on the Kāpiti Coast), U3A (leading groups on Exploring Spirituality) and helping run the Lower Hutt ecumenical centre, Wallis House. In 1995, John also finished a two-year stint as interim moderator of the Kāpiti Uniting Parish.

Following retirement, Shirley gradually retreated from the church. While John kept a loose connection with the Kāpiti Uniting Parish, he soon joined the Kāpiti branch of Quakers Aotearoa. According to friend and fellow Presbyterian the Rev Roger Wiig, John found the silence beneficial, leading to a deepening of his spirituality. "For Shirley, hymn writing and hymn playing became her main preoccupation, her life, almost to the end, including the publication of her last book with Hope," Roger said.

Alastair believes Quaker principles melded well with his father's ideas about peace and non-violence. "Dad and Mum had great faith, but that faith eventually moved away from organised religion. Mum turned away from the Presbyterian Church because of the conservative direction it was taking. Religion may have been pushed aside but their strong faith remained. They also remained strong social justice advocates, were open to differences, and to an open interpretation of the Bible."

There was time for relaxation too. Both Shirley and John were members of Peter Godfrey's Kāpiti chamber choir, with Shirley singing alto and John "a wonderful bass baritone who sang with great passion", according to friend and choir member Alida van der Velde. But, says Alida, Shirley did not stay a member as long as John. "Shirley was always a bit more reserved than John and a bit ambivalent towards people."

Murray hospitality

Alida and her partner Justin were grateful for Shirley and John's friendship. Despite a 20-year age difference, "the Murrays sort of adopted me and Justin, as part of their clan. They had always looked after the waifs and strays. John and Shirley would take me and Justin out for lunch on my birthday. They were terrific people.

"When I first met them, I had no idea they were such important people. People looked up to them and treated them a bit like royalty.

I realised how active they were politically and socially. I admired their support for gay rights and peace issues, and Amnesty International."

Alida would become Shirley's close friend and companion in her last days. "Alida became part of the family and we owe a huge debt of gratitude to her," son David would say at Shirley's funeral.

Shirley and John continued to nourish a wide circle of friends. They were particularly close to Colin and Jeanette Gibson and to Lloyd Geering and his second wife Elaine, who died in 2001. They then grew close to his third wife, Shirley, whom Lloyd married in 2004. Shirley died in 2021. Hugh and Natasha Templeton also remained close friends.

The Murrays' hospitality extended to many hymn-writing friends. In 1994, Hope Publishing president George Shorney and his wife Nancy visited them, as did Colin and Jeanette from Dunedin. John Bell of the Iona Community in Scotland visited in 1995 and again in 2009, his visits coinciding with music workshops in different parts of the country.

In 1996, Mr Methodist Music in the United States, Carlton ('Sam') Young and his wife Marj stayed with the Murrays. It was their first tour of New Zealand. Shirley had begun collaborating with Sam in 1993. Sam recalls the visit vividly in his memoir *I'll Sing On: My First 96 Years,* published in 2022. A significant moment for them both was when Sam sat at "Shirley's ancient, temperament-lacking, upright piano", and played his recently composed music for 'Star-Child Earth-Child' (see chapter 25 and 29).

In June 1995, Shirley attended a special ecumenical service in Dunedin Cathedral, broadcast on radio to honour her and Colin Gibson. "It was a bitterly cold winter night," Shirley wrote to George Shorney, "but the cathedral was two-thirds full and I was moved by the occasion."

Shirley and John spent Christmas in Melbourne with Alastair and family. According to John (writing to Colin and Jeanette Gibson), this was "the first time ever that we were not at home – and working! Shirley wonders what happened to retirement."

In 1996, Shirley and John attended, for the second time, the annual conference of the Hymn Society in the United States and Canada, with Shirley presenting on her new book *Every Day in Your*

Spirit and on New Zealand hymn writing generally (see chapter 11). They were also able to return to Toronto and renew some of the great friendships they had formed in the city during John's pulpit exchange in 1982.

In 1997, Shirley spent a fortnight in Tainan, Taiwan, speaking at the World Council of Churches' and Christian Conference of Asia workshop on music and liturgy in Asia. The workshop attracted 50 representatives of Asian churches from 26 countries. Shirley soon became aware that New Zealand was one of the first countries to have produced indigenous books of worship, two hymn books and a prayer book.

Two years later, John and Shirley attended the First National Ecumenical Hymn Conference in Melbourne where the focus was the introduction of *Together in Song: Australian Hymn Book II*. The three main speakers were the director of the Asian Institute for Liturgy and Music, Francisco Feliciano, British hymn writer Brian Wren and Colin Gibson. Shirley also took a leadership role. Among the 193 participants were New Zealanders Bill Bennett, Jock Hosking, Paulo Ieriko and Ian Render. Brian spoke of Shirley's hymn 'Touch the Earth Lightly' as a perfect blend of beauty and frugality of words – his main criteria for judging a hymn's worth.

John and Shirley had always loved the arts and continued going to concerts and exhibitions. They also gave generously to the arts, and actively supported the establishment of a new public library in nearby Paraparaumu. This opened in November 2002.

In 1999, John started lobbying the Kāpiti Coast District Council for a celebration of Waitangi Day [New Zealand's national day commemorating the signing of the Treaty of Waitangi – te Tiriti o Waitangi – between Māori and the British Crown] on the coast. This ambition was finally achieved seven years later in 2006.

Experience of ill health

In 2000, Shirley experienced serious ill health when she was diagnosed with breast cancer. This necessitated two operations, six weeks of radiotherapy and a year of being ill. "I now have a clipped wing," she told Alastair, who had recently moved back to New Zealand from Australia.

Hospital chaplain the Rev Ken Irwin, who died in September 2022, remembered visiting Shirley at Wellington Hospital, following her operation for breast cancer. "We were able to speak directly with each other about what was going on. We talked about death. She was optimistic and was walking towards the future purposefully – she could face whatever life offered. We enjoyed each other's company and were dear friends. Both of us loved words and poetry, and were playful with language."

Shirley wrote a number of hymns that year, as well as collating what she had written in previous years. But she found it easier to write about life, rather than sickness. Never one to wallow in her own troubles and frailties, she remained hopeful of a return to good health, expressing these experiences in her hymns. 'Simply to Be', written in 2005 and with the tune KĀPITI by Colin Gibson, encapsulates her strong faith:

> *Simply to be, to be in stillness,*
> *simply to trust that God is here,*
> *simply to know the Holy Presence,*
>> *is to be blessed:*
>> *so am I blessed …*

The pain and fear she experienced in 2000 is revealed, however, in her 2006 hymn, 'O God, to You I Cry in Pain'. Her good friend Jillian Bray wrote the music that same year and called it AFFLICTION.

By 2001, Shirley was well again. That year, she became a Member of the New Zealand Order of Merit (NZOM), the first person in New Zealand to receive a Queen's birthday honour for 'services to hymn writing'. Her grandson Alex described it as "a hugely proud moment for our family", although Alida said Shirley liked to joke that she got the award because she was good at making scones! There is no doubt, however, that Shirley was pleased to receive this honour.

John had become an Officer of the NZOM the previous year for his services to the community, while Colin Gibson was awarded an NZOM for services to literature and music in 2002.[3]

Shirley celebrated her 70th birthday in 2001, with a 'this-is-your-life' celebration in St Ninian's Presbyterian Church Hall in Karori. Her whole family was there, plus many of her friends from around the country. Among her many gifts was a special offering from her long-time hymn-writing friend, Swedish composer the Rev Per Harling. His greeting weaves together many of Shirley's song titles. (For more on Per Harling, see chapter 23.)

To Shirley

Come, celebrate the woman,
who brought the Church to song. *
Faith has set her on a journey,
creative, humble and strong.
In every corner sing,
let gratulations ring,
sing a happy alleluia
to this earth-child of Aotearoa!

Dear Shirley, my friend of ten years. Canberra, you remember? From one of the furthest corners of the world, I sing a happy alleluia for all the wonderful gifts that God has put into your mind and heart. God and the world Church need your sound theological reflection and poetical creativity for many more years.

God speed you on your way,
and especially today.
Let your spirit always sing,
a wish from me, Per Harling!

* to be honest the church has been singing before Shirley Murray, but not always with such good theology before…

Changes arouse anger

The Church of Scotland published a revised fourth edition of its *Church Hymnary* in 2005. Referred to as *CH4*, it includes 22 hymns by Shirley, the largest number of any contributor next to Scotland's John Bell. It also includes contributions from Jillian Bray, Christopher Norton, Bill Wallace, Marnie Barrell and Colin Gibson. Although this was something to celebrate, Shirley's enthusiasm waned a little when she discovered that eight of her hymns had text and layout changes she had not approved.

The Very Rev Pamela Tankersley recalled John Bell coming to New Zealand in 2009 to do some workshops. "He had to apologise to Shirley for publishing some of her hymns in a way she did not like. Shirley was always particular about her work, e.g. leaving out a verse when published. She wrote her hymns as a whole, with each verse progressing to the next," she said.

The story of Shirley's displeasure over how her work was published in *CH4* was mentioned by a number of interviewees for this book.

In his 2006 review of *CH4*, John Murray wrote: "Though *CH4* was compiled by a committee, it is John Bell's book – his inspiration, his guiding hand is there and he is its main contributor. ...There are, more seriously, changes made to texts without acknowledgement."[4]

A formal apology was published in the first issue (2008) of the Church of Scotland's new quarterly publication, *Different Voices*. At the end of an interview with Shirley about her work, the editor noted: "Singers of Shirley Erena Murray's hymns should be aware that some alterations were made to her hymns before inclusion in *CH4* that she did not authorise. The editors and publishers have expressed their regret at this discourtesy. Further, the English version of an Asian text at 571 ('author unknown') is also by Shirley Murray."

Despite this furore, John Bell is clearly proud of the decision to include so many of Shirley's hymns in *CH4*. "I was keen to expose people to Shirley's writing, both for its own integrity and as an encouragement to prospective writers here in Scotland," he emailed the author on 4 November 2021. "Shirley's hymns have had great acceptance, particularly her songs on issues of ecology, peace, and a lovely wedding hymn for an older couple, 'Let's Praise the Creator'. In *CH4*, it has been set to a Scottish folk melody."

John Bell added that the recently published Methodist hymnal in the United Kingdom, *Singing the Faith*, included 11 of Shirley's texts, while the Church of England's 2013 publication, *Ancient and Modern: Hymns and Songs for Refreshing Worship*, included six.

In 2005, John and Shirley moved to a smaller house at 325B Rosetta Road, their home for another 12 years. "Our marriage has often teetered on the brink when it comes to chucking out and keeping things – J. being the keeper and I being the heartless chucker-out," Shirley emailed her Canadian friend Ron Klusmeier in 2013.

John became a member of the board of The Right to Die with Dignity New Zealand in 2005. He had earlier helped set up a local branch of the organisation.

Both Shirley and John supported the establishment of a National Centre for Peace and Conflict Studies Te Ao o Rongomaraeroa at the University of Otago, headed by their friend Kevin Clements. "The Murrays provided the funding – sufficient for the next five years – to bring artists and musicians together to explore issues of war and peace through their art," said Kevin. "We were grateful for their generosity."

The Murrays also reached out to Algerian politician and refugee Ahmed Zaoui, inviting him to their house for dinner. This was shortly after he had been released from prison after serving a sentence of nearly two years. "They were generous with money, supporting the Zaoui family – his wife and four children were then living illegally in Kuala Lumpur, Malaysia. They put their heads on the block for the causes they believed in," said Alida.

Honours and awards

Awards began to accumulate for Shirley over the next few years. In 2006, she was named an Honorary Fellow of the Royal School of Church Music (RSCM), becoming the first person to receive the award for words, rather than music. The Fellowship was one of the very few awarded worldwide at that time to a woman.

The Fellowship, which honours "achievements in church music and/or liturgy of internationally recognised significance", is considered the equivalent of a doctorate. It was presented to Shirley by RSCM New Zealand president Paul Ellis at St Paul's Cathedral, Wellington in September that year. Wellington branch chair, the Rev Alison Pitts, noted in an RSCM newsletter that "Shirley's words certainly reflect contemporary theology, and use images and metaphors from modern society and New Zealand nature and culture, held in balance with the traditions of our Christian faith."

In thanking the RSCM for the honour, Shirley said: "What delights me most today is that the RSCM has chosen to honour the words that we sing. Words are so powerful – and can be dangerous! There are far more composers ... than writers, possibly because it takes a certain nerve to expose new ideas, and hope that ordinary congregations will own them."[5]

That same year, hers was the theme song sung at the WCC Assembly in Brazil, 'God, In Your Grace', to a tune by Per Harling.

In 2007, her hymn 'Leftover People in Leftover Places' won the biennial prize from the Hymn Society in the United States and Canada. Set to the music of Colin Gibson, the hymn took as its theme the phrase 'The least of these' (Matthew 25:40).

In June 2009, Shirley painted a picture of John's and her life in an email to Ron Klusmeier:

> I am still writing, but often because of occasions for other people rather than my own desperate expressions of despair with the churches and the impact of new ideas which excite me.
>
> John and I have discovered that there's no such thing as 'retirement', just a change of direction. He is working to create a new law on the difficult issue of euthanasia in our country and to strengthen our nuclear-free stance – more possible now with President Obama. I try to find time for more reading, keeping up with our six grandchildren and learning to pace things better. John got a pacemaker for last Christmas after a scary cardiac episode and a mild stroke.

In July that year, Shirley was named a Fellow of the Hymn Society in the United States and Canada, becoming the first woman and the first person outside the US to become a Fellow. The incoming Hymn Society executive director, Deborah Carlton-Loftis, presented Shirley with her Fellowship in person at the New Zealand Hymnbook Trust's national hymn conference in Palmerston North in October.

"Despite her frustrations with the church, this writer remains committed to working on its behalf and her positive, ebullient nature dominates her work," a Hymn Society press release stated. "Her hymns are ecumenical in their theology and inclusive in their expression.

They embody themes of justice, peace, human rights, nature and the integrity of creation."

The national hymn conference explored the theme Peace, Justice, Creation. It was the NZHBT's first and only national hymn conference. Speaking at the conference and later visiting Shirley and John were the American hymn writers and composers Jim and Jean Strathdee. Over the previous decade, Shirley had often sent them texts to set to music. Her relationship with the Strathdees continued until the end of her life (see chapter 22).

It was a big year for John, too. In early November, a large party gathered at Kāpiti Uniting Church Hall to celebrate his 80th birthday. A mini choir performed and sang a special song Shirley had composed. "Wonderful, considering the crisis of last December," Shirley wrote in a Christmas letter that year.

On 5 December 2009, Shirley received an Honorary Doctorate in Literature from the University of Otago. She was nominated by emeritus professor Colin Gibson who wrote, in his citation: "Her hymn texts show a remarkable range, from tender carols to solemn litanies of confession, from expressions of anguished social concern to confident faith and joy. They are distinguished by their inclusive language and their innovative use of Māori, their bold appropriation of secular terms and their original poetic imagery drawn from nature and domestic life; but equally by the directness with which they confront contemporary issues."

In an interview with the author in March 2021, Colin said: "We wanted her to be acknowledged in New Zealand, not only as a hymn writer, but as a poet who had done much to shape the language. At the time, awards were being dished out to sporting people, to people in the scientific community, but arts were hardly being acknowledged at all. Otago is a literary place. It has a long tradition of honouring writing – think of the plaques round the Octagon honouring writers. Dunedin is also a UNESCO city of literature – it all fitted very well. Shirley was pleased and surprised by these awards, but not greatly flattered."

And her son Rob observed: "Mum didn't like a fuss and in many ways was a private person. Even at her Hon Doc investiture, she declined to speak as would be traditional."

In 2009, Shirley wrote the theme hymn for the 13th Christian Conference of Asia Assembly, held in Kuala Lumpur the following year. 'Out of Strange Unlikely Places', with music by Lim Swee Hong, drew on Asian images and was based on the Charter for Compassion, which English author Karen Armstrong launched on 12 November 2009.

At the end of the year, Shirley wrote in her Christmas letter: "Some long-time routines take more effort, though both John and I still drive, which is great. Saying final goodbyes to friends, or preparing to, has become more frequent.

"There seem still to be ideas for hymns in the making. I am so grateful to my composer friends, beyond expression."

Notes

1 Verse 1, 'Go Gently, Go Lightly', written in 2001 for her good friend Rosemary Lawrence who was moving from Wellington to Auckland to take up a school chaplaincy role. "It was a generous gift which I treasure and which I find challenging and comforting," said Rosemary. The hymn was published in Hope's *Faith Makes the Song* with music by Carlton Young, called ROSEMARY. It has been set by many other composers, including Colin Gibson, Ron Klusmeier and Marnie Barrell.

2 Murray, 2016.

3 In the New Year Honours 2024, Marnie Barrell was named a member of the New Zealand Order of Merit for services to hymn writing. She began writing hymns in 1986, shortly after meeting Shirley and being encouraged by her. Still a board member of the NZHBT and a lay preacher in the Anglican Church in Christchurch, Marnie has written texts and set some of her own and other hymn writers' work to music. She and Shirley are believed to be the only hymn writers in New Zealand to be honoured for hymn writing.

4 Murray, J. (2006) Buying a new hymnbook? A review of the *Church Hymnary Fourth Edition*. *Music in the Air*, Summer.

5 News report. (2006) In Recognition of Distinguished Services to Church Music, Shirley Erena Murray, FRSCM, *Music in the Air*, Winter.

17 – Too many goodbyes

Sing for life and all its goodness,
days of joy and deep delight,
sing through times of grief and sadness
when our world has lost its light,
bring into this time of parting
all our hearts would wish to say:
tears and laughter on this day.[1]

Shirley's next milestone birthday, her 80th, was celebrated at St Ninian's Presbyterian Church Hall, Karori, on 26 March 2011. Guests ranged in age from her youngest granddaughter, Rachel, nine, to her oldest friend, Lloyd Geering, 93. Shirley was also thrilled her childhood friend and bridesmaid Faith Williamson (née Skene), whom Shirley always called Fayo, was able to be there too.

One of her presents included a caricature portrait by Wellington newspaper cartoonist Jeff Bell. Commissioned by her sons, this charmed Shirley greatly. A few days after the party, she described the picture in an email to Colin Gibson. "The attached portrait is more true to life than my disrespectful sons, who gave it to me, will admit. I adore the pearls – quite like HMQ, don't you think?" (See photo p205.)

Colin's present was a Margaret Mahy (New Zealand children's writer) medley he had composed, entitled 'When I Am Old and Wrinkled Like a Raisin'. He dedicated it: "For my dear collaborator Shirley Murray on the occasion of the eightieth birthday … and she isn't even wrinkled yet!"

"I truly love this 80th birthday present," Shirley wrote to him. "Whenever things get low – and believe me, they do – I shall hie me off, metaphorical red-striped stockings pulled on, and belt it out … The thought that in the true South are such dear friends who would do this for me is very precious."

John asked Ron Klusmeier to send Shirley something special for her birthday. This resulted in a CD with 17 tracks of their hymn writing collaborations, sung and recorded by "a small, rag-tag group of singers, who simply loved the words and music Shirley and I created together," Ron explained.

Jim and Jean Strathdee also sent Shirley recorded musical tributes for her birthday. In an email of thanks, Shirley described turning 80 as "awful, wonderful and unreal".

Over the next few years, Shirley maintained a steady stream of correspondence with her many hymn-writing friends and collaborators around the world, sharing the intimacies of her life and hymn-writing achievements.

In December 2012, she wrote to Colin: "Am about to have a minor, but highly inconvenient op. on my right hand [a melanoma] and something mysterious but benign removed from my back."

That Christmas, John and Shirley were looking forward to having all their family together "for the first time in ages".

The following Christmas was a different story. "We're having a quiet little old folks' type of celebration this year; all our three families having scattered to other places. But we gather up our long-distance friends like you to enlarge the circle," she emailed Ron Klusmeier on 23 December 2013. She described 2013 as having been "a marvellous year for me to do with hymns and their travels".

Ron and his partner Christina Bogucki were due to visit the Murrays in April 2014. The trip had taken months of planning and was much anticipated by all concerned. This was to be the two couples' first and only face-to-face meeting, despite Shirley and Ron having collaborated as hymn writers for more than 30 years.

Before Ron and Christina left Canada, Shirley sent them a slight warning: "I'm having to concede to a heap of things I can no longer do, and though John doesn't readily admit it, he is having to give things up as well. You'll find us a funny old pair."

Despite having eye surgery in March 2014, Shirley was more interested to talk about the White Poppies for Peace appeal which she and John continued to support. With Anzac Day (25 April) looming and the centenary of the outbreak of World War I not far away, peace issues were top of her mind.

"Since our churches are notably passive about this [appeal], except for the Quakers, it takes some energy to get a response on the ground. Peace Movement Aotearoa is committed but rather disorganised. This doesn't suit John!" she emailed Ron on 8 March.

Ron and Christina's arrival and first meeting with Shirley and John made a lasting impression on them, beginning with their struggle to find the Murrays' house on Rosetta Road, despite John draping a Canadian flag over the letterbox.

"I will never forget the way Shirley met us when we finally found their home," said Ron in an interview with the author in June 2022. "She was so animated. I somehow expected a larger person. She came bounding out of the house, following John who came out first. She began pirouetting and dancing. It was incredible. It kept going on and on and on. I held out my hands to her. I can't dance, but we grabbed each other's hands and we just twirled.

"She said: 'If I ever settle down in the next little while, you must come and see my Ron shrine' – this included all kinds of things of mine to welcome me there, e.g. symbols, lots of the projects we had done together and a candle in the centre that she had lit for our arrival and which she lit each day we were there. It was so touching. The combination of that and the Canadian flag – Christina and I just could not stop talking about it."

Over the next few days, the couples spent as much time as possible together, "with John and Shirley both correcting my Māori pronunciation – especially of the word Erena. They took us through a map of the North Island telling us how to pronounce the Māori place names."

Ron recorded several video interviews with Shirley and John (see chapter 11), who arranged for their visitors to meet other New Zealand hymn-writing luminaries such as Colin Gibson and Jillian Bray.

On his return to Vancouver Island in late June, Ron emailed Shirley: "It was, without question, a profoundly meaningful journey for us and the sense of kindred-spiritedness we experienced with both of you was beyond our hopes and expectations."

In December that year, Shirley continued to sort through piles of hymn books to send to Colin, to join the growing hymnology collection at the Dunedin Public Library, now numbering 2200 items. Initiated by Colin in 1985 and named after him, it is now the largest collection of hymn-related materials in New Zealand.

"Already Advent and not a baby in the house washed, nor the dismantling of this heap of hymn books reaching skywards, which I rashly promised to despatch to you … I must mine the collection for what's relevant," she wrote.

John's sister Noreen had recently died. Shirley wrote of "a fairly intensive time managing John's sister's final days and funeral … 1000 things sit waiting on this desk when what I should be doing is reassembling leftovers for the next meal."

In February 2015, Shirley discovered she had a rare blood platelets condition, which had to be adjusted by some "fiendishly awful drugs". Fortunately, the condition settled fairly quickly. Meanwhile Shirley continued "to tidy up her life", throwing out papers, sending hymnals to Colin's library in Dunedin, and going through old photos. She complained to Colin that John tended to vet her chucking out and often reinstated things!

That year Swedish composer Per Harling visited Shirley and John, and the Gibsons in Dunedin. For Per, too, visiting Shirley in her own home was like a dream come true (see chapter 23).

Although both Shirley and John were now on "life-sustaining drugs", John continued his efforts in support of the campaign to legalise euthanasia in New Zealand. He was greatly supported by friend Alida van der Velde.

"I helped John a lot on the euthanasia debate, as he wrote letters to papers and organised public meetings on the Kāpiti Coast, which he chaired," said Alida. "He had charisma, so people would come. This work went on for five years."

Shirley shared her thoughts about this campaign in an email to Ron Klusmeier on 11 October: "John gets 100 per cent for attitude and last evening held a group ecumenical seminar with a local RC priest and two nuns present to discuss what Pope Francis is doing and changing (or not). It seems important that J. keeps doing what he's always done, except that he gets extremely tired after this sort of thing. He's off to Parliament on Wednesday to help present yet one more petition for a conscience vote on End-of-Life Choice. We both joke that it had better get through in time for us to benefit!"

However, in the end, John was too sick to go and Alida refused to take him. "He was angry with me that I would not take him, but it just was not realistic," she said. "He was a stubborn old fool."

Shirley admitted she hadn't been writing much that year "but rather doing small projects around hymns".[2] However, there were successes and milestones. Her hymn, 'All Who Walk the Christian Journey', ('A Hymn about St Paul' published by Hope in her last collection *Life into Life*) came first in an international hymn competition run by St Paul's Cathedral in Melbourne. And she wrote the theme song for the 14th Christian Conference of Asia Assembly, held in Jakarta – 'The Household of God'.

She was most pleased, however, with 'It Is Time, A Song about White Poppies for Peace'. She was spurred to write the hymn, she told Ron on 21 February 2015, "by the next wave of excessive promotion of WW100 [World War I centenary] memorials here and hope our country will get red poppy fatigue and sign up for white ones". Verse one reads:

> *It is time! Let the white poppies bloom*
> *and the blood of the past stain no more;*
> *it is time … for the sowing of seed*
> *that will outgrow the jungles of war,*

Ron sent a tune for this a few weeks later, which she was grateful for. "This is important to me, as to others, so thank you again for such an immediate adoption of the theme," she emailed him.[3] "I don't really want to think about our crazy government right now sending off 'mentoring' troops to Iraq. Who would believe that?"[4]

However, it was a tune by Colin Gibson that accompanied the hymn's publication in her last collection, *Life into Life*.

John's health continued to be poor, with low kidney function. Alida would sometimes take him to hospital, if Shirley was happy with that, and she would often bring her back flowers. "I knew that John was getting demanding and a bit grumpy. That was quite hard for Shirley," she said.

Later that year, John suffered a severe bout of bronchitis, followed by an extreme reaction to an antibiotic. The family feared it could have been fatal.

"John's renal specialist told us there was little he could do to improve J's poor kidney function and that the usual things (dialysis et al.) were not possible. So we've had to change gear a little, look at a different timeline and have a good life while we're at it. Apart from that, our friends keep falling about or taking off to final destinations," she emailed Ron in September 2015.

Shirley tried to get Hope interested in putting together a collection of 'green' hymns but was told such collections didn't sell. When she took a close look at Hope's Online Hymnody, she noticed how many themes were missing. Again, she expressed her frustrations to Ron (September 2015): "There is no mention of money, sex or refugees – all of which we might be singing about and changing society! No listing of drugs, sport or technology/science either. Which world are they in?!"

Another Christmas passed. "For most of my life, I've wanted to do away with Christmas – the run-up, the bustle of parish arrangements, the overdose of sentimentality v. the reality, family dynamics, the grumpiness of being exhausted and mad with each other, the whole human mess."[5]

And the following year, 2017, a similar reflection: "As I recall the utter exhaustion of John after taking Christmas services, I've no nostalgia about the season – just look forward to New Year when we're all going to catch up."[6]

In January 2016, Shirley was preparing to speak to a local group of clergy and spouses about hymns. As she prepared for this, she wondered "why congregations are so passive about what is dished out to them in sub-standard liturgy and prophetic thought. Why clergy are so poorly trained in some aspects of ministry (Communication! Listening!! Confidence in leading singing or promoting it!!!)."[7]

Throughout that year, John's health declined steadily as he suffered increasing renal failure. "I'm OK and our family have rallied round amazingly," Shirley wrote, "but I'm a bit weary on it. Still, we draw together our small bits of understanding about it all and feel so thankful for the life we have."[8]

John was not in pain, but simply growing more tired as the weeks and months went by. "Sometimes he is his old self (give him an issue!) and I love it when things seem 'normal'. We're restricted to home and short outings … We joke that the funeral service has been re-drafted 1000 times."[9]

Despite his increasing frailty, John continued to get frustrated when he thought about all his unfinished projects. Shirley was still looking after him at home, with other family members taking rostered care of him to give her breaks. "At present, he is engaged with the hearing of his submission to the End-of-Life Choice Bill in Parliament – irony of ironies!"[10]

In November, Shirley described John watching TV all day and being totally engaged in the "unfolding horror" of the presidential election in the United States. This saw Donald Trump defeating Hillary Clinton and becoming the 45th president.

A week later, Shirley wrote about the Kaikoura earthquake. At 7.8 magnitude, this devastated parts of New Zealand, tearing through fault lines, demolishing houses, ripping up roads and railways, and causing massive landslides as it travelled – an upheaval equivalent to the impact of Trump on America, some might say.

And in December that year: "John went into respite care to give me a break and is coming home tomorrow. It's been a strange separation and I find I'm not overly good at 'respite', but he is showing signs of such utter weariness and sometimes breathlessness, that I would wish him peacefully asleep. I never thought I could say that."[11]

By January 2017, Shirley was still nursing John at home but admitted that "an 85-year-old nurse is not the greatest support system in the world!"[12] The GP recommended more respite care.

This was given in early February, and he died of kidney failure on 17 February 2017, in the palliative care unit at Sevenoaks Retirement Village in Paraparaumu. His son David described him as "looking peaceful and ready to die. He had prepared himself well for this moment."

Shirley's hymns, read and sung, expressing gratitude, acceptance and inclusivity, bound together his funeral service at Kāpiti Uniting Church on 21 February. John's oldest friend, Hugh Templeton – one of the "three musketeers" from King's High School in Dunedin – described John, the youngest and the "bright shining star" of the musketeering group, as "a prince of our church in this country's Elizabethan age". Having achieved the miracle of salvaging the oldest Presbyterian church in New Zealand, he then took St Andrew's to the city and to Parliament. "John was at the forefront of our battles in this country. He was a wise and deeply outspoken leader of the faith."

John also gave Sir Lloyd Geering a national platform, Hugh said, then he took Shirley Erena Murray's poetry of peace to the wider world. Theirs was a creative partnership to be grateful for.

The promotion of Shirley's work and the establishment of the NZHBT were, arguably, John's greatest achievements in a life of so many.

Notes

1   Verse 1, 'Sing for Life and All its Goodness', a farewell song for John, written especially for his funeral. For verses 2 and 3, see appendix 2.

2   Email to Ron Klusmeier, 19 September 2015.

3   Email to Ron Klusmeier, 2 April 2015.

4   Email to Ron Klusmeier, 2 April 2015.

5   Email to Ron Klusmeier, 16 January 2016.

6   Email to Ron Klusmeier, 24 December, 2017.

7   See note 5.

8   Email to Ron Klusmeier, 5 July 2016.

9   Email to Ron Klusmeier, 17 August 2016.

10 Email to Ron Klusmeier, 16 October 2016.

11 Email to Ron Klusmeier, 21 December 2016.

12 Email to Ron Klusmeier, 13 January 2017.

18 – Living without John

This is our faith:

trouble may break us,
grief overtake us,
sickness and death
this is our creed:
no place so distant
God is not present,
knowing our need,

Nothing, nothing in all creation
can separate us from the love of God.[1]

Soon after John's death, Shirley moved into a "pleasant villa" at Sevenoaks Retirement Village, feeling exhausted and overwhelmed with visitors. John missed the move by 11 days. Nursing John during his last months had been really tough for her, son David said.

Shirley emailed Ron Klusmeier in Canada only a few weeks after John's death: "Since then, of course, as you understand, my whole world has changed. It has been an awfully slow journey."[2]

15 Lloyd Place would be Shirley's home for the last three years of her life. Thanks to the Presbyterian Church pension fund plus government superannuation, she was able to live "in style", she told the Strathdees. She appreciated the village's trees and gardens, and being near the beach along the northern part of the coast from Rosetta Road. And she expressed gratitude for the many good friends and family who supported her.

The Rev Roger Wiig, who helped lead John's service at the Kāpiti Uniting Church, was a frequent visitor to her new home. "She wasn't obviously grieving but I think she did that in her own quiet way. I would hear her at the piano when I came to visit."

Though the family had done all the hard work of the move, Shirley admitted to feeling "totally ragged. It's more than a little daunting to look at all the cards and letters that arrive daily, but John deserved every one of them! … Too many visitors at this point are kind of wearing me down, to be truthful … Strangely, I feel that John prepared me well for all this and so far, I'm still vertical."[3]

Alida van der Velde now took a more active role in caring for Shirley, visiting often and taking her shopping or to the library. "John had asked me to look after Shirley after he died. Shirley accepted this most of the time. I would take her out sometimes – she enjoyed going to the op shop and buying a few things – similar to the stuff she already had. She liked this cheap entertainment. It was a simple pleasure."

As time passed, Shirley said she was getting used to living differently and not as sad as she had expected to be. Seeing how peacefully and "wonderfully" John had died – and needed to die – was a comfort to her.

She was getting through the winter not too badly. "Hymns always help me connect with John, so without getting maudlin but actually feeling cheered up, I often play a couple before going to bed. Sundays get to me somewhat, so I often go to hymnals for connection."[4]

In August, she told the Strathdees that she had written very little in the last months. Her own health issues and a year and a half of John's illness had taken all the energy she could muster. "I'm supposed to lead a quiet life!"

New Zealand had a general election in October 2017. Shirley rejoiced in the victory of new Prime Minister Jacinda Ardern who had only become Labour Party leader seven weeks before the election.

"It's been the most exciting and nail-biting election ever for those of us who support the Labour Party and/or the Greens," she emailed Ron. "How John would have enjoyed and contributed to the result! Jacinda Ardern is impressive, not just because she's young, smart and politically decisive, but she has a real empathy that transmits.

"She's had a meteoric rise to leader – has rescued the Labour Party from dismal despair and put new heart into everyone. Though no longer one, she was brought up Mormon (not common here) and has a strong line on social justice as opposed to the last government. I just hope she succeeds with the coalition she has agreed to – the third party [New Zealand First] a bunch of old, tough cookies, but I trust her good sense and political nous. There – that's my take!"[5]

In January 2018, Shirley attended the wedding of her grandson Alex to Sophia in New Plymouth. She also wrote them a special song for the wedding, something she did not find easy (see chapter 15).

Shirley's correspondence stretched wider than her hymn-writing friends. Others, nearer at hand, got a look-in too. She and old school friend Pam Laytham (née Norris), living in Auckland, continued their easy rapport, as they shared their experiences of increasing frailty and ongoing health complaints.

"Yes, we are all shrinking a bit," she emailed Pam in January 2018. "I lost 15kg in the time John was ill but haven't regained them despite doctor's orders to do so. No point wearing a bra, though I do for some reason. All my knickers began to fall off."

And the following month: "I have spent the day chucking out old papers. Had a family council of the three sons last weekend and discussed my funeral, headstones and footstones and which photos to get rid of. After I'd enjoyed seeing them, felt absolutely exhausted at the emotional energy required! They blithely deferred a lot until I've fallen off the twig, anyway."

Only a week later, on 13 February, Shirley had a stroke. Although she was only in hospital one night, this was to have an ongoing and profound impact on her quality of life over the next two years.

"It was a bitter blow for her," said David. "Mum had a few months of good health after Dad died and we remember her having a great time at Alex and Sophia's wedding in New Plymouth in January. The next month, she suffered a stroke. She lost the ability to speak clearly, a terrible thing for her. She struggled to play the piano. It was upsetting for her and us, but she battled on. Further strokes ensued. Mum never got to die at home, how she wanted. She never got to spend those last years in good health. It was such a disappointment."

Alastair recalls her beautiful script, which she developed early in life, despite being born a left-hander and being forced to write with her right hand. "After the stroke, her handwriting began to go. It became wispy and inaccurate – she would have hated that. She was also very lonely towards the end. I was not living close enough, and David was in Australia. She resented people dropping in. She became more private in her last months and had fewer and fewer visitors. She would love to have taken a pill and died earlier. She wanted to die."

Alida painted a similar picture. "Everything became too much for her. She was angry at her mental and physical decline. People were quite disappointed when she did not want to see them, even John's niece Marion. She did not play the piano anymore and had ceased writing."

David does remember her finishing off her last book, *Life into Life*, published by Hope, "just in the nick of time. Mum was often ambivalent about her books – they were all brilliant, of course."

Shirley was still able to email, however, and told Ron that she was ready to go. "But while I wait, there seem to be more things to do! The stroke, which is more severe than I thought, is slow to respond and I can't readily talk or write but I'm getting help."[6]

By May 2018, Shirley was no longer driving and had given up her car. She was grateful for friends who delivered shopping to her and managed her library books.

Despite her physical restrictions, her mental powers remained strong. That month, she and Pam Laytham, who was preparing a sermon for Bible Sunday, were emailing each other about theological issues and biblical interpretations.

"When on earth is/was Bible Sunday?" wrote Shirley. "I have always stood by what Colin Gibson said: that the Bible should be chucked out until people understand what a collection of literary artifacts it is … My typing is improving even if my handwriting is deplorable – so, good on the computer for rescuing me!"[7]

In July, Shirley was enjoying looking through old photos and recalling memories: "Having looked through a heap of old photos with a view to chucking them out, there you are," she emailed Pam. "Were the good old days always so good?! I get much pleasure out of sorting through the heaps of them and then wondering who on earth is going to recognise these winsome creatures.

"The winter has been dire and still is, my visitor list has shrunk though I have lots of phone conversations, but these are limited a bit by my croaky voice, due to the stroke, which keeps coming back to haunt me, though there's plenty to do around here. My feeble attempt at gardening has even made the blue and orange pansies show their colours."[8]

Her correspondence with Ron continued: "The fact is, I don't seem to 'get on' with things. It is a real nuisance not to be able to talk properly, but on the other hand, one is spared my expostulations. Thank goodness for the computer!"[9]

And again, 11 November: "It's Armistice Day here and I feel very ambivalent about it. I would like to dismiss it all, but I remember the uncles who went and were forever changed and never spoke about it."

In December, an email to Pam Laytham: "My speech is still affected by the stroke, and I don't go for long walks and keep falling asleep at inconvenient times. This is anti-social. I have taken to throwing out many old photos and am astonished at how lissom and beautiful we once were and also what stages we have been through – many and varied.

"This is a maundering note and hardly puts together what I've been thinking. I am ready to go at a moment's notice and my ideas on God have undergone several changes, but I don't get the call – yet! I would like a painless exit! Not asking a lot, am I?"[10]

In January 2019, she wished Pam a happy 88th birthday: "Would that we could see each other – I'm half the size I used to be and I bet you are not much less. I appear as a quaint old thing, wearing out the last best clothes I own and with dyed hair into the bargain, though I do have one of Wellington's best hairdressers who comes for the pleasure of my company. She has had a stroke too and knows what it's like."

Shirley's email prompted Pam to suggest her daughter might drive her down to Raumati so the two old friends could meet in person. But her hopes of seeing Shirley again were soon dashed when Shirley said the effects of her stroke and general lack of energy prevented her from contemplating the idea. Her only connection with Pam would have to be via the computer.

A month later, there was bad news about Colin Gibson. "The latest and alarming news is that Colin has had a heart attack," Shirley emailed Ron. "This is not surprising but infinitely distressing … I feel nervous but what does one do with a character like him? He is brilliant but unpredictable."[11]

Despite the shrinking of her world – and her body – on a day-to-day level, Shirley remained fully engaged in current affairs, both locally and internationally. Two weeks after the 15 March attacks on two mosques in Christchurch, in which a lone gunman killed 51 people and injured 40, she wrote to Ron: "[the attacks] have shocked/rocked our slightly smug feelings of being so far away from it all and how the feelings have come out for the Muslim community. The national memorial service has just finished as I tap out these words. There is a long way to go yet before racism is finished with! … But Jacinda Ardern is a winner and she's got my vote along with many others. She is compassionate and pragmatic, an agnostic brought up as a Mormon."[12]

In August, Shirley was delighted that a two-year campaign, spearheaded by Alida and other local activists, to save an accessway leading from Groves Road, Raumati, to the beach, was finally successful. Shirley managed to attend the opening of the lane, named the Very Reverend John Murray Way in honour of all John's contributions to the Kāpiti Coast over 25 years. (See photo p206.) Maintaining public access to the beach had always been an important issue for him. He had earlier led a long and arduous campaign to win back another accessway, Bert's Way, at 181 Rosetta Road.

That same month, Shirley also attended a screening of *Camino Skies,* the documentary her grandson Fergus had made about the Camino de Santiago pilgrims' trail (see chapter 15).

As Shirley's health continued to decline, her thoughts turned increasingly to arrangements for her funeral. Roger Wiig always knew he would be conducting this, as Shirley had often reminded him of how good a job he had done conducting John's. Shirley also made sure Roger knew exactly what she wanted.

"Shirley gave me two foolscap sheets of instructions shortly before her death," he said. "'These are the hymns I want and this is the order.' She knew the end was coming. She was realistic about her death: her theology aligned with Geering's in this regard. Life has its complexities and life ends in death."

Fergus and his father David got to spend time with Shirley before she died. "On Christmas morning, 2019, we pushed her in her wheelchair around Sevenoaks, before travelling up to join Alex and his in-laws in New Plymouth for Christmas Day."

In her final days, Shirley ceased speaking altogether, said granddaughter Anna. "But near the end of her life, she gave me a little quote and one for my sister Rachel too. Mine said, 'Sometimes naughty, always lovely.' Rachel's quote said, 'Be free like a bee.' My quote made me realise how much Grandshe understood my wild teenage years. She was always there for me, supportive and understanding. I should have shared more with her."

Shirley died at Metlifecare in Paraparaumu on 25 January 2020. She was 88. Alastair regretted she was unable to be admitted to the palliative care unit at Sevenoaks where John had died, but unfortunately the room was occupied by someone else at the time. So she had to be moved to another rest home a few kilometres away.

Alida was the last person to see her before she died. "John and Shirley would have chosen euthanasia if it had been an option, especially Shirley. She just stopped eating and drinking in the end – what else could she do?"

Shirley's funeral service was held at Kāpiti Uniting Church on the last day of January. It was, of course, a very musical event featuring some of Shirley's finest hymns – two of them read aloud by family members.

"Mum laid down some strict rules in my talking today," said Alastair in his eulogy. "'Make it happy, make it short'. Mum did not like a fuss, was absurdly modest and wouldn't want us to make such a big deal about all of this. So she is out of luck today.

"Despite all the achievements in the literary world, Mum always valued two things – her friends and her family," he continued. "Her top group of friends go back as far as Standard Two, when she was eight years old. They remained in touch all these years and I tip my hat to you, Pam Laytham, for your kind words and your lifelong friendship."

David described his mother's early life and Rob paid tribute to his mother's work, the full extent of which he had only come to appreciate in the last couple of months. "Mum's songs considered many aspects of life – peace, the church, compassion, equity, inclusiveness, all contemporary issues of the day and I hope for many tomorrows. She was saddened by congregations continuing to bang out the hymns of 300 years ago. She was infuriated when the New Zealand Defence Force, when singing her Anzac hymn, dropped out the third verse [about conscientious objectors]. She was always good for a very good foot-stamp when warranted."

Rob was overwhelmed by the hundreds of messages of condolence the family received from all over the globe – an astonishing outpouring, he said. He was touched by one from the Motueka Uniting Church in the South Island: "Be assured that as long as people have voices that can sing, she will never be forgotten." That was a legacy Shirley would like, he said.

Alex emailed from Boston:

Grandshe was a thoughtful and introverted woman who spent most of her life surrounded by extroverts. As the wife of minister Grandjohn, it must have taken at times strength and patience that I find hard to imagine. She drew her power from books, moments of quiet and contemplation, as a fiercely intelligent and independent freethinker.

She cared deeply about education. She was the one I worried about reading the bad reports most. She fostered my love of music and I have fond memories of sitting with her at the piano in Raumati singing. She had a revolutionary spirit, using her words to spread peace, to stand up to the establishment, and fight injustice and intolerance where she saw it.

Growing up, I had little idea about this side of her. Later, when I became interested in reading and discovering her work, I discovered how truly badass my grandma was.

Before I moved to the States, she told me of her own travels to America and I learnt how widespread and respected her work had become. Although she did not enjoy flying and did not travel often, she brought our country to the world with hymns that celebrated the precious taonga [treasures] of New Zealand. I am immensely proud to be her grandson, very sad that she has left us, fortunate to be able to still spend time with her in a world so often loud and full of noise. We are truly blessed to have the quiet virtue of someone like Shirley Murray.

Colin Gibson's memorable eulogy wove together the first lines of dozens of Shirley's hymns to honour her and her work. "You lived a life of deliberate commitment to the perfection of your craft ... you created a body of hymns and songs whose integrity, beauty, truth and originality have won you a world-wide reputation," he said.

Shirley also captured the deep love she had for her own country. "You showed us that the languages of science and te reo [the Māori language] could meet and kiss in poetry, poetry that is full of beauty and truth, but also sparkling with brilliant new metaphors, from small paper lanterns to lasers and lovers ...

"*Kua hinga te tōtara o te Waonui a Tāne* – indeed a very great tōtara has fallen in the forest of Tāne."[13]

In an interview with the author, Alastair reflected on the legacy of both his parents. "They were a power couple for the church. Sometimes the conservatives would try to shut Dad up as they saw him as a radical upstart. Mum and Dad encouraged each other in their different fields. They both said to each other, 'You can do this!' Mum then produced the goods and went from strength to strength.

"Shirley's words are so good, they will be remembered and continue to be sung. Her themes about the human condition are timeless and universal. This is her legacy. Many of her hymns will continue to be relevant, because she sang the praise of life."

When prophets are dead and languages shed,
with knowledge all vanished, and mind's endeavour,
there still will be faith, there still will be hope,
and love, always love, that will last forever.[14]

Notes

1 Verse 1, 'Nothing, Nothing in All Creation', written in 2005 and based on one of the maxims of the seventh century Byzantine hieromonk Hesychios of Sinai. In *Hope is our Song*, the hymn is set to REASSURANCE by Barry Brinson. There are other settings by Jillian Bray and Colin Gibson. In *Touch the Earth Lightly*, the setting by Jane Marshall is called HOPESONG.

2 Email to Ron Klusmeier, 15 March 2017.

3 See note 2.

4 Emails to Ron Klusmeier, 19 July and 16 September 2017.

5 Email to Ron Klusmeier, 21 October 2017.

6 Email to Ron Klusmeier, 9 August 2018.

7 Email to Pam Laytham, 26 May 2018.

8 Email to Pam Laytham, 28 July 2018.

9 Email to Ron Klusmeier, 18 September 2018.

10 Email to Pam Laytham, 1 December 2018.

11 Email to Ron Klusmeier, 3 February 2019.

12 Email to Ron Klusmeier, 28 March 2019.

13 Colin's eulogy can be found in full in appendix 2.

14 Verse 4, 'When I Was a Child', written in 1994 and based on 1 Corinthians 13. The words from Corinthians suggested to Shirley a 'world come of age' and the need for Christians to grow up from a childish dependence on God and other doctrinal certainties.

John and Shirley cutting their
35th wedding anniversary cake at
Wallis House, 21 July 1989

Shirley and John enjoying a ceilidh
at St Andrew's on The Terrace,
marking the 150th anniversary of
St Andrew's and of the national
Presbyterian Church, 1990

A social gathering at the manse, Talavera Terrace, Wellington, 1980s.
From left: Robin Lane, Natasha Templeton, Lloyd Geering, Hugh Templeton,
Shirley, Pam Ormsby, Jack Somerville and Elaine Geering

Shirley with George and Nancy Shorney, Chicago, 1992

Shirley outside the Hope Publishing Company office in Carol Stream, Illinois, 1992. From left: Jack Schrader (editor), Bill Shorney (vice president), George Shorney (president), John Shorney (art director) and David L. Weck (Handbell music editor)

Shirley and John celebrating *Carol Our Christmas*, its accompanying CD and "a southern sunny summer season". (Photo by Jo Head, *The Evening Post*, 8 December 1997. Reprinted with permission)

Colin Gibson and Shirley setting off the United States, c1996

Shirley becomes a Member of the New Zealand Order of Merit,
Government House, Wellington, 2001.
From left: Alastair and David Murray, Governor-General Dame Silvia Cartwright,
Shirley, John and grandson Fergus Grady

Shirley is made an Honorary Fellow of the Royal School of Church Music
at the Wellington Cathedral of St Paul, September 2006

Shirley with a copy of *Alleluia Aotearoa*, *Carol Our Christmas* and
Faith Makes the Song, Raumati 2007

Grandshe and Grandjohn celebrating Fergus Grady's 21st birthday,
with their grandchildren.
From left: Anna Murray, Alex Grady, Rachel Murray, Fergus Grady,
Elizabeth and Isabella Murray, June 2007

Shirley and John at the beach, Kāpiti Coast, c2007

Members of the New Zealand Hymnbook Trust's first editorial committee reunite at the national hymn conference in Palmerston North, October 2009. From left: John Murray, Cecily Sheehy, Colin Gibson, Jillian Bray and Shirley

Shirley receiving her honorary doctorate at the University of Otago, December 2009, with university chancellor John Ward

Cartoonist Jeff Bell captures Shirley in a commission marking her 80th birthday.

Christmas Day, 2016. John's health had begun to decline steadily during this year.

Very Reverend John Murray Way

Kāpiti Coast
DISTRICT COUNCIL

Shirley beside the Very Reverend John Murray Way, Raumati. The walkway and sign were officially opened in August 2019, attended by more than 50 people.

Part V – Working with Shirley

19 – An instinctive poet

Where the star enlightens,
light is shared around.

God has drawn no borders,
faith sees common ground:

Peace the hopeful journey,
justice without bar,

God's illumination
from the Christmas star.[1]

Hymn writer and composer Colin Gibson variously called himself Shirley's friend, collaborator, conspirator and the Sullivan to her Gilbert. He had no doubt she was New Zealand's greatest hymn writer, because of the range of her material, the number of hymns she wrote and the power of her poetry.

Colin first met Shirley in the 1970s, shortly after working on a television hymn competition with her husband John. In the late 1970s, Colin joined the first editorial committee of the New Zealand Hymnbook Trust, which had set to work to provide a New Zealand supplement to the Australian publication *With One Voice*.

Although Shirley had published *In Every Corner Sing: New Hymns to Familiar Tunes in Inclusive Language* in 1987, she soon became dissatisfied with using these familiar tunes. What she needed was some original music.

In this chapter, drawn from interviews with the author in March 2021, Colin describes how he and Shirley worked together to find the perfect settings for her texts, and what makes her hymn writing so distinct.

Very early on, as Shirley began writing hymns, she also began looking for new tunes. She began to realise that a traditional tune establishes a traditional text in half the mind of the singer, no matter what you do. That text is still sitting there behind the new words, and being more important, in the end, than what is being sung. So she decided to branch out and find somebody who could write tunes for her.

Despite being a very competent musician, she wasn't confident to write her own tunes. She wrote one for her hymn 'Alleluia Aotearoa', the first song published in the collection of the same name. However, her own musical ability made her quite capable of criticising and judging the tunes of other people. She knew whether a tune matched or didn't match her lyrics. She knew what her words were intending to do and she wanted to be sure that whatever music was used supported that.

She used to post me down a little envelope with what she called an "orphan text". Could we find something that would work for it? she would ask. That's how the first connections between us as hymn-writing collaborators began.

I have probably set to music at least 300 of Shirley's hymns, but they have not all been published. I was always thrilled to work with one of her beautiful texts. A Shirley Murray text almost immediately distinguishes itself by its freedom from cliché and tired biblical slogans; one comes to look forward to fresh images and vivid words in her writing.

I would tear open the envelope (later fax, then email) and rush to the piano and start setting straight away. In the first ten minutes, I might get the perfect tune; other times I would send something to her and she would not necessarily be happy with it. We would go back and forth on a tune. Sometimes I would give her something quite unexpected, and she would like it; other times I would not satisfy her expectations. I would either get it on the second hit, or I wouldn't, then I would leave it at that.

There are so many choices one makes musically – it becomes instinctive after a while. Sometimes she would abandon a text if no one could get the music for it. I would try my tunes out on my own congregation at Mornington Methodist Church, Dunedin. I was lucky enough to have that sounding board. Shirley, too, had the sounding board of St Andrew's where she and John would often try out her new hymns.

Initiating the New Zealand Hymnbook Trust

Both Shirley and her husband John felt equally frustrated with the church. By and large, it was still singing from an 18th century British theology. Sheer frustration with this led to the establishment of the New Zealand Hymnbook Trust (NZHBT).

Scripture in Song, a music recording and publishing brand, was founded in New Zealand in the late 1960s by David and Dale Garratt. The NZHBT ran alongside this charismatic renewal movement, with the church divided along the two theological lines of liberal and conservative. Society, too, was dividing, e.g. between those who supported the Springbok rugby tour of 1981 and those who didn't. These sorts of divisions were happening all over the world. We are still dividing, e.g. between those who support and those who oppose Covid-19 vaccination. Society is driven by these sorts of divisions.

The world was opening up to a whole range of new ideas and Shirley was there at the right time. Our pop music was the songs of

Paul Simon, Leonard Cohen and Bob Dylan. This was a time of social upheaval that was in tune with the younger generation.

Soon after the publication of *With One Voice with New Zealand Supplement (WOV)* in 1982, John decided it was time we created our own, independently published hymn book. A working group was formed, meeting two or three times a year at the Murrays' house in Wellington. This is when I really met Shirley who would dart around playing secretary to the group. We formed an instinctive friendship.

We weren't just a publishing group; we were a crowd of composers, text writers, just the kind of creative mêlée that you might want, with John officiating over it all, deciding grandly which hymn would be included and which would not. Not long thereafter, John found a backing publisher for *Alleluia Aotearoa (AA),* largely on the grounds of our success selling *WOV*. He also found Colin Daly from the Salvation Army who became our typesetter. Finally, we had the computer technology to print our music and share it easily.

Shirley and John would gather a list of 15 to 20 new texts and send them around the committee. We would discuss their worth and one or perhaps two of us would write a tune. Then the group had to decide which tune fitted best.

Creating *AA* was years of work. There were hymns left over from *WOV* that we hadn't managed to include. The only one who wasn't contributing a great deal then was Methodist hymn writer Bill Wallace. We weren't familiar with his work at that time.

I see John as the father of New Zealand hymnology and am grateful for that. He had that dynamic presence. You didn't cross him lightly but, on the other hand, he had a good instinct. He was determined that *AA* would not only have Pākehā [European] material in it but would also include Pasifika and Māori work. We recognised John's mana and authority, but we negotiated much more with Shirley.

AA deliberately included the broadest spectrum of theological beliefs, from evangelical to the most liberal. We were trying to find out who we were and we wanted to be inclusive. Seven years later, when *Faith Forever Singing* was published, hymns for and by evangelicals had vanished. Basically, the book comprises new writers and a new body of work. We had discovered who was out there, though Shirley's work often made up a third of a book.

Very few evangelical churches have adopted Shirley's hymns because her theology was so different. Hard-line conservatives prefer to stick to the exact words in the Bible. But scholarship was cracking open the biblical texts. We no longer saw them as a divine dictation pad.

Shirley knew there was resistance in some parts of the church to her hymns – she was talking about things some people did not particularly want discussed. This resistance made her write even more strongly about particular subjects – she wanted to break down these barriers. But she never turned on the church as an institution; she lived within its limitations.

The multi-faith element came in very late, almost at the end of this run of publications. Shirley's 'Now the Star of Christmas' or 'Three Faiths Carol' was published in *Hope is our Song* in 2009, the Trust's last major production. Because it acknowledged Islam and the Jewish faith as well as Christianity, it incited a lot of anger among conventional singers and no one would sing it. It was an attempt to bridge the faiths, but it seems we don't want to leave our bastions. I think Shirley was slowly moving in a multi-faith direction.

A generation of ministers bought our books and sang the new hymns. *AA* was an enormous success, but as the Trust published more books, congregations had less money to buy them. Whether the next generation does the same, is another matter. And of course, the internet allows you to download pretty much whatever you want. The church, however, is still labouring to get into it.

Writing hymns that made a difference

Shirley was intensely creative, enjoyed what she did and worked hard and consistently at it. She never faltered – she went on writing about things that mattered to her. She would sooner offend or disturb her singers than make it easy.

She realised her hymns were making a difference and she wanted to go on making that difference. The art of the word pleased her immensely and she never gave up. Right to the end she was creating text of one sort or another.

She had some strong opinions about a number of things, as shown by her insistence on including words like justice and peace in her hymns. She was passionate about the work of Amnesty International and was tender-hearted.

Shirley talks about what is real and this can be uncomfortable for some people. Religion frequently dodges the hardness of life. It often prefers to tell us that all is ok because God is in charge. There is an urgency in Shirley's writing. Her writing mattered to her and she was hurt when people did not like it.

I don't think Shirley ever saw herself as a feminist, rather as someone who sought to be inclusive. She honoured women and the feminine element in spirituality. She would get a 'she' in whenever she could. Hers was a quiet feminism. She put her heart on her sleeve and made herself vulnerable. She was self-effacing, but immensely talented.

Some New Zealand hymn writers have written more than Shirley but hers was quality writing. She wouldn't let a hymn go or find its way to a tune until she was sure it was ready. She was not prepared to have her work messed up by somebody else who didn't understand what her work was about or couldn't do it justice.

Once her hymns got to America in the 1990s, publishers like Hope wanted their own composers to write the accompanying tunes. Tunes and texts are never finally bound together. Some editors or congregations will always choose a different tune. As the centuries pass, tunes are reshaped to the most convenient and easy shape they can have. Nothing is permanent.

Editors also keep changing the words – that infuriated her and always annoyed me. She resolutely refused to change a single word. She would argue with editors and win. She protected her texts because she knew they were good. She argued with Hope a lot and wouldn't allow them to tinker about with her texts.

From the 1990s onwards, a network of writers, composers and poets gathered around her and supported her. She was a true artist in that sense. She met hosts of other creative people, making personal friends among them. She was being honoured by her peers, many of them women. Twice we went as a group to a Hymn Society [in the United States and Canada] conference – in 1992 and 1996. We were mostly well ahead of the Americans in terms of adventurous texts, Shirley's notably so, though their musical compositions were well ahead of ours. Hope Publishing Company was keen to nurture us so they would make some money out of us! We couldn't have done all this in the Covid world – we were lucky at the time. Communication was easy.

Our networks in the States and beyond grew bigger and bigger. She began working with the Swedish hymn writer Per Harling; Carlton Young became a good friend, as did American hymn writers Jane Marshall and Joy Paterson. Eventually, in 2009, the Hymn Society honoured her by making her a Fellow – she was pleased to be recognised in this way.

The Americans love her peace hymns and some of her Christmas writing. After generations of being buried in English Christmas hymns, she broke the mould entirely. If she had lived longer, she probably would have addressed Matariki [the start of the traditional Māori New Year in June]. She wrote frequently on the same subject, particularly about the barbarous ill treatment human beings offer each other – that hurt her deeply and came out of her work with Amnesty International.

On the other hand, some of her most personal hymns are also some of her most beautiful work, e.g. 'Simply to Be', a meditative piece, which came out of serious illness. It wrenches me every time I sing it. She shared her innermost feelings in her writing.

Making connections with the city

John turned St Andrew's on The Terrace to face the city and Shirley wrote hymns to back this up. Most churches made no connection with the city around them, instead focusing on theological issues of little relevance to the world outside. Shirley was determined that what she wrote must mean something in terms of real life.

Some of the hymns she wrote about the crucifixion, e.g. 'O Christ, You Hang Upon a Cross', are gruesome, they are not comfortable singing at all. Yet through her involvement with Amnesty International, she knew of the gruesome things happening in the world. I see two sides to her writing – the gentle, womanly treatment; the other a harsh account of real life.

She often wrote hymns for particular situations and particular people, but what she wrote was applicable to almost everybody. Take, for instance, her song of blessing 'Go Gently, Go Lightly', which she wrote in 2001 for her friend Rosemary Lawrence, who was leaving Wellington and moving to Auckland. It's been published in several hymn collections, including Hope's *Faith Makes the Song* and the NZHBT's *Hope is our Song*. It is a hymn of universal significance, so perfect for anyone leaving or beginning a new venture. It has been set by many composers, including me, and translated into German.

Shirley was so good at reaching out to modern references, e.g. laser beams, cursors and flight paths. So often we pull down the blinds when we go to church, and only hear church words rather than language from the working world. The two so rarely meet. How do you put a word like iPhone into a hymn? Yet, these are the sorts of words we use all the time.

Shirley also slipped in references to Māori and used some Māori words in a quiet way – words she was comfortable with and which are now generally accepted. I doubt any Australian hymns include Aboriginal words. She was way ahead in those respects.

The divine presence

Shirley and I wanted to write about a presence, a love, a sustaining, something that is more than simply human. She wrote hymns that cried out to a God, without defining what that God was. It could be a human consciousness, but at least it was something beyond us or our individual experience. Finding a way to degender God in our hymns was also difficult. This is a language problem. We needed words that cover both/all genders. We seldom wrote about "God the Father".

I think Shirley did look to a life beyond this one. I believe she had a sense of not going alone into death – that is as far as either of us got, but she didn't imagine she would be meeting John again. She had a strong sense, until the end, of a universal presence – this was a comfort to her. She had no time for evangelical sureness about these things. She found Lloyd Geering interesting, but this was not her theological cup of tea either.

Both the Murrays and I felt that Lloyd had gone one step further from where we were comfortable. We were happy to reimagine any deity, rather than dismiss the existence altogether. Lloyd imported Gaia as a God substitute. Shirley constantly invented different metaphors for God, but she did not throw away the notion of a divine presence. You will find nothing about atonement or being saved by the blood of the Lamb in any of Shirley's or my hymns.

Evangelicals, on the other hand, are drawn to the notion of atonement. This is a major point of difference between them and more progressive Christians. The figure of Jesus is central for all of us, of course, not the risen man, but the simple Galilean peasant who did lots of useful things. Shirley did not throw away the terms Christ or Lord – nor did I. They were useful terms that rhymed, but they are all terms heavily loaded by centuries of tradition. Shirley just wanted to bring a fresh and different view to them.

Shirley avoided much of the traditional church language because it carried with it generations of standard, traditional theology.

Her hymns have been affirming/reaffirming for many people who were sitting poised to leave the church, and who found in her words and their new tunes a sign of life in the old body. One of her hymns – 'Faith Has Set Us On a Journey' – is about the struggle to leave behind old ways of thinking. It acknowledges those who have found the limitations of the church too much and who have left – she offers no word of praise or blame for this action.

One of my great disappointments is that most clergy are profoundly ignorant about matters musical and hymnological. Theological colleges spend their time talking about how to create a sermon – and that's about it. But for consumers or churchgoers, a third of every service is musical. Sadly, there has been little recognition of this in the training of ministers over the years.

Ministers who are old and retired know what they like – usually 18th and 19th century hymns. Why should they change and learn new hymns? There are whole groups of people in the church who either reject Shirley theologically or they know nothing about her hymns.

When a church leader does decide to introduce a new hymn, this needs to be done carefully (see chapter 14). John knew that what a congregation sang they would remember – that's why he chose the hymns for his services. He knew his congregation might not remember his sermons, or even the ideas behind them. But singing gets the message inside the soul, which is why some congregations are so resistant to singing anything new. Most congregations and ministers choose to sing the same hymns over and over again. It's a brave worship leader who challenges that often.

Shirley's poetic skills

Shirley used all the traditional poetic skills, including imaginative use of rhyme and rhythm. She experimented with poetic forms and metrical patterns, inventing new metres, often to the despair of her composers. The 17th century English poet George Herbert also used interesting metres and never confined himself to the standard. Shirley's use of verbs was most insightful, often through using a whole string of powerful verbs. Take the hymn 'God Weeps', where each verse begins with a new verb – God bleeds, God cries, God waits. That can be a bit tough for consumers and publishers alike but was brave of her.

She applied language precisely, like a weapon. Her use of metaphors was outrageously inventive and brave. She was an instinctive poet. Think of her wonderful hymn, one of her earliest, 'Loving Spirit'. Its image of a child hoisted up on a father's shoulders to depict one aspect of God is totally original. It has never appeared before, in any poetry, in any hymn, yet now it seems such a natural image. Other hymn writers are still trying to catch up.

Shirley used rhyme a lot, mostly masculine, one-stress rhymes rather than feminine rhymes. Rhymes help lock stanzas together, with the tune the tool to make it easier to remember. However, she did not allow rhymes to become a shackle. She was good at discovering rhymes that no one else had thought of. She did not allow the language to shut her down.

She reached out into science – astronomy, chemistry, into the ordinary and the extraordinary – areas that people had not explored much. She was like Herbert in that respect. Her poems were finished in the way a Mozart sonata was finished, completed in her head before written down. Her hymns had that sense of being well thought out, well understood, before being committed to paper.

She did not write many stanzas. Congregations often get uncomfortable singing more than four verses. Shirley understood what a real congregation was and was not capable of. She stretches them through her choice of language and she subtly manipulates them at the same time. She loves alliteration. You can't say much in a small space like a hymn – it has to be intense and concentrated, a bit like a sonnet.

Sometimes the tone of one verse can be quite different from that of the next. This can be difficult for the composer, as you only have the one tune. Even changing to a minor key can be difficult for congregations. Congregations can't cope with too many changes in the harmony.

How many of her hymns will survive? Charles Wesley wrote about 6000 hymns, but there is hardly a word about looking after mother nature. It was not under any threat, as far as he could see. For us, we have to write about what is around us. What hymns survive will be very individual. A hymn is like a fishing line – it has all sorts of hooks but they don't all catch. Shirley was good at opening a hymn in a way that arrested your attention immediately. You knew you were going to go somewhere because of the quality of the writing.

She was intellectually tough but could be too tough for some people. She is an acquired taste. Young people may grow into her when they are tired of the loud, happy-clappy stuff, when they become more interested in the words they sing.

It is hard to predict the future. Perhaps the Hymnbook Trust will end. These days, there's a huge number of secular composers out there writing requiems and other religious music. The future probably lies with people like Welsh composer Karl Jenkins, who writes religious music using multicultural texts and multicultural music.

In the end, Shirley's hymns will be seen as a significant body of poetry in the New Zealand context as a whole, not just in the context of the church. Poetry, if it's good, stands away from and beyond the lives of the people who use it or write it.

Note

1   Verse 4, 'Now the Star of Christmas', 'The Three Faiths Epiphany Carol', written
    in 2008, is the first New Zealand carol to deal with an interfaith theme. Verse 3
    acknowledges the wisdom found in the three Abrahamic faiths of Christianity,
    Judaism and Islam, and Jesus' status within each, while verse 4 explores the image
    of light as enlightenment. Colin Gibson's tune KUPE, published in *Hope is our
    Song*, recalls the first Polynesian explorer to discover the islands of New Zealand.

20 – Liberated from patriarchy

God weeps
at love withheld,
at strength misused,
at children's innocence abused,
and till we change the way we love,
God weeps.[1]

The Rev Ian Render regards Shirley as one of the most memorable people in his life. He developed a deep respect for her when he joined the New Zealand Hymnbook Trust's editorial board in 1992, as an Anglican representative. During his eight years on the board, he wrote the music for some of her best loved hymns. The following comes from the author's interview with him in February 2023.

My background as a teenager and young adult was conservative, evangelical and fundamentalist. Shirley's background was quite different from mine, developed through the Student Christian Movement and from a much more liberal theology. Being exposed to her faith was helpful to me.

In my evangelical/fundamentalist days, I had a band or two and realised I had a talent for writing songs. I had always been musical thanks to my Welsh mother. But so much of the hymnody of the church had felt rather dull and passé. So I was keen on being part of a project that set out to gather hymns that reflected our local context. As vicar of Newlands-Paparārangi, Wellington, I had developed a good music ministry. I had a point of reference with a live congregation and could test new hymns out on them. Parish work and being on the Trust seemed a zeitgeist for me.

Shirley stands out for me because of the huge warmth of her personality and her generosity of spirit. Considering her tremendous gifts as a writer and the fact her work had been published long before anyone else's, her lack of ego was remarkable. She wrote because she wanted to offer the church a resource that reflected who we are in Aotearoa. She also wrote out of necessity because she and John could not find traditional hymns that suited what they wanted to say. Shirley was incredibly consistent as a person and it was a joy to work with her.

Shirley's faith was not separate from her as a person. It shone out from her. She wanted to be inclusive. She understood a God big enough for everyone and everything. She almost expressed God in an interfaith way. She did not tell us how to be. She challenged the church but she did it in a way that included herself somehow.

Along with her great warmth, there was a toughness and resilience, a sense of conviction about what she was doing and why. She would take criticism of her writing on the chin and, if she thought it was worthwhile, she would go back and have another crack at it. Shirley had strong opinions and a good analytic quality. She could critique melodies as well as words.

I remember her saying about her own work: "This is the point I wanted to make and I don't want to resile from that." Sometimes, I think her desire to be contemporary did not quite work. Take, for example, the phrase 'Christ our internet of care' from the hymn 'Christ Has Changed the World's Direction', published in *Hope is our Song*. I felt this clunked – it was trying too hard to be relevant. Sometimes, she experimented with imagery that might not stand the test of time, but none of our work is perfect. We do the best we can.

John, on the other hand, could be quite bossy. If he wanted to put his foot down, he would. He and Shirley were two very different personalities, but the Hymnbook Trust was his show. John sometimes did not listen to what people were saying. If he had the bit between his teeth about how something should be, he would mow everyone else down. He had that force of personality. Most of us on the board wanted a numbered index for *Alleluia Aotearoa*, for example, but he absolutely refused.

Shirley worked out what her place in the relationship was. She managed him and steered him a little.

Musical contributions

Some of the earliest tunes I contributed were for texts by Joy Cowley – 'Jesus Comes to Me as a Springtime Tree' and 'May the Mystery of God Enfold Us', a tune that came to me in the middle of a meeting. 'Who is Moving Through the Silence', by John Weir, is another of my compositions.

I am glad one or two of my tunes have stuck with Shirley's work. 'Who Is My Mother?' her hymn about inclusivity, and my tune BRONWEN have stuck. This is one of the first pieces of music I wrote for her. My setting LEONARD for 'When We Lift Our Pack and Go', the song for travellers, has also stuck. This tune also came to me easily.

One of my compositions was for Shirley's 'God Weeps'. Called EMPATHY and written in 1999, it was published in *Faith Forever Singing* in 2000. The tune just seemed to leap out at me. It's always the words that come first. If the words grab me, then the chances are a tune will follow or at least the intimations of a tune. A tune must recreate the feeling I have inside about a hymn. 'God Weeps' is a good example of this. I could hear how it went harmonically in my head the moment I read the words. I just had to translate that as quickly as possible onto the sheet music.

Colin Gibson describes 'God Weeps', written in 1996, as "an extraordinarily powerful hymn". Shirley wrote it as a protest at violence of every kind, especially that inflicted on the totally vulnerable – children, women and the created world. Colin explains further:

"What stands out for me is its profoundly Christian concept of a God who is victimised alongside the human victims of injustice and abuse, who shares and feels the sorrow and the hurts, who – unlike the all-powerful, punitive God of some writers (including some that exhibit a thirst for vengeance and retributive justice among the Book of Psalms) – waits patiently for us to understand the full implications of Christ's life and teachings."[2]

In his book *Hymnwriters Downunder*, the Rev Terry Wall praises an audacious and daring text "that employs anthropomorphic language to breaking point".[3] God weeps, bleeds, and cries out, even as Jesus did on the Cross.

Other commentary has noted:

Verse 4, beginning 'God waits', reinforces the message that it is up to us all to change – the way we love, the way we win, the way we care. Peace is 'seeded': naturally, apparently randomly, caught as it were by the wind; but also because we plant it, because we 'understand the Christ' and act intentionally as a result.[4]

Like Render, Presbyterian minister and composer the Rev David Dell was deeply moved by the words for 'God Weeps' when he came across the hymn in 2019. A tune for it began to emerge almost immediately. "I stayed up till midnight completing this tune. I loved it and sang it at the service at St Ninian's Uniting Church in Karori, Wellington, the next day. Other members of the congregation were also deeply affected by it. I had thought of taking it to Shirley, and I had others I wanted to share with her. But she was pretty frail by then and I talked myself out of it."

Ian Render continues:

Shirley made a great contribution to inclusive language in the church. She offered us new imagery for God and other people through her consummate use of language.

We are changed by her writing which provides us with the opportunity to critique what came before. A lot of the traditional language was patriarchal and power-dominated, with a God up there somewhere. Her body of work was to critique this 19th century material, which was often used for sentimental rather than realistic reasons or because people wanted to avoid another fight over the music.

I believe her greatest contribution to church hymnody is the Easter song 'Christ Is Alive', with a magnificent tune, HEARTBEAT, by Jillian Bray. I love to use this at Easter with the organ on full throttle.

One that grips me personally is 'In What Strange Land', published in *Hope is our Song*, with a setting called MYSTERIUM by Colin Gibson. It seems a deeply personal hymn, but works so brilliantly during Lent and Advent. Maybe it was about her own journey through cancer, about going through the unknown – the last verse certainly strikes me that way.

John hardly wrote anything, but he did write 'For the Hurt that I Create', a prayer for forgiveness, published in *Faith Forever Singing*. Jillian Bray and I both wrote tunes for this, and both are included in *FFS*. I enjoyed setting John's words and wrote a tightly woven melody, called FIVE SCRUPLES, that is meant to evoke the tension of our awareness of the hurt we create.

The future of ecumenical hymnody

As the mainstream churches continue to retrench and become increasingly fragile, the question about what will happen to our ecumenical hymnody becomes a real concern. Will it just get swallowed up by worship songs from Australia and other more traditional denominations? It would be tragic if only people overseas were singing Shirley's hymns, but it could happen.

Shirley was a trailblazer with so many of her themes. She was one of the leading writers covering the care of creation in hymnody. She could do the expansive and the tiny. She could be intimate too, without falling into the trap of sentimentality. Her own spirituality emerged through her texts. Some writers wag their fingers at the church, saying how terrible we are and that we have to do better.

People don't want that; they want to be inspired to make change and to live lives in a Christian way. Shirley was so gifted in that respect. Her hymns take us with her.

Her legacy is the establishment of the sense of the church in the Southern Hemisphere. She unapologetically wrote so it reflected our lived experience – the bicultural, the seasonal, the struggles for social justice. She enabled us to look at ourselves compassionately but critically and she also gave us language for God that liberated us from patriarchy. She was passionate about extending the language for God, plus rooting her hymns in the Southern Hemisphere. These are her two great gifts.

Notes

1 Verse 1, 'God Weeps', written as a protest at the violence humanity metes out against the most vulnerable in society. It was first published in *Faith Forever Singing* in 2000, with Ian Render's setting. It has been published in other collections with settings by Carlton Young and Jim Strathdee. It is included among 'All-time Favourites' in Shirley's last book, *Life into Life*.

2 Gibson, C. (2011) Building Jerusalem: New Zealand Hymns on Social Justice. *Music in the Air*, Winter/Spring.

3 Wall, 2022, p35.

4 God Weeps at Love Withheld. *Singing the Faith Plus*, The Resource Hub. Methodist Church UK. https://www.methodist.org.uk/for-churches/resources/hymns/god-weeps-at-love-withheld-stf-700/

21 – Weighting the love side

Where church tradition gags and binds,
roll the stone away,
where words exclude and bias blinds,
roll the stone away.

Stand up, Mary,
daughter of ancient wisdom!
Tell of your suffering
to roll the stone away.[1]

Canadian hymn writer Ron Klusmeier has worked in full-time music ministry for the United Church of Canada since 1971. He began writing tunes for Shirley's hymns in the early 1990s, but it wasn't until 2014, when he and his partner Christina Bogucki made their first and only visit to New Zealand, that they met in person. This chapter is based on the author's interview with him in June 2022.

It was hymn writer Brian Wren who first alerted me to Shirley's work. Shortly thereafter, Hope Publishing Company began to promote her work in the United States and Canada. Initially we did a lot of our writing and co-writing by email before we eventually met face to face.

The two of us hit it off immediately. We had a similar, wry sense of humour, especially about writing and the church. Neither of us was terribly fond of birthdays and similar calendar markers. Yet when I turned 60 in 2006, Shirley sent me a special birthday message which I cherish to this day. John reached out to me when Shirley was approaching her 80th. He and the family wanted to put on a surprise event for her. I gathered some of our singers together to record a selection of our collaborations and sent over a CD, which Shirley adored (see chapter 17).

In the late 20th/early part of the 21st century, I was ready to pack in the church. Were it not for being deeply moved by Shirley's thoughts and words, I am quite certain I would have left. The impact of her hymns was so great that I decided to hang in there.

Shirley and John commiserated with me and Christina a fair bit about our relationship to the church. I share a similar love/hate relationship with the institution and that fuelled many conversations for all of us. I revelled in our friendship which became close over the years – I didn't think about the how and why.

Shirley weighted the love side of the church for me in this love/hate dichotomy. She did that by using language that was not archaic. For me, her concentration on issues of peace and justice were as important, if not more so, than anything else she addressed. She could turn a well-known phrase on its head. Hymn writer Fred Kaan, with whom I also collaborated for many years, had that gift as well. I love that kind of creative intellectual playfulness.

Shirley's writing is beautifully layered and she always attempted to use the language of the day. Who else so deftly inserted the word 'cursor' or the phrase 'God of the galaxies' into a hymn?

Shirley was uncompromising when it came to people making changes to her work without her permission. I admired that. I once asked her if I could make some text alterations to one of her hymns – 'Where God Enlightens', otherwise known as 'Roll the Stone Away'.

She ultimately gave me permission to do so, but such acquiescence was rare. Though our relationship was close – and perhaps because of how profoundly trusting it was – there were occasionally things she would not agree to in my musical settings. She felt I had not caught her intent in three of my hymn tunes. Those occurrences were few and far between but, of course, she was right in each case.

I recall one text I had interpreted incorrectly as being gentle with a longing depth. She called me out on this. She wanted something 'tougher'. "You didn't quite catch that," she said. "Perhaps something less pretty!"

She liked my setting and my suggested change for 'Go Gently, Go Lightly'. I wanted to change the last line from "in all that you do", to "in all that we do". She enthusiastically agreed, but the song was already out there in other publications. I made the change an option in my setting.

In the mid-1990s, she sent me a letter saying how grateful she was that my tunes were enabling her hymns to reach new places. This had to do with style as much as geography. New tunes by me and numerous others began to expand the reach of her hymns through new idioms. Her metre was superbly crafted, which made them easily accessible with well-known, existing – and more traditional – hymn tunes. My settings – and I have composed tunes for more than 120 of her hymns – tend to be more lyrical.

People in New Zealand probably perceive Shirley quite differently from the way we see her in North America. Mainline churches in Canada would consider Shirley among their prime sources of hymn texts, even if it means singing them to older tunes. When I visit churches across Canada, and mention Shirley's name, there is always a 'thumbs up' and murmur of appreciation.

New directions through Musiklus

My music ministry and my company Musiklus, established in 1996 as a digital resource, have enabled me to be part of some wonderful families of faith. People I work with on Vancouver Island, where Christina and I live, and on the nearby British Columbia mainland celebrate the relationship I had with Shirley.

In 2005, Musiklus designed and produced a major event in Victoria titled *Song Circling All the Earth*. It was a musical journey through the entire church year. All my hymn-writing partners attended, except for Shirley, who was no longer travelling because of her health. The event featured a 240-voice choir and 25 musicians. Shirley may not have been there, but her input, in terms of the number of her titles included, was substantial. Her hymn 'Where God Enlightens' ('Roll the Stone Away') led to a spontaneous, standing ovation – the only hymn to receive such a response. It is a resurrection hymn with links to women's emancipation. People in Canada love it – it's become an Easter standard here.

Other Shirley texts which were sung included 'Where Is the Room?', 'Peace Child', 'I Am Your Mother' and our epilogue song, 'We Are the Singers Who Celebrate Jesus'.

The event was so popular within the United Church of Canada, it was held on three more occasions – twice on British Columbia's west coast in Nanaimo and Parksville and, later the same year, on Canada's east coast in Halifax, Nova Scotia.

Shirley and I had frequent conversations concerning the theology of so-called 'mainline churches'. I think the divisive conflict over literal biblical interpretations, at least within the United Church of Canada, is in our rear-view mirror. Theological scholarship, in my opinion, has moved beyond literal translations and descriptions. There are other denominations in Canada, of course, where more traditional understandings are maintained.

Even before the arrival of the Covid-19 pandemic, the United Church of Canada was keenly aware it was in decline. There was a sense of depression about that, feelings of dread, loss and grief. But although our numbers continue to decline, there is considerable forward thinking, with the church currently developing a digital music resource. While it will include most of the repertoire in our existing hymn books, it will also be dynamic – continually growing as new works are created.

One of Shirley's frustrations was that she did not have many opportunities or outlets to hear her words sung. This was exacerbated, of course, by her decision to do no more long-distance travelling.

During our visit to New Zealand in 2014 (see chapter 17), Shirley and I sat next to each other at the piano in her house singing and playing our collaborative work.

At one point, John looked across the room and said, "You two need to keep on writing hymns." Shirley threw up her hands in frustration and replied, "But John, who will there be to sing them?" She would ask this over and over again. The room would then go rather silent.

Ron continued to express his struggles with the church and its demands in ongoing email correspondence with Shirley. On Christmas Eve 2015, he shared with the Murrays his and Christina's feelings about Christmas, admitting it was a time they both struggled to plod on through. The concepts around Advent and Epiphany were preferable to the often sappiness associated with Christmas. In the same email, he talked about the bond he and Christina felt for their New Zealand friends – their closest friends, in fact. He wrote:

"At this time of gift-sharing, I really want to somehow impress upon the two of you just how special you are to us. You entered our lives through your words, Shirley, but we were unprepared for how quickly we experienced a profound attachment to you both, as a result of our visit to your turf. The generosity of your hosting us within your busy lives was superseded only by the wit, wisdom, and sense of being kindred spirits which enriched us. There are so many ways you enter or help to form the conversations Christina and I have with each other, as well as those with whom we share our ministries. I don't know exactly how to say 'thank you for you', but do hope you understand."

Note

1 Verse 2, 'Where God Enlightens' ('Roll the Stone Away'), written in 1989 to continue the Easter theme of the Ecumenical Decade of Churches in Solidarity with Women. When first published in *Every Day in Your Spirit*, the traditional spiritual hymn tune for 'Go Down Moses' was suggested as an accompaniment. However, this caused some offence among African Americans. Ron Klusmeier wrote a new tune, as did Joy Patterson.

22 – Affirming our faith

When all else is gone, through dark and pain,
love will still burn,
love will be born,

when our faith is gone, when hope is vain,
love moves the stone,
love, love alone.[1]

American hymn writers and music directors Jim and Jean Strathdee first connected with Shirley in 1998. Their musical collaborations flourished over the following decades, with the couple, now Musicians in Residence at St Mark's United Methodist Church in Sacramento, finally meeting Shirley and John in New Zealand in 2009. The following is taken from the author's interview with them in August 2021.

When we sing Shirley's words, we are grounded in our deepest faith. With elegant simplicity and intricate beauty, her phrases affirm our journeys, dance in our hearts, and ever call us to help create God's dream for this world.

We so appreciate her words that call us to care deeply for those in need – to show up for justice, compassion and peacemaking. We are grateful to have 'Shirley songs' in our backpack when we've had the privilege to share our music in local, regional and international gatherings of folks dedicated to these issues.

Jean: It was our collection, *Pieces of Our Lives*, produced in 1998, that brought us together. We had received permission from Hope Publishing to include three of Shirley's texts that we had set to music. We then mailed her the book and the CD. She was really pleased with our settings for 'This Thread I Weave', 'God Weeps' and 'Every Day'. Our communication went back and forth over the next decade, leading to the invitation in 2009 to present a plenary session at the New Zealand Hymnbook Trust conference in Palmerston North in October that year. This was to be our only face-to-face meeting.

Jim: Shirley and John hosted us at their home for a short while. It was a delightful time. Jeanie describes Shirley as an elf, or an imp within an elf! Our connection with Shirley stayed really strong from that point on. We would email back and forth about the music we were setting to her words. She would suggest subtle changes, a word she wanted emphasised, or a mood she wanted to capture. Occasionally, she would suggest a text or write words for us if we needed a song for a specific event.

Years ago, we were musicians for a conference on Children, Human Trafficking and the Gospel. We did not have a song on this topic, so I wrote to Shirley, basically saying "Help!" Then I stayed up late that night trying to create something that would work. In the middle of the night, I was about to turn in when 'Who Would Steal a Life?' appeared in an email from Shirley. I stayed up the rest of the night and wrote a tune for it. I left the text on the breakfast table and went to bed. Jeanie got up, saw the text and also wrote a tune. This created a minor crisis in our marriage. What were we going to do with two tunes to this powerful text? As it turns out, one tune is more a solo, the other more a congregational song. We now use both tunes, depending on the context. And our half century-long marriage was saved!

> *Who would hurt a child, lead innocents astray?*
> *Who would do this thing and bear the light of day?*
> *God, help us wipe away this evil trade,*
> *make it now your people's passionate crusade!*[2]

We think Shirley felt very keenly, very strongly about that issue.

In 1998, during the US-Iraq war, a tragic blunder in our minds, Shirley sent us a new carol, 'Summer Sun or Winter Skies'. This came shortly after Operation Desert Fox, a joint bombardment of Iraq by the US and the UK. Many civilians were killed. Being on Shirley's list of friends and composers, we received Shirley's Christmas poem each year, all of which carried a message of peace. Two lines blew me away: 'Hawks are in control of a nation's soul' from verse two and 'evil has no tooth that can kill the truth' from verse five. For those of us in the US, sometimes our neighbours from other lands can see us better than we can see ourselves. [The hymn was later published, without music, in Hope's *Touch the Earth Lightly*. "I was trying to write myself into believing that goodness will outclass the gun," Shirley noted.]

Jean: It's almost impossible for me to talk about Shirley without crying. And impossible to overestimate the effect she had on our lives – the way she could say things in such a deep way with such great skill.

Jim: Shirley's work is lyrical; it sings. She was very musical herself. For all the intricacy and complexity in the text, it still flows and somehow remains light, despite its often heavier meaning.

In my mind, Shirley's life and work had to be daily led by the Holy Spirit to produce such a sublime gift for so many of us. John, I'm sure, was a major sounding board and dance partner in the creative process.

Jean: She always had a twinkle in her eye except when she was being stern about something. She had strong feelings about almost all the social issues that we care about. Our mutual passion and compassion for others really brought us together. She also had other strongly held views, and one of them had to do with changing her words, especially without seeking permission!

We found ourselves in the middle of such a transgression. We had learned one of her songs at the Community of Hope in Oklahoma, a church with a strong ministry among people with HIV Aids. They introduced us to 'For Everyone Born, A Place at the Table'. They had scribbled out the words on bits of paper for us, but they were a little different than those published by Hope. They had created an additional verse, which included the phrase, 'For gay and for straight, a place at the table'.

In 2009, we showed Shirley what they had sung and she wasn't pleased at all, as no one had asked her permission to make this change. We didn't use it either there or ever again because Shirley had not approved it. But we did have a long discussion with John and Shirley about the importance of those words.

Four years later, Hope Publishing came out with her new collection, *A Place at the Table* (2013). This included an optional verse for the hymn 'For Everyone Born', beginning 'For gay and for straight, a place at the table'. She was clear that if you want to include extra words, write your own songs. Don't mess with mine.

Jim: Things are evolving around gender identity. For years we were involved in inclusive language issues (male/female, gay/straight) but now with so many folks who are transgendered or somewhere along the spectrum, this binary of either male or female just doesn't work. So if I had another chance to talk with Shirley, perhaps we would agree on the words 'For whomever you love, a place at the table'. Unfortunately, I don't know how to get in touch with her about that one!

[For further discussion on this hymn, see chapter 29.]

Working with Shirley on a composition

We worked in a variety of ways. The largest category would be around the Christmas carols she sent out each year. Generally, we worked collaboratively. I would send her a tune to whatever words she had sent. There might be a certain word that she would like to emphasise more strongly in terms of where the tune was going. We always honoured Shirley's request.

Then there were occasions where the text was fairly painful or dramatic and I set it in a minor key. I might decide to end it with a major chord. We would then go back and forth, discussing whether she wanted this particular text to end so sweetly. When we "got it right", she would send me a big "Ahhhh!"

It was a tremendous honour for me to have Shirley send us a text to set because I knew dozens of other composers were working on her texts too.

In the last few years of her life, she sent us several texts. We're old '60s folk singers as well as classically-trained musicians and choir directors. A lot of our tunes come from a folk tradition and a lot have a Celtic feel to them. To hear her say, "I need you to set this. I hear your work in this", was a tremendous honour.

Jean: One of the last she sent, in May 2019, was 'Where the Green Will Rise Again'. It had been around for a few years and she said, "It doesn't have a home, you need to give it one." She would send us stuff from her "bone pile", as she called it – these were often texts that needed redoing. The hymn tune we used for 'Where the Green Will Rise Again' is our arrangement of 'Wild Mountain Thyme', a Scottish/Irish folksong. I would send her an MP3 audio file but she really wanted the printed music in front of her so she could check it.

Probably the last email exchange was in November 2019, just a few months before she died. I wanted to make sure she had received our package. We had just finished our collection *A Love Story*. This has 'For Everyone Born' as the second song and includes 'Where the Green Will Rise Again'.

Jim: Shirley's hymns addressing the environment are so essential to our music ministry. 'Touch the Earth Lightly', set by Colin Gibson, is one of our favourites [see chapter 29]. We included it as a central part in a multimedia event called *Mass for the Healing of the Earth*, created in 1995. Using the traditional parts of the mass as a guide, this work includes 'earth wisdom' from many religious and cultural traditions, along with choral pieces, congregational songs, dancers, drummers, projected images, all woven together by a narrator and the song of the didgeridoo. Over the years, we took this event to more than 20 cities throughout the US and Canada as a fundraiser for local projects.

We gathered local singers, dancers, drummers and photographers for local content. All the words and music of this work are ours, except for 'Touch the Earth Lightly', which seemed to be a strong 'touching point' for all our audiences.

Jean: About the time John died, she sent us 'When All Else Is Gone'. In 2018, we did a tour in Western Canada, right at the time of a deadly bus crash that killed 16 of the junior ice hockey team in the province of Saskatchewan. So many communities were affected by the deaths of these young men. We used this song in some of the churches where the funeral services were going to be held that week. This song got us through.

As church musicians, it's our job to find the right song for the right moment and without the arsenal of Shirley Murray, we would be working a lot harder.

I put music to and created a video for 'God of Our Foremothers', which Shirley wrote for a Methodist women's conference in 1998. The video includes a women's march, filmed the day after Trump's inauguration in 2017. When I sing this song, I think of my mom, and the time when she was six years old, running into the kitchen and seeing her mother and grandmother holding onto each other and crying. She started crying too. "No honey, it's alright," they said. "We just got the right to vote!" That was 1918. Shirley's words really speak to me, particularly as we struggle today to affirm women around the world.[3]

Jim: I loved her helping us understand the cultural differences between the US and New Zealand. She and John had a real sensitivity for the Māori, New Zealand's indigenous population.

We have held a lot of music workshops in Canada where the United Church was clearly way ahead of the government in recognising the incredible harm that the residential schools have done to Canada's First Nations people. We had some really deep discussions with John and Shirley about that.

I have been worried that many of our churches are becoming increasingly irrelevant to the needs of today's world. But I am hopeful as I see some of the more traditional churches becoming more socially conscious and able to speak with some authority around a lot of issues we're struggling with.

Shirley's work continues to be so relevant for the issues we face and I believe will remain so for many years to come, but in what form and who will say or sing her hymns, I don't know. Shirley really followed her own truth. When she thought it was time to do something, she did it.

Notes

1   Last two verses of 'When All Else Is Gone', written in 2008 and published without music in Hope's *Touch the Earth Lightly*. Based on 1 Corinthians 13:13, it echoes the Māori waiata 'E Toru Ngā Mea', referring to faith, hope and love.

2   Verse 2, 'Who Would Steal a Life? A Hymn About Human Trafficking', published in *Life into Life*, with music by Lim Swee Hong and Jim Strathdee.

3   For a list of sing-along videos made by Jim and Jean Strathdee of Shirley's songs, including their online links, see appendix 3.

23 – Meeting of minds

Children, protect me – I need your trust:
my breath is your breath,
my death is your death,
ashes to ashes, dust into dust.[1]

Mutual admiration characterised the relationship between Swedish hymn writer and Lutheran pastor the Rev Per Harling and Shirley Murray. The following is from email correspondence with the author in July 2022.

Shirley is one of the most powerful and influential hymn writers of our time. This is due to her use of new, dynamic metaphors, her deep theological insights and her beautiful, genuine poetry. She has given new, important dimensions to what faith should be about in the world as well as in the church.

The first time I met Shirley was in 1991 in Canberra at the World Council of Churches' (WCC) Assembly. I was a member of the international worship committee that had prepared all the assembly worship sessions held in the big tent.

Some evenings we invited people to come together for sing-along happenings, where anyone could share new songs. One evening Shirley turned up and we were introduced to some of her songs. I remember how impressed I was by her poetic and theologically well-thought-out lyrics. I went up to her afterwards to ask her more about her writing methods. We talked for a long time. It was a deep and meaningful meeting of minds. We met several more times during the assembly, where she gave me copies of some other songs she had written.

After the assembly we started faxing each other. When I was a child and dug into my sandbox, I remember my mother telling me that if I dug deep enough, I would probably end up in China. How wrong she was! It took many years before I realised that my sandbox digging would finally take me to New Zealand!

Sweden and New Zealand are as far away from each other as you can get on this earth, but through our faxes and emails we made a digital bridge between our countries. Shirley sent me some texts asking if I could compose new melodies to them, which I happily did.

During the years since our first meeting, I have made around 15 compositions to her poems. We collaborated, for instance, in making theme songs for a couple of later WCC assemblies, as well as for other global ecumenical meetings. Her hymn 'God, In Your Grace', which I set, was the theme song for the WCC Assembly in Brazil in 2006. And for the WCC Assembly in Busan, South Korea, in 2013, she offered 'Peace Must Be Dared – It Is the Great Venture'. This hymn is based on Dietrich Bonhoeffer's words from an address he gave in 1934 on the Danish island of Fano about how to achieve peace.

In 2002, I published a new collection of my work in Sweden, called *I Varje Pulsslag Andas Himlen*. This contained 48 new songs and a translation of Shirley's 'For Everyone Born, A Place at the Table' ('För Vart Barn Som Föds'), a hymn I greatly admire.

I used some of the lines of her hymns in a special birthday greeting I sent to her for her 70th birthday in 2001 (see chapter 16).

As I grew older, my longing to go to New Zealand and meet Shirley face to face again before we both grew too old increased. Then in the autumn of 2015, my dream finally came true. I will always remember the day when my travelling companion and I visited Shirley and John in their beautiful house by the sea. It was an affectionate meeting, where I realised that my impression of her personality through our many email conversations matched so well with the 'live' Shirley. She was humble, encouraging, strong in her convictions but all mixed with a slight shyness.

We only spent one day with her, as John was not well. We then travelled south and enjoyed a few days staying with Colin Gibson and his wife Jeanette in Dunedin – a most generous invitation.

Naming a 'standout' hymn among her hundreds of texts is difficult since whatever she wrote impressed me. Many of her themes were close to my own heart and my own hymn writing, i.e. peace, social justice, ecology and human rights.

Like Shirley, I have written many hymns about the environment and climate issues. I remember the first time I read her 'Earth Prayer, I Am Your Mother', which she wrote about 1996. I wrote a melody for it, which is now in the hymnal of the Swedish Lutheran Church. The 'I' in 'Earth Prayer' refers to the earth, of course; it is not an individual's prayer. The voice of the earth is very seldom heard. Nearly half the hymns in our hymnals are based on the subject of 'I', usually in the form of an individual prayer or related to one or more of Jesus' 'I am' words.

At our meeting in 2015, I asked her about this hymn. She said:

> Most of the hymns I have written have had something to do with what I call 'green hymns', an important perspective for us living in New Zealand, where we are totally dependent on nature for both our economy and our spirituality. We are also influenced by Māori creation stories. Often our church hymns are about the creation's beauty; very few about creation's lament.

> Over a period, I wrote many 'green' hymns but few were actually picked up and sung. Thus, I decided to write a text from the I-perspective of Mother Earth as an attempt to wake people up to the alarming climate issue. Many have associated the 'I am'

words of Mother Earth with Jesus' 'I am' words. The connection with the Old Testament name of God, Yahweh (I am), and the 'I am' perspective of the creation is deliberate. The Creator and the creation are the only ones that constantly ARE.

Sometimes we discussed her texts. On occasions, I even suggested some alterations to her words, which she gladly accepted. She also helped me a couple of times when I struggled with English translations of some of my own songs.

Maybe, more than any other hymn writer, Shirley has influenced my own writing of hymns (around 1000 by now) and I thank God constantly for her honest, poetical and theological impact on the worldwide church song.

Note

1   Verse 1, 'I Am Your Mother', written in 1996 and included among Green Hymns in Shirley's last book *Life into Life*. Music, EARTH PRAYER, by Per Harling.

24 – A prophetic voice

As the wind song through the trees,
as the stirring of the breeze,
so it is with the Spirit of God,
as the heart made strangely warm,
as the voice within the storm,
so it is with the Spirit of God.[1]

Singapore-born Lim Swee Hong is a prolific Asian hymn writer and educator, currently the Deer Park Associate Professor of Sacred Music and Director of the Master of Sacred Music Program at Emmanuel College of Victoria University in the University of Toronto, Canada. He believes Shirley offers a unique voice from the Asia Pacific region, one he was proud to support through his compositions. The following is from email correspondence with the author in January, 2023.

I vaguely remember first catching sight of Shirley, her husband John and Colin Gibson back in 1987 at an ecumenical worship conference in Manila where I was studying at the Asian Institute of Liturgy and Music. Dr I-to Loh was professor of church music and ethnomusicology at that time.

Ten years later, in 1997, I met Shirley at the Tainan Theological College and Seminary in Taiwan at an ecumenical liturgy and music seminar, sponsored by the World Council of Churches (WCC). The seminar was attended by around 50 representatives of Asian churches from 26 countries, with Shirley one of the speakers. This second meeting was where I had time to get to know Shirley personally as we wandered around Tainan shops looking for a power adaptor for her husband's laptop. None of the shops that sell such accessories was open that day as it was the Lunar New Year holidays.

I was 32 years younger than Shirley. She felt like my relative, almost like my grandmother. Through the times that I have known her, she was always curious about what I was up to and where I was travelling to for workshops, to give talks or lead worship at conferences. She would talk candidly to me about church matters, ecumenical concerns and her interest in eco-theology. I found her personable and approachable. I never got to meet her again, though our email conversations continued and I often encouraged her to come to Asia.

The first text from Shirley that I set was 'Come and Find the Quiet Centre' from her book *In Every Corner Sing*, published by Hope Publishing Company in 1992. The traditional American melody it had been set to is lovely, but, in my opinion, lacks a sense of mystery. So, I crafted a new tune, suggesting an accompaniment using finger cymbals or a triangle, to be sung plaintively, and sent it to her. She liked it and said that I should offer it to Hope Publishing, who published it in 2005.[2] That was how we started working together.

Later I would send her tunes without words and ask her if she might consider writing a text for them. That was how 'As the Wind Song Through the Trees' came about – the first piece of music I sent to her without words or even a suggested theme. This hymn would be my favourite for a couple of reasons.

It was around Pentecost when I sent her the tune. She said it gave her a feeling of the Spirit, both gentle and powerful. More importantly for me, she worked in the line, 'as the heart made strangely warm' in the first stanza. This was a reference to my own Methodist roots. "I thought you would appreciate a reference to the Wesley brothers' experience of the Holy Spirit," she emailed me. I was immensely pleased with the thoughtful friendship we shared.

When I submitted it to Hope Publishing, I invited her to name the tune. She suggested the Māori term for the Holy Spirit, Wairua Tapu. It's the first hymn in her 2008 collection *Touch the Earth Lightly*.[3]

Another hymn where I wrote the tune first and asked Shirley to craft a text was 'God in Whose Memory No One is Lost', the 'Forget-Me-Not-Hymn'. On this occasion, I suggested we needed to do a song about memory loss, a growing issue in society. So within a week she came back with the hymn text. After typesetting it, I asked her whether I should name the tune, DEMENTIA. She wrote back very gently asking me whether I would consider changing the name as she found my suggestion rather daunting, a bit like the word cancer. She suggested naming it after the forget-me-not flower, which is the symbol of the Alzheimer's Society in New Zealand. It is published in her last collection, *Life into Life*.[4]

I have lost count of how many of her texts I have set. I always found them singable, succinct and insightful. Being married to a minister made her aware, I think, of what her texts could and could not do within a church context. Her hymns embraced themes relevant to our times, including social justice, ecology and peace. These were all concerns we shared.

Green theology

Eco-theology was one of her major concerns. 'The Garden of the World', her 'Lament for the Earth', was written in 2015 and published in *Life into Life* among a collection of nine 'green' hymns. As with so many of our collaborations, there was much email correspondence between us as I worked on the tune.

The garden of the world, the paradise we share,
the greening of all life is dying in our care,
> *the covenants we made are rendered null and void,*
> *the garden that is God's, dishonoured and destroyed.*[5]

In June 2015, she wrote:

> Since even the Pope now talks about global warming, maybe it has become respectable! But I fear that if we don't sing about it in churches, eco-theology will be sidelined in favour of the 'Jesus and Me' type of thing.

> I have suggested to Scott Shorney that Hope publish a collection of 'green' hymns and he has agreed to think about it. Let's see what happens. If you meet him, you might nudge him into remembering! So, rather dire as this text is, it's just one more to emphasise the importance of the issue. I think it could work well if used imaginatively so as to diffuse the dark ideas of catastrophe and disaster.

I named the tune CARTARET ISLANDS – they're in the Pacific, near Bougainville. Comprising seven small islands on a coral atoll, they have been identified as the first place in the world where the population will have to relocate due to climate change and sea level rises. Some families have already relocated but find it difficult adjusting to life away from their home. This song was the focal piece of morning prayer at the 2022 WCC Assembly at Karlsruhe, Germany.[6]

I do remember asking her to set texts on a variety of subjects, including the 2012 mass shooting at Sandy Hook Elementary School in Newtown, Connecticut, the downing of Malaysian Airlines MH17 over eastern Ukraine in 2014, the rising sea water concerns for Pacific Islands and the violence in Myanmar. She was gracious in acceding to my requests.

There were other occasions where she sent me a text and encouraged me to try to give it a tune. One of her hymns on peace-making arose out of her deep concerns for the plight of refugees from Syria, particularly children. 'Dona Nobis Pacem', published in *Life into Life*, has two different texts – one focused on world peace; the other on inner peace.

Shirley's is a unique voice from the Asia Pacific region when most hymn writers are based in Europe and North America – this, I believe, is her greatest legacy. Together, we strongly represented the concerns of our region, in particular severe climate change, poverty and geopolitical violence. Through her hymns she brought the prophetic voice of God to address the concerns of the world.

Other hymn writers have tended to focus on, and look towards the ethereal dimension of faith. Shirley advocated for God's ethos in the present world where 'now' matters. If we say we are God's people, the question must be how we are showing hospitality to and are inclusive of others. She would pointedly ask in her writings, "Who gets a say at the table about this concern?" This is Shirley's typical approach in her hymn texts.

As I continue to create new tunes, I find myself sorely missing Shirley's prophetic voice for new texts. I find her words 'sing on their own'. I basically become the 'midwife' helping deliver them to the world. Thus far, I have not been able to find another person to collaborate with as seamlessly as I did with Shirley.

Notes

1   Verse 1, 'As the Wind Song Through the Trees', 2004, written in response to a tune sent to her by Lim Swee Hong. "Its lyricism gave a feeling of the movement of the Spirit, both gentle and powerful" – Shirley's note on the tune in Hope's *Touch the Earth Lightly*.

2   'Come and Find the Quiet Centre', first published in *Faith Forever Singing* in 2000 (see note 1, Chapter 14). For a copy of the arrangement by Lim Swee Hong, see: https://www.hopepublishing.com/Images/HymnodyPDF/HM8846.15.pdf

3   For a recording of 'As the Wind Song through the Trees', go to https://youtu.be/exTRKORg0R8 The score can be found at https://www.hopepublishing.com/Images/HymnodyPDF/HM8846.06.pdf

4   A video recording of 'God in Whose Memory No One is Lost' is available at https://www.facebook.com/sweehong.lim.14/videos/1549468881881506

5   Verse 1, 'The Garden of the World: Lament for the Earth', published 2019 in Hope's *Life into Life*.

6   A YouTube version of 'Lament for the Earth' can be found at https://www.youtube.com/watch?v=8Y_WoC89Pq8 (from 33:20-36:05).

25 – Something beautiful for God

In the singing, in the silence,
in the hands expectant, open,
in the blessing, in the breaking,
in the Presence at this table –

Refrain:

Jesus Christ, Jesus Christ,
be the wine of grace:
Jesus Christ, Jesus Christ,
be the bread of peace.[1]

Prolific hymn writer and editor Carlton ('Sam') Young, known as Mr Music of United Methodism in the United States, had a collaborative relationship with Shirley for more than 20 years. In his memoir *I'll Sing On*, he described her as the most musical hymn writer he had ever worked with.[2]

Shirley and John were our dear friends for many years. Our personal/professional relationship with them began in 1994 with my composing her exquisite carol 'Star-Child Earth-Child'. This reached me via her Christmas card that year and it drew an immediate response. Shirley described my tune as "simple and lilting". It was published in the New Zealand Hymnbook Trust's *Carol Our Christmas* in 1996, and, that same year, in Hope Publishing's *Every Day in Your Spirit* [see chapter 29].

I first met Shirley at the 1992 conference of the Hymn Society in the United States and Canada, held in Washington [see chapter 11]. I shall always be grateful to George H. Shorney from Hope Publishing Company for bringing us together. Marj and I then invited Shirley and John to stay with us at the Scarritt Bennett Center, in Nashville, Tennessee. While showing them around Nashville, they asked to visit a homeless encampment. I took them to one situated underneath a highway interchange. Shirley and John talked to several in the camp and left a contribution.

In 1996, Marj and I visited the Murrays in New Zealand. Our long conversations regarding the church and its worship-song over and after meals were punctuated by a locally-produced plum brandy and dry sherry. At one point, I interrupted our conversation and played 'Star-Child' on Shirley's ancient, temperament-lacking, upright piano. She explained that she used the piano to check composers' scores for ease of playing. While viewing the printed score, the melody and (depending on the complexity of the harmony) most of the sounds entered her tonal memory. Shirley often suggested changes in my draft settings of her hymns.

Shirley's texts run the gamut of meter, metrical patterns, subjects and topics. She had the gift of compressing and lyricizing, biblical, theological, contemporary expressions, and traditional metaphors. Her texts always scan and sound like spontaneous outpourings, yet they are so well formed and crafted. With few exceptions she wrote true rhymes, but when forced would cleverly use a false rhyme or eye rhyme, rarely no rhyme.

Stanza by stanza there are few modulations from one foot to another, or false accents. Shirley was the most musical hymn writer with whom I've collaborated, short of Fred Pratt Green, and I greatly admire her musical-poetic gifts, which make composing for her words such a joy. In our decades-long association, she abided with good humor my blue notes, musical puns and parodies, turnaround endings and endings in other than tonic, jazz chords and rhythms, and mostly unison vocal lines.

Shirley wrote meditations and more than 20 Christmas carols, often with Southern Hemisphere landscapes or references. Over four decades she composed hymns on human rights, child abuse, women's concerns, justice, peace, the integrity of creation, the unity of the church, celebrating the cultural gifts of the Māori people, and in later years, her abiding trust and personal relationship with the Spirit of Deity, the latter seen in this hymn on ageing, which she wrote in 1995 as a positive response to growing older. Published in *Faith Forever Singing* in New Zealand in 1995 and in Hope's *Every Day in Your Spirit* in 1996, its fine tune, REBEKAH, is by Rusty Edwards.

Let my spirit always sing,
though my heart be wintering,
though the season of despair
give no sign that you are there,
God to whom my days belong,
let there always be a song.

In 1996, having received that evening Shirley Murray's communion hymn, 'In the Singing', I composed a six-tone diatonic melody with a five-chord setting. It premièred the next morning to an appreciative class. I called my tune BREAD OF PEACE, named from a phrase in the refrain. Shirley described it, in her collection *Every Day in Your Spirit* as a "simple and beautiful congregational setting". I've tried to keep it uncomplicated, with the notion that in time, those coming to the distribution [of the communion elements] might sing it from memory.[3]

In 2004, Abingdon Press published *Sing for Peace: The Hymns of Shirley Erena Murray*, with 18 of her songs set to tunes composed by me and by another of Shirley's great musical collaborators, Jane Marshall. Among them are 'Star-Child', 'Touch the Earth Lightly' and 'This Thread I Weave'.

There was much email correspondence between the three of us as we worked on this book. In July 2004, Jane Marshall wrote to me:

> I never laid eyes on Shirley Murray. But we have filled the cyberspace between New Zealand and Texas with email letters. I dare to say we have become sisters in the process, partly because of my admiration for Shirley's work and our common interests but especially because of who Shirley is as a person.
>
> Her letters have the down-home flavor that shows up in her use of the almost Celtic flavor of her verse. 'This Thread I Weave' is but one example. It speaks of ordinary objects that in her hand become sacramental, objects similar to those used in Celtic devotional poetry.
>
> The emails Shirley writes are economical, like her verse. Not a word is there that doesn't need to be, though the subject is thoroughly covered. What more can one say about Judas than what appears in 'Lullaby for Judas', also included in *Sing for Peace*? And words of only one or two syllables abound, a blessing for any composing collaborator.
>
> The language is fresh: we are woefully 'one-eyed', she says in 'God, We Bless You For Our Freedoms' [published in *Sing for Peace*]. Who else but Shirley could write as vivid a punch line as 'the money bag, the silver swag, and then, the knotted rope' in the Judas hymn ['Lullaby for Judas']? or the phrase 'If you passed across my screen, I might switch you out of sight', in 'Stranger, Standing At My Door'?
>
> Our idiomatic expressions suggest the differences in our continental habits. 'Who gave a toss for the man on the cross?' shows up in the song 'While Soldiers Threw A Dice' ['The Gamble'], countering my Texas comment, "Lord willin' and the creek don't rise." "I would like to apply for use of that," Shirley comments in her return email. I'll not hold my breath for that.
>
> Too late, I caught in one hymn her way of using a phrase to tighten a poem. This happened – or didn't – in 'Touch the Earth Lightly' in which she urges us to 'use the earth gently', then closes in the last stanza by praying that Christ will use us.

How I wish I had not earlier deleted some of the emails that match in flavor exactly who Shirley is with her poetry: a grandmother enjoying and enduring a visit from grandchildren, a kinswoman physically who confessed one of her legs is "listing to starboard", a musician, whether she admits it or not, who sees right through the why of my settings and describes the techniques in musical terms.

Now one final quote from a recent email: "I have just been to a theological colloquium and am exhausted by the use of five-syllable words, as well as the lack of right brain activity. One good hymn every half hour would have made all the difference! I felt brave enough to ask one contributor how he spelled Christological because one of his listeners sitting near me thought he was dealing in crystals."[4]

Jane's son, Peter Marshall, explained further in an email to the author:

A measure of my mother's regard for Shirley's work can be seen in the frequent textual underlinings, highlightings, and marginal annotations found in her copy of *Every Day in Your Spirit*, a 1996 publication from Hope. She seems particularly keen to note the use of metaphor ('Differently abled, differently labeled, widen the circle round Jesus Christ: crutches and stigmas, culture's enigmas …') and active verbs ('whistle up, shepherds! saddle up, kings! chorus up, angels, flexing your wings'). She notes also the inclusion of texts that deal with age, death, AIDS, the disabled, etc. Craft and message were always important to my mother in her own writing, and she was appreciative of those things when she found it elsewhere.[5]

Carlton Young also explains in his book, *I'll Sing On*, the inspiration for his tune HIROSHIMA, composed for Shirley's powerful hymn 'God Weeps'. He continues (quoting from p253):

On our return [from our trip to Japan in 1995], we stopped in Tokyo, visited friends and former students in Lobe and Kyoto and had a sober and revealing stay in Hiroshima. There we went to the memorial site which commemorates a US B29 plane dropping the first atomic bomb that instantly killed in excess of 100,000 innocent civilians.

Later that day I sketched a tonal remembrance of that experience for voice, cello and piano. I believe I had brought along Shirley Murray's text 'God Weeps', which predates that visit. I completed the hymn setting 6-9 August 1995, the 50th anniversary of the bombing of Hiroshima and Nagasaki. [Carlton's setting was published in Hope's *Every Day in Your Spirit*. For more on 'God Weeps', see chapter 20.]

In 2015 I collaborated with Shirley in composing two Christmas hymns, 'Bring In the Christmas That Lights Up the Ages' (this lyrically presents the new-born child's extended nativity, set to my adaptation of the Catalonian melody, 'Presents al Niño Jesus') and 'Christmas, Come Close', that I perceive is her autobiographical prayer to celebrate Christmas more personally. This begins:

Christmas come close
in a child's crumpled face,
to the ragged and raw
in a harsh birthing place,

in a surging of joy,
in a bundle held tight,
in a breath, in a cry
through the dark of the night.

Both hymns appear in our final collaboration, *Songs between Friends*, published by GIA Publications in 2016. The 17 songs in the collection resulted from "more than two decades of lyrical-musical collaboration" and "three years of sharing, via emails and occasional phone calls, words, ideas, opinions, theology, dissent; and questions about prosody, tempo, tessitura, and time signatures", as our introduction to the book states.

This book was published close on the heels of my 90th birthday with Shirley's lighter side seen in the tribute she composed for that birthday, as she did for many others. In April 2017, she wrote:

Dear friend Sam – your day has dawned as a beautiful autumn morning here and I will assume, without news to the contrary, that there will be some celebration at the 'Owl's Nest'. Just survival is sometimes a miracle! I do hope all is well with you. Life has been a little shaky for me but is levelling out to a new 'normal'. I'd like to be the first fan this year to say, 'Glad you were born, Sam!'

Much love, and greetings to Marj and Robert

Attached to the email was "an irreverent but heartfelt ditty", the first two verses of which read:

Dear Sam, ageless nonagenarian
by anyone's vote or criterion:
we're turning the mike on
to make you our icon –
hang in there till you're centenarian!

You've hymnals galore to your credit –
God knows how much stuff you did edit;
with vast expertise
you cut through the sleaze
no matter what tunes and who said it.

It is my belief that all who knew Shirley close up or encountered her through her poetic gifts would agree that her wish as expressed in her hymn, 'Something Beautiful For God', was fulfilled. This was made manifest in the way she chose to live, in how she saw the world and in what she believed and stood for.

Notes

1 'In the Singing' ('Invocation') was written in 1994 at the request of Professor Peter Godfrey, director of the Kāpiti Chamber Choir. Carlton Young's tune, BREAD OF PEACE, is set in the key of D flat major.

2 The author thanks GIA Publications for permission to quote from a tribute to Shirley in *I'll Sing on: My First 96 Years* by Carlton R. 'Sam' Young, (Shirley Erena Murray, pp298-302), published in 2022. Carlton Young died on 21 May 2023.

3 Gibson, 2021, p130.

4 Email from Jane Marshall to Carlton Young, Dallas, 9 July 2004.

5 Email from Peter Marshall, Jane's son, to the author, 11 August 2022.

26 – In tune with Asia

Son of poverty,
shame us till we see,
self-concerned, how we deny you,
by our greed we crucify you
on a Christmas tree,
Son of poverty.[1]

It was I-to Loh's encounter with Shirley's 'Hunger Carol' in 1988 that first inspired him to set her work to music. Now retired Chair and Professor of Church Music and Worship at Tainan Theological College and Seminary in Taiwan, I-to Loh believes Shirley had a unique understanding of Asian theological imperatives. This chapter is from email correspondence with the author in November 2022.

Shirley's untraditional views or interpretations of Christian faith were what initially attracted me to her work. I tried to set to music the theology of her ideas and to contextualise its meaning within the context of Asia.

Shirley has been considered the best writer of hymns in English today. To me, her hymns are tender, neat, imaginative, unconventional, provocative, surprising, and deeply moving. They have inspired me to compose interesting tunes in Indonesian, Indian, Japanese, Taiwanese and Chinese styles.

Many forces have challenged me to compose something different from Western and past traditions. There's the reality of the world during the last four decades, especially in Taiwan amid threats from China, and other internal political turmoil; our church's struggle with proclaiming the Gospel; and our long-time pursuit of contextualisation of theology, music and worship.

I began teaching at the Asian Institute for Liturgy and Music in Manila in 1982, and one of my missions was to collect and promote Asian hymns from different countries. While compiling a new Asian Hymnal for the Christian Conference of Asia (CCA) from 1986, somehow I discovered Shirley's 'Hunger Carol: Child of Joy and Peace'. The text shocked me in its confronting of humanity's inhumanities. I was struck by her warning that if we fail to share and feed the world's hungry children, then our celebrations of Christmas are like crucifying the newborn child on a Christmas tree. I have always felt uneasy, even angry with the secularised, commercialised celebrations of Christmas that exclude Christ. But it was Shirley who pinpointed the ugly and shameful acts of most people during Christmas.

After a long period of thought and prayers, I chose to compose a tune in an Indonesian gamelan pelog scale: 'mi fa sol si do'. The accompaniment is an imitation of simplified gamelan orchestration using different sizes of kettle gongs, imitating, anticipating or decorating the main melody. I named the tune SMOKEY MOUNTAIN after the huge garbage dump on the outskirts of Manila where around 5000 families once scavenged to make a living. This poignant tune was my attempt to create a different mood in a pseudo-Indonesian style and I regard it as one of my masterpieces.

Although Shirley had difficulty understanding my style, which did not use any familiar Western scales or harmony, she respected my interpretations of this and some other pieces. She herself described 'Hunger Carol' "as a protest at our consumer society, its excesses and heartlessness".

First meetings

I first met Shirley in Canberra during the World Council of Churches' Assembly in 1991. I was impressed by her cordial, warm, motherly personality. She spoke softly and tenderly. Since I had already composed a few of her hymns and had corresponded with her a few times, we became close friends immediately.

The second time we met was during the WCC Ecumenical Seminar on Liturgy and Music, which I hosted at Tainan Theological College and Seminary in 1997. She stayed at our house, and I was very embarrassed that someone broke in and stole some of her money, the only time we had ever had any theft in our house. She was very kind and did not blame anybody. We continued to communicate frequently through email though, sadly, most of these emails have been lost. I was grateful that she sent me her last collection of hymns, *Life into Life,* a few months before she passed away.

The earliest texts of Shirley's that I set to music include 'Hunger Carol', 'Child of Christmas Story', 'Loving Spirit', 'Song to the Spirit' and 'Christ Is Our Peace'. All of these are published in *Sound the Bamboo: CCA Hymnal 2000*.[2] Except for 'Hunger Carol' and 'Child of Christmas Story', the rest were specially written for a CCA General Assembly or the 1991 WCC Assembly in Canberra. *Sound the Bamboo* has 315 hymns from 22 Asian countries, with 44 languages. Shirley's contribution comprises 12 original lyrics and paraphrases or translations of 13 others. Explanations about these hymns can be found in my publication *Hymnal Companion to Sound the Bamboo: Asian Hymns in their Cultural and Liturgical Contexts*.[3]

In total, I have composed 22 tunes for Shirley's lyrics. Most of these were published in *Sound the Bamboo* and my recent hymn collection *In Christ There Are East and West,* vol. 2, 2021, and two collections of anthems, entitled *New Songs Proclaiming God's Marvelous Works*, vols. 1 and 2, 2021 and 2022.[4]

Other examples of my use of musical language and styles to enhance the theological implications of hymns by Shirley include 'Loving Spirit' and 'This Is the Mind-set of One Who Has Come' ('Mind-set of Christ'). I was impressed and deeply moved by 'Loving Spirit' which draws analogies between one's relationship with the Holy Spirit and the intimate relationships of the family. My composition uses a 'gypsy scale' which combines a variety of small and large intervals, 3 4 #5 6 7 1 #2 3, a form that is related to the Indian raga, called mayamalava gowla raga. I used Indian double drones to support the melody but developed them into a more complex style to convey the implication of mystery. Although I thought the tune would probably be too exotic and difficult for most people, surprisingly it was chosen as one of the theme songs for the WCC Assembly in Canberra in 1991.

Shirley wrote 'Mind-set of Christ' for the Asian Mission Conference in 1994. I composed the tune, named CIPANAS, in an Indonesian style. The melody is in a pelog tuning, B = 3 five-tone scale (3 4 5 7 1) and should be accompanied by a zither-type plucked instrument.

'Touch the Earth Lightly' is my favourite. It uses an Indonesian gamelan scale 'mi fa sol si do'. For the initial phrase 'lightly' and 'gently', I used half-tone progressions (Eb-D). I treated important words like 'wonder' and 'surrender' melismatically (like a word painting), to help singers think about the important messages contained in those words. The accompaniment somehow imitates or echoes some of the musical ideas to make it more interesting.

The text of 'Stranger, Standing At My Door' is striking. The melody was composed according to the natural intonation of my Taiwanese language with certain variations as needed. Shirley wrote approvingly to me about this composition in 2002: "The simplicity of your melody line gives the words good exposure. I like the way you have dealt with the last line."

Shirley also understood my intentions with my composition for 'How Shall We Find You?' She wrote: "I was instantly attracted to the mood and again, a clear, simple song-line. I think you have done a clever thing in moving between keys, major and minor, as if one were searching for answers and then ending on a question. That's how I envisage the ideas in this one, and I am glad you chose it."

In 2014, I was approached by the Lutheran Institute of Liturgical Studies in the Valparaiso University, Indiana, to compose a theme song for the celebration of the 500th year of Reformation: Liturgy Serving the Life of the Church: How Worship Re-forms Us. I asked Shirley to write the lyrics, which she did after a few weeks. For the first time after nearly three decades of co-operation, I was not satisfied with her lyrics, so with hesitation and some courage, I asked her to rewrite them. She was very kind and rewrote verse one:

> *The Spirit comes to recreate*
> *and shape our world to God's design:*
> *new psalms to sing the timeless truths,*
> *new songs to make the Gospel shine,*

Shirley's hymn implies that God continues to shape and reshape the world. New things are happening, so we should be writing new psalms to interpret God's timeless truths. Composers, too, should be inspired to set new tunes to invite all to proclaim, as in this refrain:

> *So let our worship, praise and prayer*
> *be true to all we know and share!*

Shirley's prophetic voice helps us to see that many of us have been repeating, in our worship, praise and prayer, what we knew and shared for the last few decades or even centuries, as if God only lived and worked for some people in the past. Verse three says:

> *The Spirit sighs, for we are slow*
> *to see the change that God intends*
> *the grace to sing another's song*
> *and round one table, meet as friends:*

The tune was composed with a typical Indonesian gamelan tuning of a pelog scale: 'mi fa sol si do' (E F G B C). The accompaniment resembles a simplified gamelan style, where the main melody is doubled on every strong beat, with the other notes decorating around. It builds up to a climax at the end, calling all to 'Let our worship … be true to what we know and share'.

I also composed another version with a Taiwanese, Chinese and Indonesian five-tone scale: 'do re mi sol la', but the sixth tone si (B) appears in the refrain after the climax on the word 'know' in the second line (see refrain above, p259).

Shared concerns for social justice

I have not seen any poet in Asia who has covered such wide and serious issues for social justice, human rights, ecology and peace as Shirley has done. All these issues are also my concerns. I am grateful to Shirley for inspiring me to compose in Taiwanese and Pan-Asian musical styles, to feel God's presence in the midst of our sufferings and to see images of God's glory through Asian artistic expressions.

Although Shirley was a Caucasian, she was from the Pacific or Oceania, and had much contact with Asians and Māori people. She understood Asian culture and feelings, so most Asians could resonate with her feminine, motherly, introspective yet at times bold, courageous and provocative hymns. She was the first woman hymn writer from our region to have depicted vividly the loving God, the Holy Spirit as a mother, which resonates well with Indian and many Asian concepts of female deities.

Shirley was a woman of faith, not in a traditional or evangelical way, but as shown through faith in action, the principal message in most of her lyrics. All her hymns show God's love through the realisation of human dignity and social justice. Our praise and worship should be put into action to care for God's creation. She has her poetic imagination and the special touch and inspiration as a mother that one cannot find among male poets. All my best compositions were inspired by her challenging texts, which moved me deeply.

Although some of her hymns like 'Hunger Carol' proved too provocative for inclusion in American hymnals, her creative and beautiful hymns have appeared in more than 100 collections around the globe. Her contributions and impact on congregational songs continue to grow beyond our expectations.

Notes

1 Verse 4, 'Child of Joy and Peace' ('Hunger Carol'), written in 1987 as a protest at the consumerism of Christmas. It condemns the lavish spending and selfish greed associated with the commercialisation of Christmas. The carol has been set by many composers including Ian Render. Douglas Mews and I-to Loh.

2 Loh, I-to. (Ed.) (2000) *Sound the Bamboo: CCA Hymnal*. Tainan: Taiwan Church Press; (2006) Chicago: GIA Publications.

3 Loh, I-to. (2011) *Companion to Sound the Bamboo. Asian Hymns in their Cultural and Liturgical Contexts*. Chicago: GIA Publications.

4 These publications are all available from the Tainan Theological College and Seminary Library, email: publish@ttcs.org.tw

Part VI – Shirley's Legacy

27 – Mixed responses in New Zealand

In what strange land shall I sing Your song,
O God, my God?
to what new code must my heart belong,
O God, my God?
the boundaries shift as the lines delete,
and the way back home is a tired beat:
there are new directions to take my feet
to follow You.[1]

While Shirley's hymns are widely published and appreciated abroad, in her own country she is popular mainly within more progressive, liberal congregations – though there are some exceptions. Considering her own upbringing and early influences, the theological directions she would take as a hymn writer were clearly mapped out.

One of the most formative influences on Shirley's theology was undoubtedly her involvement in the Student Christian Movement (SCM) while at the University of Otago in Dunedin. This movement shaped her progressive social gospel, as it did her husband John's, and many contemporaries who remained lifelong friends.

As fellow student and Anglican priest Paul Oestreicher said in an interview with the author in May 2021, the SCM shaped members' faith in action and helped develop New Zealand's wider liberal social Christianity. The same forces were developing throughout the Anglo-Saxon world, he said, with one of the most influential publications being *Honest to God*, written by the Anglican Bishop of Woolwich, John Robinson, and published by the SCM Press in 1963. This challenged traditional images of God and promoted notions of a secular theology. Oestreicher describes the book as a return to Christianity's radical roots.

"The message in *Honest to God* is that it is not what you believe, but what you do that matters. Almost all of Shirley's hymns reflect that idea of faith in action. English hymn writers Sydney Carter and Dutch-born Fred Kaan were similarly exploring radical expressions of faith. Carter's 'Lord of the Dance', set to an English folk song, is still widely sung in liberal churches throughout the world."

Oestreicher, a peace activist and a founding member of Amnesty International in the United Kingdom in 1961, believes this liberal tradition, still evident in some inner-city churches like St Andrew's on The Terrace, St Peter's Anglican Church in Wellington and Knox Presbyterian Church in Christchurch, needs to be rediscovered.

> Overall, modern Protestantism has gone fundamentalist and that is depressing. But even within conservative Protestantism, the Holy Spirit can break through. Some pop-up churches in Britain are radical, as are many black or ethnic minority churches. Their congregations often meet in factory halls rather than in dedicated buildings and can be deeply socially committed.
>
> I see Shirley as remaining within an orthodox tradition, and so, for much of his life, did John. Towards the end of his life, John became more of a Quaker than a Presbyterian. Shirley kept many influences from her early Methodism and turned her love of the world into good rhymes. Shirley and John moved together to recognise that traditional doctrine is a human construct to help us understand ultimate meaning. They would both say that we don't have ultimate answers. In the SCM, we learnt that God raises questions and doesn't answer them. Do we love each other deeply enough to change our lives? That's the bottom line in most of Shirley's hymns rather than any formal doctrine.[2]

The SCM's pacifist beliefs also had an enormous influence on Shirley, Oestreicher said. The great New Zealand pacifist preacher, the Rev Ormond Burton, was eventually deprived of his ministry by the Methodist Church. Years later, it was ready to apologise. Pacifism became even more pressing with the rise of the nuclear issue after World War II.

During the 1960s and '70s, social change continued to sweep through most Western countries, with 1968 recognised as the great revolutionary year.

"The attempt to radically change society failed in the end," said Oestreicher. "At present we are going through a profoundly reactionary phase. Even the feminist revolution has only partly succeeded, due to its continual portrayal by some sectors of society as being anti-male."

In the hymn world, new text writers and composers began to emerge during the 1970s, '80s and '90s, but they, too, reflected the growing divide between the evangelical and more liberal churches. In New Zealand, the three volumes of *Scripture in Song* (1979-1988), begun by David and Dale Garratt, were hugely influential among evangelicals. They are characterised by their use of biblical texts, and a focus on themes of praise and salvation, using popular musical styles. Although the content largely comprised American and English praise songs, work by New Zealanders Richard Gillard ('Brother, Sister, Let Me Serve You') and Brent Chambers was also included. *Servant Songs*, published in 1987, was the work of choir leaders Guy Jansen and Felicia Edgecombe. Many of these songs were recorded and sung by the Festival Singers of Wellington. They included some New Zealand pieces.

Wellington musician and song-writer Felicia Edgecombe sees Guy Jansen as bridging the divide between the evangelical and liberal arms of the church.

> Guy was a Presbyterian but with an ecumenical outlook. He introduced singers and congregations to Shirley Murray's stable. He also championed the folk hymns that were easy to sing, often accompanied by guitar.

> Some of Shirley's hymns don't work so well with a guitar accompaniment, yet, in the last 50 years, the guitar has been a most important instrument. Guy always thought tunes had to be suitable and simple enough for the village pianist.

As well as leaning heavily on the *Servant Songs* repertoire, the Festival Singers also recorded several New Zealand Hymnbook Trust songs including Shirley's 'Every Day I Will Offer You', 'Come Now, Lord Jesus' and 'Our Life Has Its Seasons'. As Edgecombe explains:

When I was head of music at Queen Margaret College in Wellington, we also often sang 'Take My Gifts', 'God Speed You On Your Way' and 'Christ Is Alive'.

Today, evangelical congregations sing a wide spectrum of music. The internet has also changed things enormously. At Titahi Bay Community Church, which has Brethren roots, we will sing traditional hymns, Hillsong music, folk hymns, a lot of *Servant Songs*, plus some from *Alleluia Aotearoa* and *Faith Forever Singing*.

We relate best to Shirley's songs that are based on scripture. Her songs are quite cerebral. Today, people live extremely busy lives and they need some space in the service – perhaps people don't want to be challenged too much. Some of the mega churches write their own songs. Or they find a YouTube of what they want. It's all there on the internet these days, for example sheet music, guitar chords in whatever key you want a song to be. These resources are quite cheap to access. The days of being reliant on books have passed.[3]

Presbyterian minister the Rev Mervyn Aitken believes the evangelical churches didn't quite understand the imagery in some of Shirley's writing. There was certainly some pushback to her hymns from a number of quarters and from those with more traditional theological understandings. "Shirley had to ignore negative opinions or she wouldn't have done anything. Some evangelical churches just want straightforward hymns like 'Shine, Jesus, Shine!' that anyone can sing and understand. With a Shirley hymn, you have to think about the words as you sing."

Massey University emeritus professor of (religious) history, Peter Lineham, believes Presbyterian minister and music archivist David Dell was another bridge between the evangelical and liberal musical worlds. Before the New Zealand Hymnbook Trust was established, Dell had edited *New Zealand Praise*, published by the New Zealand Christian Resource Trust in 1988. Among work by more than 70 New Zealand writers and composers are 12 by Shirley and 13 by Colin Gibson. It was the first attempt to produce a hymn book comprised entirely of New Zealand content.

Lineham believes one or two of Shirley's songs might have caught on in evangelical churches, but the sophistication of the music can make them harder to sing. "You need to make the effort to learn Shirley's songs – and Colin Gibson's – and you need skilled musicians to play the music.

"Of course, in the evangelical world, people don't sing any more, as the music is performed by bands, with the congregation just joining in a bit. Everything is tightly controlled, with the words projected via PowerPoint. In these churches, the hymn book has almost disappeared."

Lineham has noted shifts in evangelical churches, however, with some wanting to reflect New Zealand reality here and now. Some of these churches are also incorporating Māori expressions and traditions, including Māori chants. "People are finding their own way and learning to sing the Lord's song in a strange land. The shift, which began in the 1990s led by people like Felicia Edgecombe, is significant."

Lineham predicts another shift is on the way as the immigrant church continues to grow. "What hymns will these new arrivals in New Zealand want to sing and what will the shape of the church of the future be? It is hard to predict."

Lineham grew up within the Brethren Church, with his early church influences largely fundamentalist. Today, however, he is a member of Ponsonby Baptist and the Auckland Rainbow Community Church, and he is very familiar with Shirley's work. "Ponsonby Baptist is an inclusive church, which means we have to be careful about what words we sing – they must be inclusive too. Our musical diet consists almost exclusively of work by Shirley and Colin.

"We are somewhat notorious in the Baptist world for welcoming the LBGTQ+ community. Gay people marry in our church and gay people are in leadership. In Baptist terms that is very liberal. It also means we are always at risk of being expelled from the Baptist Union, but we have fought back and I think our acceptance is growing."

Another Auckland church that regularly uses Shirley's hymns is St Matthew-in-the-City, an Anglican church led (in 2022) by the Rev Helen Jacobi:

We have about 40 of her hymns in our hymn database and have about ten real favourites. Every Waitangi Day we sing 'Where Mountains Rise'; every Anzac Day, 'Honour the Dead'; every Easter, 'Christ Is Alive'; and every Christmas, 'Carol Our Christmas'. Other favourites are 'Church of the Living Christ', 'Unity of Christ', 'Every Day I Will Offer You', 'Faith Has Set Us on a Journey', 'In the Name of Christ We Gather', 'Now To Your Table Spread', 'Take My Gifts' and 'Touch the Earth Lightly'. These are so familiar; our congregation hardly has to look at the words. They are our basic staples.

We like them because they connect to Aotearoa, to our own issues and the way we think. We try to avoid concepts of God in heaven, able to fix everything for us. We shun triumphalist words and seek different images and words for God. Gender inclusivity is also important. Shirley's hymns are about community, about gathering, about God in the midst of us. Shirley is a good poet and her hymns have a good rhythm. They are simple and not overlaid with imagery. Other writers try too hard.[4]

Jacobi describes her congregation as coming from right across Auckland, from Pōkeno to Orewa. It includes people from all walks of life and level of education, though the majority are highly educated, and mostly Pākehā (of European origin). She sees St Matthew-in-the-City as the most progressive Anglican church in the country, along with St Peter's in Wellington.

"We do not define our faith. As an outward-looking church, we are concerned about climate change, have protested against things like the Springbok rugby tour and nuclear ship visits. Interfaith issues interest us. The Auckland Rainbow Community Church meets here on Sunday evenings and has done so for 40 years. It started off as a St Matthew's Bible study group but is now an independent ecumenical congregation but supported by us." (Helen Jacobi left St Matthew-in-the-City in May 2023.)

The Rev David Dell readily admits Shirley and he are from opposite ends of the theological spectrum. They never formally collaborated but Dell knows she appreciated his compositions, particularly for 'Loving Spirit' and 'Where Is the Room?' both published in *Alleluia Aotearoa*.

He agrees the Hymnbook Trust publications have not been picked up by evangelical, charismatic churches. "*Alleluia Aotearoa* is just not on the shelves. When you go into a church that expresses a particular kind of theology, you know what books to expect on the shelves. Looking after the planet and other issues of social justice are not big themes in most charismatic churches, though things are changing a bit."

Despite their theological differences, Dell greatly admires Shirley's gifts as a hymn writer. "I believe she is certainly our most well-known and talented hymn writer – she absolutely stands out. There is music in the way she put her words together. I found them easy to set to music, because of their flow. Shirley was also the loveliest person to talk to. She was warm and engaging, a gentle person, yet some of her words have a real bite. Her ability to take her thoughts and express them in a way that would touch people's hearts was amazing. One of the great blessings in my life has been to set some of her words to music. She definitely deserves to be remembered."

Retired Presbyterian minister the Very Rev Pamela Tankersley and her husband, organist and composer Roy Tankersley, concede Shirley's hymns are unlikely to become the mainstay of the church in New Zealand.

> Those for whom her hymns have profound meaning are not running the churches anymore, while those who are in charge do not recognise her gifts. Yet internationally she is incredibly well respected.
>
> Her hymns are included in so many overseas publications. The international ecumenical movements will continue to use her and so will progressive churches in New Zealand. But they only exist in pockets – they are not the mainstay. Many congregations just want to sing love songs to Jesus, or worship songs, which to us are theological nursery rhymes and not satisfying at all.

Only time will tell what hymns of Shirley's survive into the future. Even for hymn writers like Charles Wesley, who reportedly wrote up to 10,000 hymns, and the prolific Isaac Watts, only a handful are remembered and sung today. In the 1996 hymnal of the United Church of Canada, *Voices United*, there are 11 hymns by Watts, 14 by

Wesley and 12 by Shirley! Her international reputation remains strong, while her reputation within New Zealand as a national, indigenous hymn writer with a unique ability to contextualise theology continues to burn brightly, but only among largely liberal and ecumenically-minded congregations.

Note

1   Verse 1, 'In What Strange Land', written in 2005 as a meditation on Psalm 137:4, "How shall we sing the Lord's song in a strange land?" The "strange land" is contemporary society and the hymn is about finding our faith in a different sphere.

2   From an interview by the author 3 May 2021.

3   From an interview by the author 21 March 2023.

4   From an interview by the author 1 July 2022.

28 – The human cost of war

Honour the dead, our country's fighting brave,
honour our children left in foreign grave,
where poppies blow and sorrow seeds her flowers,
honour the crosses marked forever ours.[1]

Shirley composed her 'Hymn for Anzac Day', 'Honour the Dead', to reflect contemporary New Zealand sensibilities towards war and sacrifice. Bound up in its verses is respect and gratitude for those who have served their country in all wars, along with a condemnation of war's obscenity and a rallying call for peace.

The third verse honours conscientious objectors and remembers how shamefully they were treated. Shirley describes this hymn as her "boldest attempt to speak peace in my own context".[2]

'Honour the Dead' had its first public appearance on Anzac Day 2007, when it was played by the New Zealand Army Band at Wānaka, Central Otago, and by the Kāpiti Brass Band at Paraparaumu to a tune composed by Colin Gibson. Written in 2005, it had its first significant appearance in 2006, as part of an Anzac Day service at Rathkeale College, Masterton.

During all her early experiences of attending Anzac services, Shirley had only heard traditional hymns from British hymnals, such as 'Abide With Me' and 'O God, Our Help in Ages Past'. What was needed, she believed, was a New Zealand expression of our own national feelings about wars and their enduring pain.

Never one to avoid controversy in her hymn writing, she soon realised that her Anzac hymn had touched a nerve in the national psyche. Reactions came from a variety of organisations, she said –

from the Ministry of Defence, the Royal New Zealand Returned and Services Association, newspapers, church bulletins, a former prime minister and the Attorney-General.

Other countries also waded in, including Japan, Canada and the United States where the hymn had been seriously studied and used.

Verse three, honouring conscientious objectors, was omitted at the official Chunuk Bair remembrance at Gallipoli in 2008 at which then Minister of Foreign Affairs Winston Peters presided. It was at Gallipoli, western Turkey, that New Zealand and Australian troops – the Australia New Zealand Army Corps, hence Anzac – went ashore on 25 April 1915, in an attempt to open the Dardanelles to Allied shipping. The campaign did not succeed, and led to the deaths of nearly 3000 New Zealanders and close to 9000 Australians.

Emeritus professor of the National Centre for Peace and Conflict Studies at the University of Otago, Kevin Clements, says Shirley was upset by the omission of verse three, while for Clements, omitting this verse was "an outrage and a travesty. Shirley wanted her hymn to be inclusive, to help people remember the different dimensions of that war."

Clements' father, Methodist minister the Rev Les Clements, spent four years in detention during World War II because of his pacifist views. The criticism levelled at Les's wife during these years caused her to have a breakdown.

Shirley was realistic enough to realise that getting her hymn accepted by the mainstream was never going to be easy.

There were some positive affirmations, however. Former Prime Minister and Minister of Culture and Heritage Helen Clark praised it in her foreword to the New Zealand Hymnbook Trust collection *Hope is our Song* in 2009: "This hymn will make a significant contribution to the expression of our nation's identity on Anzac Day … I am sure in the years to come, 'Hymn for Anzac Day' will be sung in memorial services in New Zealand and overseas."

The hymn had first been published in 2008 in Shirley's American collection *Touch the Earth Lightly*, and in a special New Zealand Hymnbook Trust edition. This included a Māori translation by Rangi McGarvey, adapted by Whirimako Black who later recorded the hymn (see appendix 4).

Colin's strong and solemn setting of the hymn, Anzac, enhances the emotional impact of the words. The tune moves slowly and with gravitas, with certain sections sounding like 'The Last Post' played at a soldier's funeral. Shirley explained what inspired her to write the hymn in an article in *Music in the Air* in 2007:

> This hymn was not written in a vacuum. It is dedicated to, and written because I remember my two uncles, Norman and Jack Ferguson, who set off with other Southlanders of their kind to join the Otago Regiment as volunteers at the beginning of World War I.
>
> Norman was 21, Jack 20. Their elder stepbrother, Neil, had already served in the Boer War and my guess, according to my mother (their only sister), was that they couldn't wait to get away from Invercargill, to see more of the world and have an 'adventure'. That adventure was centred on Gallipoli, which they both survived, Norman invalided out, and Jack never willing to describe what he had seen and experienced. Uncle Jack lived in our household all my student days, went marching on Anzac Day, but never spoke about the war. I inherited his Gallipoli medal.
>
> Later, in my student days, I went to a Student Christian Movement conference in Wellington, where one of the speakers was [Methodist clergyman] the Rev Ormond Burton. He was a broad-shouldered, bear-like man, of impressive physical character. He became one of New Zealand's best known Christian pacifists.
>
> He had landed at Gallipoli as a medical orderly, having enlisted as a volunteer aged 21, and was described as "a gallant, even foolhardy soldier". By the end of the war, having served right through and refusing home leave, he had been wounded three times, been decorated by both the British and the French, and promoted to lieutenant.
>
> But after this war, he became an unabashed propagandist for pacifism. Due to his outspoken and charismatic speeches at Wellington's Basin Reserve and elsewhere, especially in the church, he became a prime suspect to the government, as a stirrer. He was treated despicably and imprisoned for most of World War II in Napier Prison, in solitary confinement, isolated from other pacifist colleagues.

Ormond Burton made an enormous impression on me, even though I did not know half of what a hero he had been. I could not imagine writing a hymn for Anzac Day which did not give an honoured place to those whom other New Zealanders treated brutally for their sincere beliefs.

I consider peace to be the prime issue we must deal with — from the horrors of world wars to the impersonal, but no less ghastly waste of human life by nuclear explosion and the missiles still screaming in Iraq. Whenever you sing this hymn, don't focus only on the past — think of what you can do for positive peacemaking in your lifetime, and respect those who will never commit themselves to killing another family's son or daughter in warfare.[3]

Anglican priest and peace activist Paul Oestreicher regards 'Honour the Dead: A Hymn for Anzac Day', as one of Shirley's finest poems. In an address delivered to the congregation of St Peter's Anglican Church in Wellington in April 2020, he reflected on the hymn's significance, in responses to each of its five verses:

Verse one [opening this chapter] describes our empire at war with other empires. Their sons, brothers, lovers, husbands, like ours, were under orders, like ours, to go and kill the enemy, hoping to survive. All this, to maintain the structures of power. Today the historians tell us World War I was a pointless, futile war. They said it was a war to end all wars – it was not. It fuelled the next, and once again young men were sent to kill and, if need be, to be killed. Today the grandchildren of those who fought on both sides can hold hands and mourn together on that Turkish beach. There is only one humanity.

Weep for the places ravaged with our blood,
weep for the young bones buried in the mud,
weep for the powers of violence and greed,
weep for the deals done in the name of need.

In every war, the real enemy is not the squaddie on the other side who breathes and thinks and fears like you, but war itself. War makes a mockery of humanity. War drenches the good earth with good blood. There is no such thing as Turkish blood, no Māori or Pākehā blood, no German or Russian blood. No Jewish or Muslim blood. Only human blood. Are you wounded? Ask not whose blood will save your life. You need a surgeon? Ask not the colour of her skin. If you die, they'll say your cause was holy. And if you kill an enemy, his people will believe his cause was holy. The war-makers will deck the war graves with crosses. Don't believe their lies. Truth is war's first victim. But have compassion for the liars, for 'they know not what they are doing'. Weep for the dead. Weep for the living. Work to end killing.

Honour the brave whose conscience was their call,
answered no bugle, went against the wall,
suffered in prisons of contempt and shame,
branded as cowards, in our country's name.

Those who defied public opinion and said no to World War I because they would not kill, were few in New Zealand. Their names are known. They put humanity before nation. They were treated as cowardly traitors. Let one name stand for them all: [Dunedin pacifist] Archibald Baxter. His account of the cruelty he was made to suffer in his book *We Will Not Cease* tells the bitter story well. It makes painful reading. Their number in World War II was greater. Some of them were exempted on religious grounds and the rest treated like prisoners of war. At least people now knew what conscientious objection was.

Archibald and his fellow sufferers had paid a high price for the human right to say no. There are still many countries where that right does not exist. In Hitler's Germany, during WWII, the devout farmer Franz Jägerstätter refused to kill: 'Jesus', he said, 'will not let me.' His Bishop tried to change his mind: 'You will be executed. Your children will have no father.' 'Are you saying, then, that I should kill the fathers of Russian children?' He was beheaded. Half a century later the Pope beatified him. Our churches are slow to learn.

Weep for the waste of all that might have been
Weep for the cost that war has made obscene,
Weep for the homes that ache with human pain,
Weep that we ever sanction war again.

The nations have not ceased to sanction war. Often enough on Anzac Day it is made to seem holy. It never has been, though good men have fought. Soldiers are not the problem, our mindset is. Yet long before Jesus – who taught his followers to love their enemies – the prophet Micah looked forward to the day when 'nation shall not lift up sword against nation, neither shall they learn war anymore'. Look, just for a moment, at what we, all of us humans, spend on preparing for war: the money needed to provide adequate food, water, education, health and housing for everyone in the world is about $30 billion a year. A huge sum of money. It is about as much as the world spends on armaments every week.

Lord have mercy. Christ have mercy, Lord have mercy.

Honour the dream for which our nation bled,
held now in trust to justify the dead,
honour their vision on this solemn day:
peace known in freedom, peace the only way.

Honour the dead, is where this song began. It began with our country's fighting brave. Gallipoli was over a hundred years ago, but why should our honouring, if honour we must, not go further back than this British war on a foreign beach? Why not grieve for the brave of the Māori/Pākehā wars, when the original people fought for their land, this land? Do we want to forget those wars in which our land bled? Do we want to hide, that their aftermath still bleeds? But it is the dead of all the wars of all of history that make Jesus cry. To quote him: 'They do not know what truly makes for peace.'

I leave the last words to Jesus: 'Those who live by the sword shall die by the sword.' Amen.[4]

Shirley did not believe in the popular myth that New Zealand's identity was formed or forged in the trenches of Gallipoli or on the Somme. Such attitudes, she warned, could lead to sentimental observances of wreath-laying and glorifying war. Rather, she believed our identity was formed by those early settlers who came to this country looking for a place of freedom and peace. And that imperative for peace was driven largely by women, including, during Shirley's own lifetime, union activist Sonja Davies, former High Court Judge and New Zealand's first woman Governor-General the Hon Dame Silvia Cartwright, and National Council of Women peace campaigner Dame Laurie Salas.[5]

In an article in the *Otago Daily Times* in 2015, Shirley wrote: "If the national psyche cannot hold more than the idea of remembrance and sacrifice, if the causes and cost of war are not constantly in our mindsets, we may turn our most solemn day into a military funeral parade, with youngsters wearing great-grandfather's medals and a complete lack of understanding of our own history. Then the glorification of conflict becomes a sentimental journey."[6]

Notes

1   Verse 1, 'Hymn for Anzac Day', written in 2005 and first published in Hope's 2008 collection *Touch the Earth Lightly*. In 2009, it was published in *Hope is our Song*.

2   Wootton, 2010, p301.

3   Murray, S.E. (2007) Hymn for Anzac Day: the writer of the text shares its story. *Music in the Air*, Winter/Spring.

4   This sermon by Paul Oestreicher was part of a Facebook service streamed to the St Peter's congregation on 26 April 2020, the day after Anzac Day and near the end of New Zealand's first Covid-19 lockdown.

5   Murray, S.E. (2006) A hymn for Anzac Day. *Word and Worship*, New Zealand Lay Preachers Association. Autumn, 24-26.

6   Murray, S. (2015) The courage of soldiers and 'cowards' honoured. *The Otago Daily Times*, 24 April, 13.

29 – Hymns of special note

'Where Mountains Rise to Open Skies'

Where mountains rise to open skies
your name, O God, is echoed far,
from island beach to kauri's reach,
in water's light, in lake and star.

Your people's heart, your people's part
be in our caring for this land,
for faith to flower, for aroha
to let each other's mana stand.

From broken word, from conflict stirred,
from lack of vision, set us free
to see the line of your design,
to feel creation's energy.

Your love be known, compassion shown,
that every child have equal scope:
in justice done, in trust begun
shall be our heritage and hope.

Where mountains rise to open skies
your way of peace distil the air,
your spirit bind all humankind,
one covenant of life to share!

'Where Mountains Rise to Open Skies' ('Hymn for Waitangi Day') was written in 1990 to celebrate the 150th anniversary of the signing of New Zealand's founding document, the Treaty of Waitangi (Te Tiriti o Waitangi). It was first published in *Alleluia*

Aotearoa in 1992 and in her 1996 American collection *Every Day in Your Spirit* with a setting by New Zealand Roman Catholic musician Dr Vernon Griffiths. Shirley hoped it would become a national hymn chosen for the many state and community commemorations of the Treaty held on 6 February each year.

It has been sung on many significant national and state occasions, including, in 1995, as the only congregational New Zealand hymn for the visit of Queen Elizabeth II to Christchurch Cathedral. In 2003, it was sung in Westminster Abbey at the annual Anzac Day service – believed to be the first time a New Zealand hymn had been sung in the Abbey. And in 2022, it was chosen for the State Memorial Service for Queen Elizabeth II in Wellington's Cathedral of St Paul.

Like Shirley's 'Hymn for Anzac Day', 'Where Mountains Rise' is a hymn for a public theology – a theology that embraces global issues around peace, justice and creation for people in the wider community. As close friend and former co-manager of the NZHBT John Thornley said, "Shirley felt that her legacy was to the wider, secular world as much as to the church. Her hymn texts – those that address green issues, or public occasions like Anzac Day, Waitangi Day, Hiroshima Day or multicultural festivals – have found a place in civic rituals as well as worship services. They are also sung in school assemblies in private schools and a few, such as 'Honour the Dead', in public schools."

When writing 'Where Mountains Rise', Shirley was conscious she was writing not only for a Christian community, but also for citizens of every faith and none. She set out to express the bicultural life of Pākehā New Zealanders and Māori within the natural environment of the country. Her use of the well accepted Māori words aroha (all-embracing love) and mana (power/prestige) is significant and sensitive.

The first two verses express the wonder of God's creation in the landscape, a concern for the environment and feelings of mutual respect and friendship. The darker sides of our history are captured in verse three, where the New Zealand Land Wars of the 19th century are referenced, as well as the ongoing struggle for justice for Māori. The last verse prays for God's way of peace and a covenant to bring the whole world into harmony.

Shirley pays tribute to the NZHBT editorial committee for encouraging her to write the hymn. She also sought a tune that would be recognisably New Zealand, adopting DUNEDIN by composer Vernon Griffiths. He composed it around 1935 when he was music teacher at King Edward Technical College in Dunedin. Shirley described the tune as dignified, with a "strong bone structure and confident shape", while American composer Carlton Young compared it to the work of English composer Hubert Parry, calling it "one of the finest of 20th century long metre tunes, with stanzas designed to be sung in alternation between choir and congregation".[1]

Shirley provided an interpretation of 'Where Mountains Rise' in the journal *The Hymn* in 2007:

> [New Zealand] spirituality is most at home, not in churches, but in the cathedrals of tree ferns and high mountains, places where incarnation seems natural and resurrection experienced in the springing up of life from the rotted leaves of green bush and the clear waters.
>
> Our two official languages, Māori and English, spell out our bicultural life together. The struggle for domination by colonising British and European powers has coloured our history with blood, as it has many other nations. We have cause for shame, too, that we did not honour the peacemakers, and still honour a strong warrior tradition, though that is now rather transmuted into prowess in sport. We take no little pride in having declared our country nuclear-free and are committed to keeping it this way.
>
> So, on our national day, 6 February, what can we possibly sing that would capture the spirit of all this? We are a largely secular nation, but we have our own vision and values, voiced by prophets, priests and poets, especially poets.[2]

'Star-Child Earth-Child'

Star-Child, earth-Child,
  go-between of God,
  love Child, Christ Child,
heaven's lightning rod,

  Refrain:
  This year, this year,
  let the day arrive
  when Christmas comes for everyone,
  everyone alive!

Street child, beat child,
  no place left to go,
  hurt child, used child
no one wants to know,

  Refrain

Grown child, old child,
  mem'ry full of years,
  sad child, lost child,
story told in tears,

  Refrain

Spared child, spoiled child,
  having, wanting more,
  wise child, faith child,
knowing joy in store,

  Refrain

Hope-for-peace Child,
  God's stupendous sign,
  down-to-earth Child,
Star of stars that shine,

  Refrain

Increasing concern at New Zealand's market-driven welfare system drove Shirley to write this hymn in 1993. It was first published in Hope Publishing Company's *Every Day in Your Spirit* with a setting by Carlton R. Young, then in *Carol Our Christmas*, with settings by

Colin Gibson and Young. This system was creating growing numbers of social rejects. Full of word play and adventurous imagery, the hymn has been set by many composers and is a regular feature at Christmas services around the world.

Shirley explained more at an Advent Service at Ngaio Union Church in Wellington in November 2003:

> 'Star-Child' is a favourite of mine. It's been translated into Estonian, Korean, Russian, and the traditional World Council of Churches languages, like Spanish, French and German. For me it was a breakthrough carol and the one that has travelled the farthest. There are heaps of tunes for it but Carlton Young's [see chapter 25] has 'settled' with these words.

> Though I think of the hymn as being set within a New Zealand context, there's nothing to tell you that when you look at the words, is there? Many of us attempt to write New Zealand carols, with the injections of words like pōhutukawa, which are very hard to scan. One of my first attempts to indigenise or contextualise a carol is 'Come To This Christmas Singing', which I wrote in 1983. A reworking of the biblical story of the gifts brought by the Magi to the infant Jesus, this references our own gifts of 'greenstone' and 'paua shell', which I had to reduce in the text to 'shell' and 'stone'.

> But there's another context in which we operate – it's not all visual. It's the context of the heart. I wrote 'Star-Child' in 1993, in which there were some really savage welfare cuts. There were health cuts the year before, but the welfare cuts of 1993 put us all into a downward spin. There was more unemployment, more fear, and as Christmas that year came round, I thought, 'I can't get away from the shadow side of Christmas'. There is the promise and there's all the things that, if you're a believing person, are going to happen through the incarnation. But on our own patch, what am I seeing? And so it was another sort of landscape I was describing.

> If we take a look at the structure of 'Star-Child', the first and last verses form a kind of a frame. They're a sort of theological window because there are the names of the Christ child and they culminate in the last verse in 'God's stupendous sign'.

Part of the first verse, 'Heaven's lightning rod', I stole from the wonderful French theologian Teilhard de Chardin, who said of the coming of Christ: 'From pole to pole there would be lightning strike and it would happen and we would recognise it.' The middle verses bring us into our own country with people we recognise. At least I did that year, and if you don't recognise all of them, you'll recognise some of them.

Through every verse there's something to help us identify with the child in ourselves, however old we are. Verse four refers to our rampant consumerism, and that's why I was bold enough to include the words 'spared child, spoiled child/having, wanting more'.

The refrain is just a repeated hope that whatever Christmas means to Christians, the goodness of God will be seen in some way by 'everyone alive', no matter what faith they follow. That's how I saw 'Star-Child' when I put it together.

It's important to me that we get to remember the other side of Christmas, along with the bright hope expressed in the last verse. To me, incarnation is far more important than resurrection. There is no resurrection without incarnation first, anyway. Birth and life are more important than death, and Christmas every year opens a door into our childhood, to re-examine where we've travelled.

Professor Michael Hawn, then distinguished professor of church music at Perkins School of Theology in Dallas, Texas, offers further commentary on 'Star-Child'.[3] Quoting United Methodist Bishop Joel Martinez, he says Christians cannot rely on the Christmas carols of the past, but must ask themselves, what the God who came to earth in a human form means for us today. He explains:

> Charles Dickens' *A Christmas Carol* and Hallmark greeting cards may condition us to view Christmas sentimentally. Our songs should include those that remind us that there are many among us for whom the joy of Christmas has never been experienced. Ms Murray, one of the most accomplished writers in the English language, achieves this message through a series of short descriptive modifiers before 'child'. In very economical language she catalogues children of all ages and stations of life: 'street child,

beat child', 'hurt child, used child', 'grown child, old child', 'sad child, lost child'.

All of these children are created in the image of the 'Star-Child earth-Child' of stanza one and the 'Hope-for-peace Child' of stanza five. The refrain, 'This year, this year, let the day arrive', is a petition for the presence of the 'Christ Child' for 'everyone alive'.

Carlton Young's musical setting captures the lyrical quality and warmth of a traditional Christmas carol. The beautiful melody becomes a vehicle for singing a message that fits our generation's stanza – a worthy contribution to the great hymns of the church.[4]

'Touch the Earth Lightly'

Touch the earth lightly,
use the earth gently,
nourish the life of the world in our care:
gift of great wonder,
ours to surrender,
trust for the children tomorrow will bear.

We who endanger,
who create hunger,
agents of death for all creatures that live,
we who would foster
clouds of disaster –
God of our planet, forestall and forgive!

Let there be greening,
birth from the burning,
water that blesses and air that is sweet,
health in God's garden,
hope in God's children,
regeneration that peace will complete.

God of all living,
God of all loving,
God of the seedling, the snow, and the sun,
teach us, deflect us,
Christ reconnect us,
using us gently, and making us one.

An early hymn of Shirley's addressing ecological responsibility, 'Touch the Earth Lightly', written in 1991, is one of eight 'green' hymns, published in her final collection, *Life into Life*. A prayer for the protection of the earth and its inhabitants, it also addresses human responsibility for the planet's desecration.

Taking its title from an Aboriginal saying, the hymn is a gentle plea for humanity to take better care of the planet entrusted to us. Its gentle opening turns to a darker side in the second verse when humanity's destructive power, bringing death to all living things, is described. This is a prayer of confession, with a plea that, with God's help and forgiveness, we will forestall the worst consequences of our actions. Colin Gibson's setting, TENDERNESS, changes from a major to a minor key in this verse to emphasise the destructive power of human activity.

The phrase 'clouds of disaster' in the second-to-last line of this verse refers to the nuclear testing by France in the Pacific, which New Zealand protested against at the United Nations for many years. The testing has ended, but Shirley says that "the horrific effects on communities in their testing areas are still coming out".[5] Shirley's hymn invites us to attune ourselves more empathetically to our world, its natural resources and its people, so our connections become stronger and more fruitful.

Hymn writer Brian Wren discusses the structure of 'Touch the Earth Lightly' in his book *Praying Twice*.[6] The metrical pattern is unusual, he says, with the first two lines having five syllables, followed by a ten-syllable line. This pattern is repeated in the next three lines. The longer lines, except in the second verse, have light, unstressed endings, giving gentle sounds and gentle meanings.

Wren describes the second verse as "a confession of the human race's failure as planetary guardians". In contrast, the closing stanzas, also written as prayers, return mostly to the light, gentle endings of the first. "God in Christ opposes our destructive mismanagement, not violently", says Wren, but like a teacher deflecting bad behaviour. Humanity is called to use the earth gently, even as Jesus can be trusted to use us gently. In this way, Shirley is using her poetic skills to "do theology".

Former Methodist minister and internationally published hymn writer William (Bill) Wallace, in his examination of the hymn, describes it as "an excellent example of a particular phase in the process of the greening of hymnody".[7]

Although acknowledging it contributes to a widening of green theology, Wallace suggests Shirley has not gone far enough in her condemnation of human beings' destructive nature.

> We have to move even further on the greening journey. The concept of stewardship still has within it the idea that we are superior to the Earth, and we have the right to control it. 'Touch the Earth Lightly' exhibits the beneficial side of this approach. But stewardship can easily turn to exploitation …

> The hymn exhibits two approaches to solving the ecological problems. In the main it talks of actions we must take, but it also talks of urging God to 'forestall' and 'deflect us' which I assume is a plea to God to intervene. This, I believe, is a dangerous notion which is used by some Christians as an excuse for doing nothing.

> Yes, we will need hymns like Shirley's to comfort us and to challenge our stewardship. But we will also need hymns which open our hearts and minds to the God-given wisdom of the cosmos and which also echo the words of the 13th-century Christian mystic, Meister Eckhart, who said "commerce is supported by keeping the individual at odds with himself and others, by making us want more than we need and offering credit to buy what refined senses do not want".[8]

William Wallace died in March 2024.

'Who Is My Mother?'

Who is my mother,
who is my brother?
all those who gather round Jesus Christ:
Spirit-blown people
born from the Gospel
sit at the table, round Jesus Christ.

Differently abled,
differently labeled,
widen the circle round Jesus Christ,
crutches and stigmas,
culture's enigmas,
all come together round Jesus Christ.

Love will relate us –
colour or status
can't segregate us, round Jesus Christ:
family failings,
human derailings –
all are accepted, round Jesus Christ.

Bound by one vision,
met for one mission
we claim each other, round Jesus Christ:
here is my mother,
here is my brother,
kindred in Spirit, through Jesus Christ.

Shirley's great hymn of inclusivity and hospitality arose out of her experiences at the World Council of Churches' Assembly in Canberra, in 1991. Its sentiments and allusions are drawn from several gospel passages.

'Who Is My Mother?' was published in Shirley's first American publication *In Every Corner Sing* in 1992. The following year it was published in *Alleluia Aotearoa*, subsequently appearing in many hymn collections worldwide. A hymn that extends God's gender, helping us recognise the genderlessness of God, it has been set by many composers, though Shirley favoured Ian Render's setting, as published in *AA*. He named it Bronwen after his own mother. Colin Gibson described Ian's tune as "finely crafted to match its text", with a graceful 3/4 rhythmic movement. Other compositions, he said, lacked "the sympathetic and expressive qualities of this one".[9]

Shirley's own analysis, which she delivered at a number of hymn workshops in New Zealand, explains the story behind the hymn and its many allusions.[10]

> If this hymn were a movie, I'd have to give credits for the script to two categories of people: first, the three gospel writers who gave me my opening line, and then to the two groups of people, among others, who appear in the text. These two groups of people have stayed with me ever since. They are, and I suspect sadly, continue to be, the invisible part of the Body of Christ. Sometimes they wear masks.
>
> I first met these two groups of people at the 1991 World Council of Churches' Assembly in Canberra. Daily worship was held in the great tent, where 2000 people sang, prayed and danced, with wonderful colours and sounds. It was the 'united nations' in action. Except that, outside the great tent, in the evening, two small communities worshipped on their own.
>
> The smaller of the two was the differently-abled – a label of their choosing. They felt the churches did not see them, in any recognisable way. This group not only includes the halt, the lame and the blind of the gospel stories; they are those of us who would come to worship if there were loop systems and large print hymnals, and other basic needs of access to our buildings were met.
>
> They include those who do not feel a welcome at the door if they are labelled a nuisance (as in the case of some deaf people) or a disturbance or are people with a known previous psychiatric history. And they wish to feel really included, not just tolerated. Some of us move in and out of this community, depending on our state of health and mind.
>
> Then there was the other group of the gay/lesbian community within the churches. This was a larger group of about 40, more diverse in terms of age, nationality and denomination than you might imagine. And worship always included telling the stories, the stories of Christian people unacceptable to other Christians.

This invisible community knew they would be less than welcomed at the door and especially at the table of their churches if they declared themselves. They ranged from Dutch to African American, to Asian and Brazilian.

Almost every denomination there had similar stories to tell – of searching for a family in the community of the church, when their own families had often rejected them.

But what they found was another source of rejection, either as members of the church or potential leaders of the church. There was such deep pain and alienation in that worship – lament, but also, celebration in the sharing of their life. It was unbearably moving, and I felt honoured to be accepted there.

What is there to sing that will bring all of us into the circle? That's my rationale for writing 'Who Is My Mother?' Let's look at the structure and language of this hymn, because both count here.

In terms of language, I broke the rules. Conventional wisdom tells hymn writers to use musical sounding words which do not disrupt the flow. Verse two has 'crutches and stigmas/cultures' enigmas', language designed to provoke and stir you, rather difficult to say. But also, there needs to be the warmth and welcome of the real Christian community, the one that knows we all have 'family failings/human derailings'. I see the image at the back of St Andrew's on The Terrace, Wellington, when this was our home worship site in the '80s, of our local drop-out, who chose to sit there, and who had a distinct personal fragrance problem, but yet was part of us until he died recently.

We are together for a purpose – we need each other – let's never close the circle. And let's keep our spirits high through staying close to the Christ figure we worship.

The main symbol of Christian teaching about community is a table, with people seated round it, sharing food. Not an altar, with priest and sacrificial offering, but something essentially homely, familiar, accessible. So this hymn is written to express, in contemporary terms, the meaning of the table as a gathering place, the character and identity of the people who come and the kinship of all who know God's presence there.

It also raises questions about how the churches present this symbol to the non-churched world. For example: how open is this table, really? What protocols (table manners) are expected? Are there rules about qualifying, and if so, who makes them?

One of the most poignant words of Jesus is the rather shocking question, 'Who is my mother?' (Mark 3:33). Didn't he love and respect her, as a Jewish son was bound to? Of course, he was not reducing his mother to an ordinary member of his community. Rather, he was raising the crowd to be equal in affection and relationship to his mother and family. Jesus is saying, by asking the question and giving the answer, that in God's sight, everyone who chooses to come is family except for those, who, by their own choice and action, show their rejection of other human beings.

This was the question for the Jews then, and for the majority of humankind now, because it changes the basis of our own personal identity, and more, our 'corporate' or tribal identities. The universality of Jesus's message is still a challenge, and is clearly seen in those who gather round the table.

An essential element in this understanding is shown in the story of the giving of the Spirit at Pentecost to people 'of every nation under heaven' (Acts 2:5). The more expected word in line four of verse one might have been 'Spirit-filled', but 'Spirit-blown' is a reference to John 3:8, 'the wind blows where it will', something less definable, but in this context, more powerful.

Differently abled, differently labelled' (Verse two)

Recall those stories in the Gospel about the 'halt, the lame and the blind' who came to Jesus for healing. Then list the socially undesirable in these stories: lepers, women, tax collectors, and the culturally undesirable: Romans, Samaritans, even Pharisees (a culture within a culture).

The heart of the Good News is that no one is rejected because of perceived or labelled deficiency or disability. The very nature of Jesus was to welcome people as they were, and to see them as potentially fully human. As others come into the company of the table, the circle changes shape, grows wider to include all our human variables.

Who would you feel uncomfortable sitting beside at the table? What has your church done to make its worship, the leadership in worship and the facilities accessible to differently-abled people?

'Love will relate us' (Verse three)

It is not easy for Christians to accept the universality of Jesus. Love recognises and overcomes differences which most of the time are barriers to us. We experience the reality of this inclusiveness only when faced with a specific challenge and choice. Look at Peter, preaching the Gospel of universal acceptance in Acts 2, but finding it extremely difficult to apply in Acts 10! This was the breakthrough for early Christians struggling with the acceptance of both Jew and Greek, male and female, slave and free (Galatians 3:28).

'Family failings, human derailings' (Verse four)

The things that cause us embarrassment or shame can separate us from one another. And it is not just individuals going 'off the rails', but the ways in which the family of the church lets people down. How do we explain or excuse continuing disunity among ourselves, rejection of other faiths, failure to speak out with one voice on issues of social justice, 'that the world may believe'? (John 17:21)

'Bound by one vision, met for one mission' (Verse five)

This hymn challenges us in the church to see things in the round, to face our 'pockets of resistance' – personal, cultural, theological – to see our neighbour as ourselves, and to bring in some more seats! Jesus is not seated at the head of the table (there is no head of a round table), but Jesus is the person sitting between each of us, joining us in a unity which the world desperately, despairingly, needs.[11]

'For Everyone Born, A Place at the Table'

For everyone born, a place at the table,
for everyone born, clean water and bread,
a shelter, a space, a safe place for growing,
for everyone born, a star overhead,

Refrain:

> *and God will delight when we are creators*
> *of justice and joy, compassion and peace:*
> *yes, God will delight when we are creators*
> *of justice, justice and joy!*

For woman and man, a place at the table,
revising the roles, deciding the share,
with wisdom and grace, dividing the power,
for woman and man, a system that's fair, (Refrain)

For young and for old, a place at the table,
a voice to be heard, a part in the song,
the hands of a child in hands that are wrinkled,
for young and for old, the right to belong, (Refrain)

For just and unjust, a place at the table,
abuser, abused, with need to forgive,
in anger, in hurt, a mindset of mercy,
for just and unjust, a new way to live, (Refrain)

For everyone born, a place at the table,
to live without fear, and simply to be,
to work, to speak out, to witness and worship,
for everyone born, the right to be free, (Refrain)

*Optional verse

For gay and for straight, a place at the table,
a covenant shared, a welcoming space,
a rainbow of race and gender and colour,
for gay and for straight, the chalice of grace, (Refrain)

Shirley wrote 'For Everyone Born, A Place at the Table' in 1996 when seeking a hymn that reflected a broad overview of human rights and to highlight her commitment to the work of Amnesty International. She uses the symbol of a meal table as a sign of inclusion, making it suitable as a Communion hymn but it can be used for a variety of services focusing on the themes of justice, compassion and reconciliation.

It was first published in 2000 in *Faith Forever Singing*, set to music by Colin Gibson. In Shirley's 2013 American collection, *A Place at the Table*, it includes an additional sixth verse and has a setting by Brian Mann. Shirley's last book, *Life into Life* also features it, accompanied by a new setting from Lim Swee Hong.

The last line of verse one – 'for everyone born, a star overhead' – alludes to the star that shone the night Jesus was born. This suggests, says the Rev Thomas Wesley Moore of the Presbyterian Church USA, that all people created in God's image deserve a birth that is celebrated and wanted.[12]

Verse two describes a table of equality between women and men, while the third verse depicts a table of acceptance where people's voices will be heard regardless of their age. Verse four points to a table of reconciliation where the 'just and unjust' and the 'abuser [and] abused' come together. While agreeing it is difficult to accept that those who have hurt and those who hurt can sit together at the one table, Moore says "it is what followers of Jesus should and must strive for". Healing can begin through mercy and grace and the discovery of a new way of living.

Verse five describes "a table of dignity", where "people can freely work, speak their minds and worship" in the ways they choose. It is a place where everyone has "the right to be free".[13]

For New Zealand Presbyterian minister the Rev Adrian Skelton, 'For Everyone Born' is "one of the most moving and effective of Shirley's hymns".

"Verse four really sticks in your throat. In contrast, the chorus is so joyful. This puts the onus back on us to create justice, compassion and peace and to be agents of God's work in our world. As a non-theistic Christian, I am comfortable that human beings are depicted as creators or co-creators. Inclusiveness, for me, is the central theme of the Gospel. Shirley explores this so brilliantly."

The words in verse four have proved problematic for some. Shirley was certainly aware some people found them confronting and uncomfortable. However, she argued that "under the manifesto of Jesus, even the worst abuse has to be dealt with and faced, and forgiveness requires singing about here".[14] She recognised that sometimes congregations would choose to omit this verse. Others, however, welcomed it "as exposing and recognising wounds that seem impossible to heal".[15]

(See also chapter 22 about the optional sixth verse.)

In 2023, Hope Publishing Company produced an authorised revision of 'For Everyone Born', following a number of requests for changes. Hope vice president Scott Shorney explained the background to this decision in an email to the author in March 2024.

"The alternative text came about after we heard that, while once a favorite hymn of the LGBTQ+ community, it had fallen out of favor and use, because it no longer felt all-inclusive to some," he wrote. "We also were told that on some college campuses, students were creating their own versions to address that feeling. We pursued some of the altered versions, but ultimately decided it would be best to create our own."

One of the editors of this revision, Daniel Charles Damon (a hymn writer himself), described his own struggles to embrace inclusive language in an article published in *The Hymn*.[16]

"During my life, language has changed. It is still changing, always changing, of course," he said. He argues the focus has now moved from using gender-neutral language to language that incorporates intersex and non-binary people, those who have any gender identity and any sexual orientation. New hymn writers, he says, must write about the whole spectrum of humanity. He now favours words like people, children, youth and elders rather than women and men, young and old, which can feel exclusive and polarising.

"Murray's idea and intention was to write a text that imagines all people at the great feast. Even though she later wrote a stanza for gay and straight people, this binary naming still leaves out portions of the human race." This hindered her inclusive message, he said.[17]

Damon worked with his co-editor at Hope, Carl Daw, to revise the text, with the aim to reflect God's love for all people. In verse two, the phrase 'For woman and man' reads *For all who share life*. In verse three, 'For young and for old' reads *For those we neglect*. In verse four,

'For just and unjust' reads *For you and for me*; and 'abuser, abused' reads *though wounded and sore*. In the optional last verse, 'For gay and for straight' reads *For all who have breath*. Shirley's original version will continue to be made available, Shorney said.

Whether Shirley would approve of these changes is impossible to say. But judging by her struggles over many years to maintain the integrity of her texts, it is doubtful. However, Shirley also understood, as noted in chapter 13, that "the politics of inclusiveness" are "subtle" and language "inherently dangerous".[18]

Shorney admits it is unlikely Shirley would approve Hope's revisions of 'For Everyone Born'. "I never once knew Shirley to accept someone else's reworking of a hymn text of hers. If she felt there was just cause to make an alteration, she would always do so herself to satisfy the request. So if she were still living, she would probably offer her own rewrite instead of this one."

'Lift High the Cross'

Refrain:

*Lift high the cross, the love of Christ proclaim
till all the world adore his glorious name!*

*Come, Christian people, sing your praises, shout!
if we are silent, even stones cry out.*[19]

"I have never been able to sing the original words of G.W. Kitchin's 'Lift High the Cross'," said Shirley, "because of the military imagery and now inappropriate theology. My adaptation locates the emphasis on the Holy Week story, the cost of conflict and the gospel imperatives of peace making."[20]

English hymn writer George William Kitchen wrote his popular hymn (originally 12 verses long) in 1887. It was later modified by Michael Robert Newbolt. In 1984, nearly 100 years after it first appeared, Shirley wrote her adaptation, while retaining the musical setting, CRUCIFER, by Sydney Nicholson. It was published in her private collection, *In Every Corner Sing*, in 1987, and has since been included in many hymn collections. Shirley retains Kitchen's refrain, though substitutes the word 'glorious' for 'sacred'.

Churches today have found in Shirley's adaptation a theology more relevant for the third millennium than that found in the traditional words, says Methodist lay preacher and then NZHBT co-manager John Thornley:[21]

> Gone is the imagery of substitutionary atonement and, in its place, there is an eloquent plea for the contemporary Christian and church to be peacemakers.

> The original hymn draws on images of the triumphal return home by victorious Roman generals, following success in warfare. The procession is led by standard-bearers, holding unit emblems, and by a reclining statue of the god Jupiter. Take verse two:

> > *Led on their way by this triumphant sign,*
> > *The hosts of God in conquering ranks combine:*[22]

> In Shirley's version, this becomes:

> > *Jesus, you wept to see our human strife,*
> > *Teach us compassion for each human life …*

> In omitting all the imagery of warfare rituals, whether of Roman or contemporary times, Shirley's words highlight the drama of the Holy Week events: the mob acclamation of Jesus turning so quickly to cries for his death; Jesus' words, saying that if his disciples were silenced in their acclamation of him even 'the stones will cry out' (Luke 19:39-40); the tears of Jesus over the fate of Jerusalem (Luke 19:41-44); and references to the many words of Jesus to his disciples on the cost of following his way of suffering love.

> Here is a God not of 'power' and 'might', but one suffering with us, in the 'powerlessness' and 'frailty' of our humanity.

> Verse three in the original reads:

> > *Each newborn soldier of the Crucified*
> > *bears on his brow the seal of him who died:*

> Shirley's verse picks up her favourite theme of peace:

> > *Peace was your plea and peace your loving theme*
> > *let peace be our passport, peace a living dream.*

The imagery of peace as our 'passport' is a contemporary reminder of our global village and the ever-present debates around whom we accept and whom we reject as migrants and refugees.

As Shirley's words make clear, the Gospel of Jesus is found in the lives of those who follow and live the faith journey today. The dramatic events around Easter are just the beginning of the journey, not its end point.

The choruses of 'praise and worship', so popular in some sections of the church today, extol the might and power of God and the victory of love, but do not often sing about the pain and conflict involved in following God's way of suffering love. It is a 'costly discipleship', to use the phrase most closely associated with the life and writings of the German Christian pastor, author and martyr Dietrich Bonhoeffer.

Shirley's words challenge us for our lives today: 'teach us compassion for each human life', 'let peace be our passport', and 'great is the cost of walking on this road/to follow and suffer with the Son of God'.

In the original words, the focus looks back to the events of the past … Kitchin's last verse reads:

> *From farthest regions let them homage bring,*
> *And on this cross adore their Saviour King:*

Contrast this with Shirley's last verse:

> *Worlds to be born and children yet to be*
> *come, take up this song into eternity.*

Shirley's words emphasise the shift to the present and ourselves as bearers of this message today – a transformative experience for those willing to walk the path of Christ.[23]

Notes

1 Gibson, 2021, p257.

2 Murray, S.E. (2007) Hymn Interpretation. "Where mountains rise to open skies" *The Hymn*, vol 58, no 1, 51-53. The Hymn Society in the United States and Canada.

3 Hawn, C.M. (2013) History of Hymns: "Star-Child". Discipleship Ministries, The United Methodist Church, 17 December. https://www.umcdiscipleship. org/resources/history-of-hymns-star-child

4 See note 3.

5 'Touch the earth lightly' by Shirley Erena Murray. Methodist Church UK, The Resource Hub. (2016) https://www.methodist.org.uk/for-churches/resources/ posts/touch-the-earth-lightly-stf-729/

6 Wren, B. (2000) *Praying Twice: The Music and Words of Congregational Song.* Louisville, Kentucky: Westminster John Knox Press, pp293-295.

7 Wallace, W. (2009) Hymn Interpretation. The Greening of Hymnody? "Touch the Earth Lightly", *The Hymn*, vol 60, no 1, 24-26. Winter.

8 See note 7.

9 Gibson, 2021, p263.

10 Murray, S.E. (2007) Who is my mother? – origins and biblical sources of a hymn. *Music in the Air*, Summer, 7-9. Reprinted with permission.

11 See note 10.

12 Moore, T.W. (2016) History of Hymns: "For Everyone Born" by Shirley Erena Murray. Discipleship Ministries, The United Methodist Church. 29 June. https://www.umcdiscipleship.org/resources/history-of-hymns-for-everyone-born-by-shirley-erena-murray

13 See note 12.

14 Hall, L. (2012) Hymn Interpretation. "For Everyone Born, a Place at the Table". *The Hymn*; vol 63, no 3, 42-44, Summer.

15 See note 14.

16 Damon, D.C. with Johnson, E.M. (2023) "For everyone born": A hymnwriter struggles to address all people. *The Hymn*; vol 74, no 3, 25-27, Summer.

17 See note 16.

18 Wootton, 2010, p295.

19 Verse 1, 'Lift High the Cross', published in *Alleluia Aotearoa* 1993, adapted by Shirley from G.W. Kitchin. Music by Sydney Nicholson. Also published in 1992 in her American collection *In Every Corner Sing*.

20 Gibson, 2021, p151.

21 Thornley, J. (2005) 'Lift high the cross' – reflecting on 'good words' with Shirley Erena Murray. *Music in the Air*, Summer, 25-27. Reprinted with permission.

22 *With One Voice: A Hymnbook for All the Churches with New Zealand Supplement* (1982) London and Auckland: Collins.

23 See note 21.

Final word

I first interviewed Shirley Murray in 1989 when working for the Presbyterian/Methodist newspaper *Crosslink*. Nearly three decades later, as I near the end of writing this biography, my feelings are a mixture of gratitude and some sadness. One reason for my sadness is that Colin Gibson did not live long enough to see his wish fulfilled – a biography written about his dear friend Shirley.

Entering Shirley's world as intimately as I have done for the past five years has been an enormous privilege. I now know her and many more of her greatest hymn poems in a way I never knew before. Of course, the hymns featured in this book are only a fraction of her vast body of work. I hope, in time, a full bibliography will be undertaken – something quite beyond the scope and purpose of this book.

Shirley's hymns have anchored me to the church and to the Christian faith, as they have done for so many who have contributed to this biography. They have been like a cord/chord threading and resonating through my life for the past 30 years, but even more so during the last five.

Shirley wrote hymns as a way of writing herself into faith and of stating her faith. She wanted to right the balance in the sorts of themes expressed in most hymns. She addressed the missing themes like inclusivity, the pursuit of peace, justice and human rights, the plight of refugees, the feminine element in spirituality, care for the environment, to name just a few. Then there's the gap between good words and good music that she set out to balance, as well as filling in other theological cavities. And she went on doing all of those things, from the perspective of someone from Aotearoa New Zealand, from the regions of Asia and the Pacific, almost until her death.

But I am sad, too, that Shirley's hymns are not more widely known and sung in New Zealand. Jesus had something to say about prophets and how they are not honoured in their own countries, didn't he? Her work probably earns her greater respect outside New Zealand, in Asia, North America and parts of Europe. The liberal, mainstream churches – in New Zealand at least – continue to shrink year by year, with younger, more liberal-minded people mostly absent. The Rev Ken Irwin believed that if ministers and church leaders had more clearly expressed the kind of theology Shirley was expressing through her hymns, these younger people might have stayed.

Churches, he said, have failed to speak directly about the things that matter, like what happens after you die and what we believe and don't believe about that.

Shirley was able to tap into our deepest feelings, hopes and fears, as in the haunting hymn 'Nothing, Nothing in All Creation'. Irwin regarded this as a sermon in itself. And the simple parting blessing, 'Whatever This Life Has Been'. These hymns, written so insightfully and skilfully, are about the transcendence of hope and the human spirit being absorbed into the framework of the universe. They are deeply personal and intimate works, yet universal in their significance.

Reading her hymns closely, it is clear Shirley believed the church's true spirituality would help shape a wider societal morality, providing real leadership. As her friend Roger Wiig said, she didn't just want to write nice poetry for the church, but instead was always looking out to the community, addressing the issues most pressing to society, and addressing them firmly but never stridently. She was disappointed churches were not more adventurous in their choice of which hymns of hers they sang. Most chose and continue to choose a fairly narrow range. Maybe this book will help right that balance a little and contribute to a greater awareness and appreciation of her rich poetical talents.

Hymn singing appears to have a diminished presence in most mainstream churches, even at many funeral services. There is a greater reliance on recorded music downloaded from the internet. Maybe the future for many of Shirley's hymns will be as spoken words, as poetry, rather than sung as hymns.

Shirley knew that hymns teach theology. She knew that hymns are the place for new ideas, new metaphors, new politics and for all our faith expressions to be held.

They give us the poetic language to respond to and deal with both the good things and bad things happening in the world around us and in ourselves. Singing with others is also a sensory, corporate experience. When we lose this custom, we are the poorer for it.

In his memoir *Barefoot in the Dust*, Brian Wren writes: "Whether hymns will be sung in 2050 is impossible to predict, though one can safely say that if they are, some will need revision. I can safely predict, however, that in almost every act of public worship, people will want to sing. As long as the human voice is part of our anatomy, people will be singing together."[1]

Hymn singing is a rich tradition that Shirley helped renew and refresh, along with many other great hymn writers of the 20th and 21st centuries. Now is the time to value and retain that tradition before it is lost forever.

Shirley leaves the choice to us, as expressed in one of her last hymns, 'Who Will There Be to Sing', published in *Life into Life*.[2] Written as both a plea and a rallying call, Shirley says it's up to us whether we choose to keep singing the gospel truths, to sing out for justice, to call out evil, greed and selfishness whenever and wherever we see it, and to hold fast to faith. Or not.

'Our Life Has Its Seasons', a hymn she wrote decades earlier, reinforces this message – 'so there's never a time to stop believing, there's never a time for hope to die, there's never a time to stop loving, these three things go on'.

'Who Will There Be to Sing'

Who will there be to sing
if we do not sing well,
if all we know as true
has now no sounding bell?

    Let's sing, my friends!
    We make the choice
    in disarray
    or with one voice.

Who will there be to know
the Story in the song,
the soul food of our life
that makes the church stand strong?

    Sing from our hearts
    to tell and teach
    by tune and text
    where faith may reach!

Who will there be to hear
if we do not sing plain
that want of peace and bread
creates the world's deep pain?

    Sing justice, friends,
    to right the scales
    where powers oppress
    and greed prevails!

Who will there be to speak,
when silence is our song,
to state the Gospel truths,
provoke the powers of wrong?

    Sing out, each voice!
    One band, one choir,
    be instruments
    of God's desire!

Notes

1 Wren, B. (2017) *Barefoot in the Dust: A Hymn-Poet's Memoir.* Eugene, Oregon: Cascade Books, p88.

2 'Who Will There Be to Sing', written in 2015 and published in *Life into Life* in 2019, is set to music by the 18th century English clergyman and hymnodist John Darwall. This is the plaintive setting he wrote for Psalm 148, known as Darwall's 148th. The fact his second wife, Mary Whateley, was also a published poet and hymn writer would surely have appealed to Shirley.

Appendices

1 – 'Sing for Life and All its Goodness' – a farewell song for John (Verses 2 and 3)

Sing this life well-lived for others,
strong to stand, to lead and teach,
ministries of care and kindness,
talents of the mind and speech;
praise his life's creative spirit,
vision of a better way:
thanks and blessings on this day.

No sad songs for him we honour:
raise the hymns of faith held fast,
music that will carry onwards
now that death itself is past;
keep within our memory's treasure,
all he gave us on his way:
thanks and blessings on this day.

2 – Eulogy by Colin Gibson

This eulogy for Shirley Erena Murray was delivered at her funeral service on 31 January 2020.

Dear friend

Where shall I begin?

Shall I begin with the bald fact that, almost completely ignored by the media (who were too busy lamenting the death of an American basketball player), New Zealand's greatest hymn writer, member of the New Zealand Order of Merit, honorary Fellow of the Royal School of Church Music London, Fellow of the Hymn Society in the United States and Canada, Erik Routley Fellow of the Presbyterian Church of America and University of Otago Honorary Doctor of Literature, you died just under a week ago.

You were never one for titles, and I'm sure this list of some of the international awards you have won and the honours you have received will keep you smiling. As Professor Kevin Clements, your longtime friend, recalls, "your smile always lit up every room you were in; your entire life was a love and a blessing for others."

Shirley, you lived a life of deliberate commitment to the perfection of your craft – your intricate metrical and rhyme schemes were often the despair of your musicians – and you lived a life of intelligent dedication to the service of God and the church. 'Every day I will offer you, loving God, my heart and mind; every way I discover you in the work your hand has signed. Help me see I'm your image and you have dreamed what I might be, every day in your Spirit, I'll find the love and energy.' In your poem 'Something Beautiful For God', which as you yourself said you wrote as a hymn of personal dedication, occur the lines:

Something beautiful for God,
  in my seeing,
  in my being,
something beautiful for God
let the Spirit make of me.

Something meaningful and true,
in my living
and believing,
Something meaningful and true,
Something beautiful and new.

It is the measure of your achievement that you did indeed create a body of hymns and songs whose integrity, beauty, truth and originality have won you a world-wide reputation. I am the bearer of too many messages to read them all out: messages of admiration and sadness from Australia, from England and Scotland (in particular the Iona community), from Sweden, from Canada and from the United States.

Having tried teaching languages, producing radio programmes, acting as religious affairs co-ordinator for the New Zealand branch of Amnesty International and doing parliamentary research work for the Labour Party, you found the truest way to express your inner life, as well as your major life's work, when you took up your ministry of hymn writing at the Presbyterian church of St Andrew's on The Terrace, responding to John, your dearly-loved husband's urgent need for modern hymns that would address the contemporary issues with which both of you were passionately concerned.

And you discovered that you were good at it. Your very first little publication, privately printed at Wellington and provocatively titled *In Every Corner Sing: New Hymns to Familiar Tunes in Inclusive Language*, already contained 'Come to this Christmas singing! Come to a birthday, bringing gifts from our country's treasure, beauty of shell and stone', 'Faith has set us on a journey past the landmarks that we know', 'Now to your table spread we come, each one, in faith that you alone provide the words of life and death ... Here is our common wealth in sharing what is good, as though all humankind around one table stood', 'God of freedom, God of justice, you whose love is strong as death … touch our world of sad oppression with your Spirit's healing breath', 'O God, we bear the imprint of your face: the colours of our skin are your design, and what we have of beauty in our race as man or woman, you alone define,' 'Loving Spirit, loving Spirit, you have chosen me to be – you have drawn me to your wonder, you have set your sign on me.'

In the same little book, you set out your first manifesto: "Singing our faith in the present tense means having to stock some corners of the Christian household with new themes. For me, human rights and racism, women and peacemaking all need singing about, and words to sing are hard to find … Some corners need refurbishing, since the word styles of the past do not always express the theological emphasis we now value … I take it for granted that inclusive language is the mode in which Christian people must express belief."

And you went on to write words that have rung true for modern Christians throughout the world, creating new classics, and a whole new landscape of hymns for we New Zealanders, and in turn the world, to sing. I think of 'Honour the Dead', undoubtedly our country's greatest war hymn, and one that daringly for its time, upholds the conscientious objectors we treated so shamefully.

I think of 'Where Mountains Rise to Open Skies', your noble Hymn for Waitangi Day, the nearest we have to a truly contemporary national anthem: 'Where mountains rise to open skies, your name, O God, is echoed far, from island beach to kauri's reach, in water's light, in lake and star. Your people's heart, your people's part be in our caring for this land, for faith to flower, for aroha to let each other's mana stand.'

I think of that universal musicians' song, 'For the Music of Creation', now set by a positive crowd of international composers. And I think of 'Touch the Earth Lightly', one of the finest hymns advocating for the respectful treatment of the environment we and the world have.

And in all of this what shines through is your heart-felt love for your own country. Not some distant anonymous heavenly landscape, but the clear skies, the mountains and lakes of this bush-clad, bird-rich land, our own Aotearoa New Zealand. 'Carol our Christmas, an upside-down Christmas. Snow is not falling and trees are not bare. Carol the summer, and welcome the Christ child, warm in our sunshine and sweetness of air.' 'Come to our land, come to our hearts, Spirit of life, breath of new birth, teach us to care for water and air, nourish the seed and cherish the earth.' (How prophetic that sounds now, as we scramble to remediate our human impact on pristine nature!)

And you laid open your own heart of compassion and maternal care, for all to see – 'Like a mother you enfold me, hold my life within your own, feed me with your very body, form me of your flesh and bone'. 'For everyone born a place at the table, for everyone born clean water and bread, a shelter, a space, a safe place for growing, for everyone born a star overhead. And God will delight when we are creators of justice and joy, compassion and peace: yes, God will delight when we are creators of justice and joy, compassion and peace.'

And you shared with us your keen-sighted faith; a faith that faced the world as it really is, singing your song of love into its darkness: 'Shine through our winter grey, break through depression's day, live in the little deaths we die in growing: meaning for whom we grope, home of our strongest hope, power and peace through all creation flowing.' 'Rid the earth of torture's terror, you whose hands were nailed to wood; hear the cries of pain and protest, you who shed the tears and blood; move in us the power of pity, restless for the common good.' 'Peace Child, in the sleep of the night, in the dark before light you come; in the silence of stars, in the violence of wars, Saviour, your name. Peace Child, to our dark and our sleep, to the conflicts we reap, now come; be your dream born alive, held in hope, wrapped in love, God's true Shalom.'

In the end you wrote hundreds of hymns, whose quality and precisely directed passion are acknowledged throughout the Christian world, ranking you with the best in our whole heritage of Christian religious song. You showed us that the languages of science and te reo (the Māori language) could meet and kiss in poetry, poetry that is full of beauty and truth, but also sparkling with brilliant new metaphors, from small paper lanterns to lasers and lovers.

And you memorably urged us never to give up on the faith, even though you were often personally ashamed of the behaviour of individuals and groups within its institutions: 'There's never a time to stop believing, there's never a time for hope to die, there's never a time to stop loving, these three things go on.'

Shirley, you may have been taken into the Presence of the loving God you trusted to the end, but your spirit (in the words of another old hymn) goes marching on. Your friend and fellow hymn writer Marnie Barrell has said, "You have left a legacy of hymns for the church that is to be." Let us continue to sing them. There is no better response to the grief we feel at your passing.

Kua hinga te Tōtara i te Waonui a Tāne

Indeed, a very great Tōtara has fallen in the forest of Tāne.

3 – Video renditions of Shirley's texts by Jim & Jean Strathdee

Here are links to view video renditions by Jim and Jean Strathdee of Shirley's texts.

- **At the Door of the Year:**
  https://strathdeemusic.com/AtDoorYear.html

- **Christ, Let Us Come with You:**
  https://strathdeemusic.com/ChristLetUs.html

- **Christmas Come Close:**
  https://strathdeemusic.com/ChristmasComeClose.html

- **Every Day in Your Spirit:**
  https://strathdeemusic.com/EveryDay.html

- **God of Our Foremothers:**
  https://strathdeemusic.com/GodForemothers.html

- **God Weeps:**
  https://strathdeemusic.com/GodWeeps.html

- **Make Spaces for Spirit:**
  https://strathdeemusic.com/MakeSpaces.html

- **Now the Star of Christmas:**
  https://strathdeemusic.com/NowStarChristmas.html

- **Loving Spirit, Loving Spirit:**
  https://strathdeemusic.com/LovingSpirit.html

- **Peace Child:**
  https://strathdeemusic.com/PeaceChild.html
- **Sing a Happy Alleluia!:**
  https://strathdeemusic.com/SingHappySlides.html
- **There is No Child So Small:**
  https://strathdeemusic.com/ThereNoChild.html
- **This Thread I Weave:**
  https://strathdeemusic.com/ThisThread.html
- **When All Else Is Gone:**
  https://strathdeemusic.com/WhenAllElse.html
- **Where the Green Will Rise Again:**
  https://strathdeemusic.com/WhereGreen.html

4 – Himene mō te rā o Anzac

Kia ikeike te wāhi mō te māia
ka tīraha ki whenua kē
taku pōkai-tara te pua o te pōuri
ko te rīpeka hei tohu i tō mate.

Tangihia mō ngā toto o te toa
mō ngā kōiwi o te māia
mō ngā mōreareatanga o te ao
mō ngā ritenga mōrikarika.

Whakatūria te toa ki tōna taumata!
nā te hīinga ngākau te wae i takahi
whakapirau atu te mauhere
kīia ai koe he ware, kai nā te ahi.

Turuturu ngā roimata auē te moumou
ko te hekenga o Maruiwi ki Te Rēinga
tangi taukurī ai ngā kāinga
auē te moumou! Tangi taukurī e.

Kei waikura te ōhākī nei
i rere te toto o ngā toa
whakamaua te kitenga kia tina
kei waimeha te kura o Rongo.

© *Translation by Rangi McGarvey 2007, adapted by Whirimako Black*

5 – Timeline of Shirley's life

1929   John Stewart Murray born in Dunedin, 5 November

1931   Shirley Erena Cockroft born in Invercargill, 31 March

1933   Brother Bruce born

1935   Attends Invercargill Middle School. Dux in 1943

1938   Begins piano lessons with Mrs Boyd

1944   Starts at Southland Girls' High School (SGHS)

1947   Alliance Française competition in Dunedin. Shirley beats John. Colin Newbury wins. Shirley accredited for University Entrance

1948   Shirley head prefect SGHS. Completes Teachers' LTCL in piano

1948   Obtains Secondary School Teachers' Bursary

1949-52   Attends University of Otago, joins the Student Christian Movement and the A Cappella choir

1950-51   John lectures in University of Otago Classics Department

1951   Shirley gains her BA in English, Latin, French, Music and Greek, taking Latin and French through to Stage 3

1952   John and Shirley engaged in February

1952   Shirley begins honours degree, moves in with John's parents, completes MA 2nd class honours in Latin and French

1952	John sails to Britain to study theology at Cambridge. Shirley teaches at St Hilda's Anglican School for Girls
1954	Shirley and Faith Skene travel to Britain
1954	John and Shirley marry in Westminster College Chapel, Cambridge, on 21 July
1955	John gains a Diploma of Ecumenical Studies at the Bossey Ecumenical Institute, Geneva, Switzerland
1956	John and Shirley return to New Zealand. John appointed minister at St David's Presbyterian Church, Taihape
1957	David Stewart born
1961	Alastair John born
1962	John appointed ecumenical chaplain at Victoria University of Wellington and Wellington Teachers' College
1963	Robert Bruce born
1967	Lloyd Geering 'heresy trial'
1967	John becomes minister at Knox Presbyterian Church, Christchurch
1974	John has study leave in the US, Washington DC
1975	John appointed to St Andrew's, Wellington
1978	Family moves to 11 Talavera Terrace. Shirley begins writing hymns
1978	Shirley initiates an Amnesty International group at St Andrew's
1979	NZ Hymnbook Trust (NZHBT) founded. Shirley becomes secretary to its editorial board
1981-88	Shirley works for the Labour Party as a clerk/researcher
1981	Amnesty International launches its Campaign Against Torture. Shirley becomes Amnesty's religious affairs co-ordinator
1981	The Springbok rugby team tours New Zealand

1982	John has three months' study leave and pulpit exchange in Toronto. Shirley attends hymn conference in Ottawa. Shirley and John travel to Italy, attend Amnesty International council at Rimini, visit the Taizé Community in France, then London and Cambridge
1982	*With One Voice with New Zealand Supplement* is published, including Shirley's hymn, 'Come Now, Lord Jesus'
1985	St Andrew's on The Terrace declares itself nuclear-free
1987	Shirley publishes *In Every Corner Sing*
1987	New Zealand declares itself nuclear-free
1988	John gets a Winston Churchill Memorial Trust scholarship to study central city churches in Britain and North America
1988	Shirley works with I-to Loh, Colin Gibson, Douglas Mews and Roy Tankersley
1988	Br Ghislain of Taizé and British hymn writer Brian Wren visit the Murrays
1988-89	Shirley prepares scripts for Radio New Zealand's *Hymns For Sunday Morning*
1989	John and Shirley attend the World Council of Churches' (WCC) workshop on worship, music and the arts in Melbourne
1990-91	John serves as Moderator of the Presbyterian Church of Aotearoa New Zealand (PCANZ)
1990	Shirley works with I-to Loh on *Sound the Bamboo*
1990	150th anniversary of St Andrew's on The Terrace and the PCANZ. A busy year of hymn-writing for Shirley
1991	WCC Assembly in Canberra. Shirley's hymns 'From the Waiting Comes the Sign', 'Spirit of Love and Spirit Who Broods', 'Spirit Who Sings' feature
1991	PCANZ General Assembly rejects the rights of homosexual people in the church. St Andrew's declares itself an inclusive congregation

1992	Shirley presents at the annual meeting of the Hymn Society in the United States and Canada in Washington DC. Hope's first collection of Shirley's hymns, *In Every Corner Sing,* published
1993	NZHBT publishes *Alleluia Aotearoa*
1993	John retires from St Andrew's on The Terrace
1993-2005	John and Shirley live at 168 Rosetta Road, Raumati
1994	John works as a peace monitor for the ecumenical monitoring programme in South Africa's general election
1996	NZHBT publishes *Carol Our Christmas*
1996	Shirley is the Routley lecturer in hymnology at Montreat, North Carolina. She presents her new Hope publication, *Every Day in Your Spirit*, at the Hymn Society conference in Oberlin, Ohio
1997	Shirley speaks at the World Ecumenical (WCC/CCA) Workshop on music and liturgy in Asia, in Tainan, Taiwan
1999	Shirley and John attend the first Australian national ecumenical hymn conference in Melbourne, with Shirley as a leader
2000	John becomes an Officer of the New Zealand Order of Merit
2000	NZHBT publishes *Faith Forever Singing*
2000	Shirley has breast cancer – a year of being ill
2001	Becomes a Member of the New Zealand Order of Merit, the first New Zealander to be honoured for services to hymn writing
2001	Shirley celebrates her 70th birthday
2001	WCC announces Decade to Overcome Violence
2002	NZHBT publishes *He Came Singing Peace: Songs to Overcome Violence*
2003	Hope publishes *Faith Makes the Song*

2003   Management of the NZHBT transfers to John and Gillian Thornley. *Alleluia Aotearoa* celebrates ten years

2004   *Sing for Peace*, Shirley's hymns set to music by Jane Marshall and Carlton Young, published by Abingdon Press

2005   John and Shirley support the establishment of an Aotearoa NZ Peace and Conflict Studies Centre at the University of Otago

2006   Shirley made an Honorary Fellow of the Royal School of Church Music, the first person to receive the award for words, rather than music

2007   Receives biennial prize from Hymn Society in US and Canada for her hymn 'Leftover People in Leftover Places', with a tune by Colin Gibson

2008   Hope publishes *Touch the Earth Lightly*

2008   John has cardiac episode and mild stroke

2008   NZHBT publishes *Hymn for Anzac Day*

2009   NZHBT holds a national hymn conference in Palmerston North, attended by Jim and Jean Strathdee. *Hope is our Song* is launched. Shirley becomes Fellow of the Hymn Society in the United States and Canada, the first woman and first person outside US to become a Fellow

2009   Receives honorary doctorate from the University of Otago

2009   John turns 80

2009   Shirley writes a theme hymn for the Christian Conference of Asia

2011   Shirley turns 80

2013   Hope publishes *A Place at the Table*

2014   John and Shirley promote the wearing and selling of white poppies to counteract the WW100 anniversaries

2015	Shirley wins an international hymn competition run by St Paul's Cathedral, Melbourne – 'All Who Walk the Christian Journey'
2015	Shirley writes theme song for the CCA Assembly – 'The Household of God'
2015	Shirley writes 'It Is Time! A Song About White Poppies for Peace'
2015	John's health poor with low kidney function
2017	John dies on 17 February, aged 87
2017	Shirley moves to Sevenoaks Retirement Village, Paraparaumu, 11 days after John's death
2018	Shirley has a stroke
2018	Prepares her last book with Hope
2019	Hope publishes *Life into Life*
2019	The Very Reverend John Murray Way in Raumati South is opened
2020	Shirley dies on 25 January, aged 88

Acknowledgements

Bringing this biography to birth has been dependent on the willing and enthusiastic help of a great many people, both in New Zealand and around the world.

First and foremost, I thank Shirley's closest hymn-writing collaborator Colin Gibson, who sadly died in December 2022. Colin gave generously of his time on a four-day visit I made to Dunedin in March 2021, even hosting me in his home. That he was in his late 80s with his own health issues while also caring for his wheelchair-bound wife Jeanette is a measure of his beneficence and commitment to the project. It was Colin's belief and urging that a biography be written that inspired me to take up the challenge.

I am grateful for the support of and the opportunity to interview a number of Shirley's close friends, namely the Revs Roger Wiig, Ken Irwin, Mervyn Aitken, Pamela Tankersley and George Armstrong; Ian Harris, Kevin Clements, the Honourable Hugh Templeton, John and Gillian Thornley, Rosemary Lawrence, Lesley Aitken and Roy Tankersley. Emeritus professor Peter Lineham also backed the project and contributed to it.

Ian Harris, founder of the Wellington Ephesus group, and Lesley Aitken were my closest mentors and the first to read the manuscript. Both provided invaluable editorial critique and encouragement when my energies began to flag. I also thank my near neighbour, historian and editor Julia Stuart for reading the near-finished manuscript and providing valuable advice.

I thank Shirley's family for their support over the past few years. Clearly, I could never have written this book without their blessing and assistance. I have interviewed Shirley's sons, David, Alastair and Rob, and three of her grandchildren, Fergus, Alex and Anna. Alastair's wife Lynda and David's wife Janelle Grady also contributed. I cannot thank the family enough for sharing with me their precious memories, photographs and historical documents. I only hope I have done their mother, mother-in-law and grandmother ("Grandshe") the justice she so richly deserves.

Family friend Alida van der Velde spoke to me via WhatsApp from the Netherlands. Her insights into Shirley's last years, when she was her regular companion, are much appreciated.

Enormous thanks go to Hope Publishing Company in the United States and vice president Scott Shorney for their help throughout the research process. Thank you, Scott, for always answering my emails promptly and candidly, and allowing me to quote from Shirley's texts liberally and without charge.

Shirley's hymn-writing collaborators overseas are numerous. I conducted lengthy interviews with Jim and Jean Strathdee, Ron Klusmeier, Brian Wren, I-to Loh, Carlton ('Sam') Young, Per Harling and Lim Swee Hong. I especially thank Ron Klusmeier and his partner Christina for their friendship and advice, and for sharing with me much of their many-years-long email correspondence with Shirley. In addition, I thank Christina for her work on a concept for the cover. Scottish hymn writer the Rev John Bell also provided useful comment.

My thanks to Peter Marshall, son of Shirley's friend and American collaborator Jane Marshall, for allowing me to include email correspondence from his mother.

Then there are Shirley's New Zealand hymn-writing collaborators. In addition to Colin Gibson, I thank David Dell, Ian Render, Shona Murray, Marnie Barrell and Felicia Edgecombe.

Members of St Andrew's on The Terrace, Wellington, have contributed to the book in so many ways. Along with those already named, I thank Pat Booth, Sheila Irwin, Pam Ormsby (who died in 2023), the Rev Barrie Keenan and former minister the Rev Susan Jones.

My gratitude to Shirley and John's long-time friend Paul Oestreicher. Thank you, Paul, for your recollections of your friendship with the Murrays over many years and for allowing me to publish your reflection on Shirley's 'Hymn for Anzac Day'.

I am grateful for contributions from the Rev Adrian Skelton, Sir Lloyd Geering, the Rev Helen Jacobi and *Hymns on Sunday* producer Robyn Jaquiery. I thank Robyn for her personal support and for continuing to bring Shirley's hymns to the wider listening public.

Volunteer archivist at Southland Girls' High School Barbara Clark assisted me most enthusiastically, searching out old photos and Shirley's contributions to the school magazine. Having your various packages arrive in the mail always added a shine to my day, Barbara. Thank you.

Several of Shirley's lifelong friends feature in the book. Sadly, a number died either before Shirley did or within a year or two of her death. With the help of some of their children, I was able to paint a picture. I thank Shirley's god-daughter, Judith Eastgate, daughter of Nigel and Lindsey (née Harrington) Eastgate; Mark and Fiona Williamson, children of Faith Williamson, née Skene; and Jacqué Mandeno, daughter of Pam Laytham, née Norris. All have contributed important and often amusing insights and memories.

I appreciate the help of archivist staff at the Presbyterian Research Centre, Knox College, Dunedin. Their attention to detail and prompt service helped me immeasurably.

My husband, Sandy Lang, has been my technical and administrative go-to person and general all-round encourager on this long research and writing journey. Thank you, Sandy. And I acknowledge the efforts of my publisher Philip Garside in working with me to bring the finished book together.

Finally, enormous thanks to the Justice-Compassion Trust Aotearoa New Zealand, the New Zealand Hymnbook Trust and the Central Presbytery of the Presbyterian Church of Aotearoa New Zealand for their generous support that has made publication of the book possible.

Anne Manchester, July 2024

Bibliography, sources, abbreviations and illustrations

1982 *With One Voice: A Hymnbook for All the Churches with New Zealand Supplement* (1982) London and Auckland: Collins.

1987 *In Every Corner Sing: New Hymns to Familiar Tunes in Inclusive Language by Shirley Murray.* Privately printed.

Publications of the New Zealand Hymnbook Trust

1993 *Alleluia Aotearoa, Hymns and songs for all churches.*

1996 *Carol Our Christmas, A Book of New Zealand Carols.*

2000 *Faith Forever Singing: New Zealand Hymns and Songs for a New Day.*

2002 *He Came Singing Peace: Songs to Overcome Violence.*

2008 *Hymn for Anzac Day: Himene mō te rā o Anzac.*

2009 *Hope is our Song: New Hymns and Songs from Aotearoa New Zealand.*

Shirley collections published by Hope Publishing Company, Carol Stream, Illinois

1992 *In Every Corner Sing: The Hymns of Shirley Erena Murray.*

1996 *Every Day in Your Spirit: Shirley Erena Murray. New Hymns Written Between 1992 and 1996.*

2003 *Faith Makes the Song: Shirley Erena Murray. New Hymns Written Between 1997 and 2002.*

2008 *Touch the Earth Lightly: Shirley Erena Murray. New Hymns Written Between 2003 and 2008.*

2013 *A Place at the Table: Shirley Erena Murray. New Hymns Written Between 2009 and 2013.*

2019 *Life into Life: Shirley Erena Murray. New and Collected Hymns.*

Further sources

Church Hymnary, Fourth edition. (2005) Church of Scotland. Norwich, UK: Canterbury Press.

Sing for Peace: The Hymns of Shirley Erena Murray set to the tunes of Jane Marshall and Carlton R. Young. (2004) Nashville: Abingdon Press.

Songs between Friends: Seventeen Hymn Tunes by Carlton Young for Texts by Shirley Erena Murray. (2016) Chicago: GIA Publications.

Correspondence between George H. Shorney and Shirley Erena Murray. George H. Shorney papers, 1974-2002, Pitts Theology Library, Emory University, Atlanta, Georgia. Accessed December 2022.

Edmond, Rodney Stewart. (2013) *Migrations: Journeys in Time and Place.* Wellington: Bridget Williams Books.

Gibson, Colin. (2021) *Knowing The Song: A Companion to the Publications of the New Zealand Hymnbook Trust from 1993 to 2009 together with the New Zealand Supplement to With One Voice (1982).* The New Zealand Hymnbook Trust in association with Philip Garside Publishing Ltd.

Loh, I-to. (Ed.) (2000) *Sound the Bamboo: CCA Hymnal.* Tainan: Taiwan Church Press; (2006) Chicago: GIA Publications.

Loh, I-to. (2011) *Companion to Sound the Bamboo. Asian Hymns in their Cultural and Liturgical Contexts.* Chicago: GIA Publications.

McEldowney, Dennis. (Ed.) (1990) *Presbyterians in Aotearoa 1840-1990.* Wellington: Presbyterian Church of New Zealand.

Meehan, Norman. (2013) *Jenny McLeod: A Life in Music.* Wellington: Te Herenga Waka University Press.

Murray, John Stewart. (2016) *The Story of St Andrew's on The Terrace 1975-93: The Ministry of the Very Rev John Stewart Murray.* Wellington: St Andrew's on The Terrace.

Murray, Shirley Erena. (c2014) *My Story – Shirley Erena Murray. Notes for My Family.* Unpublished.

Wall, Terry. (2022) *Hymnwriters Downunder: Methodists sing the praise of God in Aotearoa New Zealand.* Tuakau Union Parish.

Wootton, Janet. (2010) *This Is Our Song: Women's Hymn-Writing.* Eugene, Oregon: Wipf and Stock.

Wren, Brian. (2000) *Praying Twice: The Music and Words of Congregational Song.* Louisville, Kentucky: Westminster John Knox Press.

Wren, Brian. (2017) *Barefoot in the Dust: A Hymn-Poet's Memoir.* Eugene, Oregon: Cascade Books.

Young, Carlton R. 'Sam'. (2022) *I'll Sing on: My First 96 Years.* Chicago: GIA Publications.

Music in the Air: Song and Spirituality, a biannual journal published and edited by John Thornley 1996-2015.

The Hymn, quarterly journal published by the Hymn Society in the United States and Canada.

Audio and visual sources

Pacific Landfall documentary. 150th anniversary of the Presbyterian Church in New Zealand from St Andrew's on The Terrace, Wellington. Directed and produced by Gil Barker. Aired 25 February 1990. Ngā Taonga Sound and Vision.

Video interview conducted by Sam Young and George Shorney, 12 July 1996, recorded on Shirley's second visit to the US. Hope Publishing Company.

Association of Presbyterian Women. Sheila Irwin interviews Shirley Murray, 26 November 2001, 7 November 2002, 19 November 2002 and 22 November 2002. Audio tapes held by Presbyterian Research Centre (Archives), Knox College, Dunedin.

St Andrew's on The Terrace oral history project. Interview with Shirley Erena Murray conducted by Margaret Pannett, 7 November 2006. National Library of New Zealand.

St Andrew's on The Terrace oral history project. Interview with John Stewart Murray conducted by Ann Barrie, September-November 2006. National Library of New Zealand.

Video and audio interviews with Shirley and John conducted by Ron Klusmeier, Raumati Beach, August 2014.

Abbreviations

AA: *Alleluia Aotearoa, Hymns and songs for all churches*

Anzac: Australia New Zealand Army Corps

APW: Association of Presbyterian Women

ATCL: Associate of Trinity College, London

CABTA: Citizens' All Black Tour Association

CARE: Citizens Association for Racial Equality

CCA: Christian Conference of Asia

CH4: *Church Hymnary, Fourth Edition* (Church of Scotland)

NZHBT: New Zealand Hymnbook Trust

OE: Overseas experience

RSCM: Royal School of Church Music

SCM: Student Christian Movement

SGHS: Southland Girls' High School

U3A: University of the Third Age

UN: United Nations

WCC: World Council of Churches

WOV: *With One Voice*

Illustrations

All photographs are courtesy of the Murray family, except where noted otherwise.

Additional photos:

Chapter 19: Colin Gibson, by Stephen Jaquiery, published in the *Otago Daily Times*, 20 April 2007. Reprinted with permission

Chapter 20: Ian Render, by Bishop Andrew Hedge

Chapter 21: Shirley with Ron Klusmeier, by Christina Bogucki

Chapter 22: Jean and Jim Strathdee, by Jay Hart

Chapter 23: Per Harling with Shirley, by Johannes Stenberg

Chapter 24: Lim Swee Hong with Shirley at the Tainan Theological Seminary, 1997, photographer unknown

Chapter 25: Carlton 'Sam' Young, by Mike DuBose, published in the *United Methodist News*, 3 September 2020. Reprinted with permission

Chapter 26: I-to Loh with Shirley at the World Council of Churches' Assembly in Canberra, 1991, photographer unknown

Index of names and subjects

Index of hymn names and first lines

About the author

Journalist Anne Manchester began her career working on the Presbyterian and Methodist newspaper *Crosslink,* and later served as editor of the nursing journal *Kai Tiaki Nursing New Zealand.*

She has published two books for children – *Toughen Up, Andrew!* and its prequel *Andrew Down Under, The story of an immigrant dog* – and a memoir, *Memory Stick*, in 2020.

(Photo: Simon Hoyle)

(Anne is also an actor and director for her local theatre troupe. In 2023, she directed and narrated a photographic tribute and film of Katherine Mansfield's story *At the Bay.*

She lives in Eastbourne, across the harbour from Wellington, with her husband Sandy, and near her son James and two grandchildren.

Praise for *Peace is Her Song*

"This biography is grounded in Aotearoa New Zealand, anchoring Shirley's hymns in the life and the faith that inspired them. It will ensure the woman who wrote them is remembered as she deserves to be. Shirley's work continues to have a huge impact on the way Christianity is experienced in Aotearoa. She gave us something to sing that captures what shalom is about within the contours of our landscape and our churches."

– John Bluck, retired Anglican bishop and writer

"Shirley's works display the concern she has for people, for peace, and for the planet. It is God's truth that compels her writing, and we are pleased to be part of her wider ministry."

– Scott Shorney, Vice President, Hope Publishing Company, United States

"Anne Manchester presents many rich sources of material on Shirley's life and legacy. Shirley's own recollections, together with those of her colleagues and friends, paint a fascinating picture of her emergence as a leading poet of the church in Aotearoa New Zealand and the world.

This book is a fine tribute to a woman who has given us the words and images we need today to act justly, love mercy and walk humbly with God."

– Marnie Barrell, MNZM, hymn writer and
board member of the New Zealand Hymnbook Trust

www.ingramcontent.com/pod-product-compliance
Lightning Source LLC
Chambersburg PA
CBHW051003140626
46546CB00016B/137